THE
FAILURE
OF SUCCESS

OTHER BOOKS BY ROBERT THEOBALD

THE RICH AND THE POOR   1959
THE CHALLENGE OF ABUNDANCE   1960
FREE MEN AND FREE MARKETS   1963
THE GUARANTEED INCOME   (ed.) 1966
SOCIAL POLICIES FOR AMERICA IN THE SIXTIES   (ed.) 1968
AN ALTERNATIVE FUTURE FOR AMERICA II   1970
ECONOMIZING ABUNDANCE   1970
TEG'S 1994   1972 (with F. M. Scott)
HABIT AND HABITAT   1972
FUTURES CONDITIONAL   1972
MIDDLE CLASS SUPPORT   1972

THE
FAILURE
OF SUCCESS

Ecological Values vs Economic Myths

edited by Robert Theobald and
Stephanie Mills

THE BOBBS-MERRILL COMPANY, INC.
INDIANAPOLIS   NEW YORK

The Bobbs-Merrill Company, Inc.
Publishers: Indianapolis / New York
Copyright © 1973 by Robert Theobald and Stephanie Mills
All rights reserved
ISBN 0–672–51695–0 cloth
ISBN 0–672–51818–X paper
Library of Congress catalog card number 72–9883
Designed by Jack Jaget
Manufactured in the United States of America

Contents

BIBLIOGRAPHIES:

Preface

What is success?

Until very recently, Western nations believed that they possessed the answer to this question. The rich countries have seen success as the production of more goods and services as well as the ability to gain greater control over the environment. The individual saw himself as successful if he had attended university, if he was married and had several children, and if he was earning a large income.

Suddenly, we are no longer sure that these patterns constitute success. We have become aware that raising the production of goods and services increases pollution. We also know that our desire to dominate nature may damage the environment and our self-interest. In addition, universities are increasingly seen as irrelevant to education, while the pollution costs of large, rich families are more and more recognized.

We are suffering from future shock. We have achieved the successes for which we have striven and they have turned to ashes. Those who have been most successful in industrial era terms often seem most threatened by the new conditions which they themselves have created on the basis of man's increasing power.

The shock we are suffering is increased because Americans—far more than people in the rest of the world—have believed that their success criteria were valid for all time and for all countries. They have failed to recognize that criteria of success will necessarily be relevant only to specific times and places. As a result, they are particularly shocked because the success criteria valid for America's past are no longer retaining loyalty in the present or serving as valid images for the future.

It is critically important that we come to recognize the magnitude of the differences between our values and those of others. For example, many cultures have seen their lives as part of an endless cycle with man being unable to change significantly the patterns of events in which he is involved. Some cultures have valued the family which gave away all its goods. The roles assigned to men and women vary widely in different parts of the world. In some cultures anger is seen as necessary, even desirable; in others it is deplored. The anthropological record shows societies which have counted their wealth in cows, in stones, in women.

Human nature is widely flexible. Some societies are profoundly cooperative in their styles of behavior, and some deeply competitive. In some cultures both men and women play with their children; in other cultures children are largely left alone. In most cultures the old are revered, but harsh reality may still compel their abandonment when they can no longer contribute to the life of the tribe.

It is critical that we remember the extent of variation as the Western world tries to choose new success criteria relevant to the conditions which it has brought into existence. What should we try to achieve at a time when we have the power to do *any*thing that is vital—but not *every*thing that we want. What is worthwhile and feasible in a world which is so closely interconnected by communications that we are moving out of the competitive industrial era into the cooperative communications era?

This book looks at how we should change our success criteria. Because there are as yet no tidy answers, it provides you with the raw materials which you can use in creating your own personal viewpoint. Fiction, science-fiction, poems, songs, advertisements, social science, etc., are juxtaposed so that they will hopefully add depth or questions to the pieces which precede and follow them.

Such an organization makes assumptions about the future and your own capacity to create meaningful new criteria for your own life. It assumes that life is not merely a hopeless blur—nonsensical and depressing. It assumes also that the patterns of reality are not so completely determined that your decisions cannot alter the shape of the world in which you and we live. This volume is based on the belief that each individual affects the events in which he takes part, and that the more he understands the patterns behind the events, the greater may be his impact on the world in which he lives.

Authors and editors usually bury their assumptions about their fundamental beliefs in their writing. We have stated our key belief above in arguing that man is neither completely free nor completely determined in his actions and that the primary human and intellectual goal of our time must be to discover how to be creative in such conditions. We are hampered in our efforts to achieve such a goal because both our language and our styles assume the existence of dichotomies—black or white, free will or determinism, etc.

Given this basic pattern of dichotomies, it will necessarily be difficult for us to see ourselves as part of an environment by which we are constrained but which we can nevertheless alter by intelligent action. It is our hope that this book will help you to understand the present clash between economic and ecological views of the world and also facilitate the process by which you will discover the skills you need to live in the new world we are all creating together.

Perhaps the hardest reality which each of us has to grasp is that our present criteria of success may not be suitable either for the survival of the planet or for our own self-development. It is already recognized that striving for the maximum increase in Gross National Product may be counter-productive. We are only just beginning to understand that our personal success criteria are caught up in the same competitive, goal-oriented patterns as those of the total society.

In a profound sense, each one of us is booby-trapped by the patterns within which we were socialized. It is going to be much easier to perceive intellectually the changes in socio-economic priorities which are required by our new environmental understandings than to make the necessary changes in our personal lives. The building of an ecologically sound society requires the creation of a new style of human being.

The process of discovery implied in this last sentence is made more difficult by the fact that it is now known that the communications era will be one of diverse values where there will be no single lifestyle appropriate for all of us. The communications era can only come into existence as each person—and organism—is able to fulfill his success criteria to the maximum possible extent. The intermeshing of success criteria—and consequent synergy—provides the potential for continued individual, societal and environmental development.

This book has five parts. The first examines the nature of the clash between economic and ecological values. It shows how our assumptions about the possibility of continued economic growth have been destroyed by our growing ecological understanding. It shows that we are now confronted with a massive socio-economic crisis resulting from the obsolescence of our mechanisms for distributing rights to resources.

The second section examines the implications of the clash between economic and ecological understandings in the context of the poor countries of the world. Up to now we have been trying to convince—and often to coerce—the poor countries of the world to follow the route which the rich countries took during the process of industrialization. It is now clear that this route into the future is infeasible. What other options are open?

The third section aims to resolve the clash in thinking between the economic and ecological approaches. It shows that we must value everything and everyone for the contribution that they can make—that there is a possible coordination which can be achieved without the use of structural authority if we are willing to work toward it rather than strive to prevent it.

The fourth section suggests some of the issues which we shall have to deal with as we move forward into the communications era and try to discover social and human patterns suitable for the new era. There is little we can do here except to suggest a program of further reading which moves you out of your present set of assumptions and permits you to steep yourself in the alternative assumptions which are already emerging—even if they have not yet taken final shape.

The final section is quite different from all the others. It assumes that you need to discover yourself before you can really start changing your own success criteria. Each of us needs at some point to take a leap of faith, to move from the industrial-era side of the mirror to the communications-era side. This is always an intensely personal moment which you can only achieve for yourself, but with, of course, a little help from your friends. (We should acknowledge here the help from our friends which enabled us to complete this book—it is impossible to acknowledge the contributions specifically, for some of the most significant are certainly those of which we were least conscious.)

Books are poor ways to start the process of experiencing yourself and your environment. It is urgent that we discover more effective routes. Nevertheless, this book does aim to open up the future so that you can take hold of it and shape it.

ROBERT THEOBALD AND
STEPHANIE MILLS

June 1972

THE
FAILURE
OF SUCCESS

PART I.

Economists vs Ecologists

MAN has moved through two major transformations in his history: from hunting and gathering to agriculture, and later from agriculture to industry. These transitions have been accompanied by the collapse of cultures as they attempted, unsuccessfully, to deal with the profound shifts in success criteria.

We now face a third transformation: from industry toward cooperation and communications. It is essential that this transition be managed more successfully than the previous shifts, because we now live in a global culture and we cannot afford the collapse of this culture. Such a collapse would, at the very least, end any chance for a movement toward true humanity. It could all too easily destroy the planet.

The necessity of the third transition has been proved, most obviously, by the environment/ecology movement. Western man came to believe during the industrial revolution that his success criteria should be based on his ability to produce more, to control nature more completely, to raise his standard of living. Believing this, industrial man built a system which was ideally designed to ensure continued growth. Unfortunately, it is no longer functional now that we have decided we cannot make economic growth the first priority.

Perhaps the primary requirement for the effective functioning of any culture is that it provide rights to resources to those within it. The industrial era growth model assumed that most people should earn their income by holding a job, that this job should provide enough money to buy necessary/desirable goods and services and that the demand for goods and services would ensure the availability of enough jobs, closing the circle.

The requirement for economic growth emerges from the fact that there will necessarily be an increase in productivity and efficiency in any functioning system. This increase in productivity means that fewer people will be needed to produce the same amount of goods and services. Thus new jobs must be opened up if they are to be available for all, and this can *only* be done by increasing the demand for goods and services. It was this sort of pattern which led Professor William Gomberg to categorize industrial-era systems as "whirling-dervish economies dependent on compulsive consumption."

The impossibility of long-run continuation of the present system has been known for many years. Professor Dennis Gabor, a recent Nobel Prize winner, stated in the early sixties: "In today's world all curves are exponential. It is only in mathematics that exponential curves grow to infinity. In the real world, they either break down catastrophically or they saturate gently. It is our duty as thinking men to strive toward a gentle saturation."

Not until the emergence of the environment/ecology movement was the infeasibility of ever-continued growth really perceived. The finiteness of planet Earth has now been demonstrated over and over again. We are increasingly aware that we cannot afford economic growth, but we are still unclear about the new options open to us or about the route by which we can move from the present set of values which encourage economic growth to another set which will ensure ecological sanity.

Indeed, one of our problems is that much of the environmental/ ecological writing suggests that we only need a shift in priorities rather than an alteration in values. It has been argued that we can stop growth and return to an earlier and simpler life. Many of those in the environmental/ecological movement are profoundly anti-technology or neo-Luddite—they believe that technology is at the root of all our present complex of problems.

This viewpoint is unrealistic, and indeed immoral, in a profound sense. Man has now unbalanced his economic, social and political systems so completely that he cannot suddenly step aside and argue that he has no obligation to manage the mess he has created. The starving people in the world can only be fed, clothed and sheltered if we learn how to make decisions far more effectively, if we learn how to use technology far more successfully and if we learn to accomplish more while using less resources.

As always, there are explicit success criteria behind this statement. We, the authors, believe that our only hope of survival will vanish if people come to feel that there is no hope of success for themselves and their children. It is for this reason, as well as an outraged sense of humanity, that we must reject the idea that it makes sense to starve whole populations. Such a policy would create such despair and such levels of tension between rich and poor countries that destruction of the planet would then be certain. If we are to achieve short-run and long-run success we must find ways to care for all on this earth with increasing success while at the same time recognizing that this is only possible on the basis of massive shifts in value systems.

We do not believe that the transition from the industrial era to the communications era can be achieved without grief and pain. We recognize that the costs and disruption of the transition will inevitably be so high that we can only prevent them from overwhelming us by paying full attention to all the means by which the grief and pain can be kept to levels which will not destroy our attempt to create a more human future.

It is hard to understand—and even harder to accept—that solving our problems is impossible within the present value system. Fundamental inequality is necessary for the survival of the industrial era— we can only produce a world in which each individual can maximize his potential by abandoning the goal of equality and replacing it with success criteria based on diversity. If we are to succeed in building a better world we must change the successes we hope to achieve rather than continuing to accept the obsolete success criteria of the industrial era.

Clues Reveal a Better Economy*

ART BUCHWALD

Washington—You're going to hear a lot about "economic indicators" this year. An economic indicator is a clue to what is really happening to the economy.

From these hints, economists can make fantastic predictions of which way the country will tilt in the next 12 months.

A man who works with nothing but economic indicators is Dr. Fredrich Strasser, who is in charge of the Input-Output Institute of Sensuous Economics.

A visit to Dr. Strasser's Institute produced some very interesting but frightening information.

Dr. Strasser said that at the moment all his economic indicators were pointing up.

"More people are starting to travel on the airlines, which is a very good thing," he told me. "At the moment, though, it's still possible to book a flight without difficulty and have a comfortable ride without people sitting on your lap.

"But if things keep getting better, the airports won't be able to handle the traffic. The planes will be overbooked, baggage will be lost and the airlines will have a very good economic year."

"Wait a minute," I said. "Are you trying to say that if the economy gets better in this country, things will get worse?"

* Reprinted from *Arizona Republic,* January 21, 1972. Used by permission.

"Of course I am. Everyone knows the price of a good economy is a breakdown in services that the economy provides. The more refrigerators people buy, the less chance they have of getting them repaired.

"The more cars that are sold, the bigger pollution and traffic problems you have. The more the country consumes, the less opportunity there is of getting rid of the garbage."

Dr. Strasser said one of his best economic indicators is the behavior of shop clerks, hotel reservation people and headwaiters.

"The nicer they are," he said, "the more trouble the country is in. During the recent recession we found shop clerks, hotel people and headwaiters the most courteous they had been since the economic doldrums of the early sixties.

"This indicated to us that things were very bad. Lately we've been spot-checking, and we've discovered that the hotel people are getting snippety again, the clerks in stores are starting not to give a damn, and in some good restaurants the headwaiters, for the first time in two years, are becoming their old obnoxious, patronizing selves. This shows that things are picking up, and the country could be in for a good year."

"It's fantastic how you people arrive at your conclusions," I said.

"*What's happened* now?"

"Wait a Minute"*

MAURICE STANS

When I was asked to speak today, I was told I could talk on any subject of my choice. I realize that Secretary Morton has already covered many of the topics that would be of interest to you—energy policy and matters of that type—and for that reason I would like to take a broader subject to explore, one that is of direct interest to your industry but that also has an extension far beyond the oil industry and relates to American business throughout the economy.

I am speaking of the matter of environment and the antipollution movement in the country. It is a very emotional one in many quarters. It is a political one in many quarters. The public is demanding action; actively, vocally, impatiently demanding immediate action. And this is what presents the difficulties.

Now, we all know that the environment ultimately has to be cleaned up, that pollution has to be dealt with.

President Nixon has declared that the nation has been long overdue in halting its abuses of the air, land and water. He has made a commitment to eliminate pollution and to cleanse the atmosphere and conditions in which we live.

The question is, how do we go about doing this? And in the most sensible way?

* Address by the Honorable Maurice H. Stans, delivered before the 25th Anniversary Meeting of the National Petroleum Council.

9

Priorities

Understandable as the public's interest is for immediate solutions, and justified as the impatience of the public may be, we have the obligation to see the problem in the whole, not just piecemeal.

We cannot have single track minds in which the environmental issue overrides everything. But that is how some of the people would have us look at our problems.

If we settle for quick, immediate solutions to one set of problems, we can catapult ourselves into others that are much more serious, and we are beginning to find that out.

So we have to begin to look a little farther down the road.

I think it is high time for the entire nation to weigh the needs against the demands and say: "Wait a Minute, what are our priorities?""

We need to weigh the requirements against our resources and say: "Wait a Minute, which can we afford? Which can we achieve?"

We need to weigh technological capabilities against the timetables and the options and say: "Wait a Minute, how can we get there from here?"

We need to weigh environmental goals against economic reality and say: "Wait a Minute, how do the benefits compare with the costs?"

Problems

In other words, the problem is: how do we develop public and private policies in which economics and technology are factored into every environmental assessment?

Let me start at this point.

Industry has been indiscriminately accused by some of ignoring the pollution problems of our times and being responsible for most of them.

The charge is dead wrong and it is unfair.

The fact is, without denying industry's responsibility, most polluters are outside of industry—municipalities, other governments, agriculture, and the public itself. Witness the fact that hundreds, perhaps thousands, of American communities pour untreated sewage into waters every day.

Response

Moreover, American industries, almost across the board, have launched vastly complex and expensive efforts to help clean up the air, water and landscape of the country.

For example:

The chemical industry in 1970 spent $600 million for pollution abatement.

The iron and steel industry has spent more than a billion dollars on air and water facilities, and almost two-thirds of that in the last two years.

The automobile industry currently is investing a quarter of a billion dollars a year in pollution research and development.

The electric industries will spend two-thirds of a billion dollars on pollution control this year alone.

Your own petroleum industry is spending more than $500 million in pollution control this year, and in addition is developing expensive facilities in other countries to reduce the sulphur content of fuel oils being shipped here.

The oil and tanker industries are working closely with the government to eliminate oil discharges and accidental spills into the oceans.

The fact is that, on average, American companies will have increased their pollution control spending by almost 50 percent this year over last year. They will spend some $18 billion over the next five years to meet the requisite standards.

Unfortunately, business has failed to make these achievements credibly known to the American people, and the idea still persists in many quarters that business is doing nothing and what it does do is only because it is being dragged across the line. Neither is true. Business has been working at pollution control for a long time.

Pressures

So we have come to a troubled time by a very direct route.

Critics press the public to insist upon quick solutions to these complex problems.

The people, in turn, press the Congress. Timetables have been imposed, and regulations applied, giving some people a false feeling that the problems will all go away if we put enough squeeze on business to act.

The trouble is that in the development of these pressures reason sometimes gets lost and extremes become the result.

Many of the results have been beneficial, to be sure, but some have been ill-conceived and harmful to people, to business, and to the country.

Phosphates

I would like to give you a few examples, starting with detergent phosphates—the washday ingredient that has recently come to typify the pollution villain.

State and local governments all over the country have begun to ban the sale of detergent phosphate on a crazy-quilt basis, geographically.

But in the rush, perhaps someone should say: "Wait a Minute, what are we really doing here?"

Laws to ban phosphate detergents may give the public the notion that the problem is solved, while nutrients, including phosphates, continue to flow into the lakes and rivers from other sources—agricultural and natural as well as manmade. And some of these cannot be controlled.

So if people assume that just a legal ban on phosphate detergents will do the job, they may only lull themselves into neglecting far more significant scientific efforts to help purify waters through phosphate removal techniques in municipal waste treatment plants.

Dangers

Then—and this is perhaps even more important—some hastily devised phosphate substitutes can be more harmful and dangerous than many people believe the phosphates are.

One substitute developed by manufacturers, at a cost of many, many millions of dollars, was temporarily put aside at the request of the government because there were concerns it might create some health hazards. Additional safety tests are now being completed and the situation may be changed.

But some of the other substitutes now reaching the public contain caustic materials that are dangerous, especially to children. If those products get in their eyes, they can blind—or if they are accidentally ingested, they can maim or even kill.

To limit these risks, the FDA has instituted labeling requirements for caustic detergents.

Unfortunately, the fact is that small children creeping on the floor next to the washing machine can't read those labels.

Some chemical substitutes for phosphates also wash out the flameproofing in children's cotton sleepers which the textile industry has been working hard to develop.

Now, my purpose in citing these points is not to defend phosphates, or the industries that use them, or the products that contain them.

Instead, it is my way of saying:

"Wait a Minute." Before we rush helter-skelter into immediate responses to such problems of nationwide concern, isn't it prudent first to take the time to know what we are doing? To weigh all the factors and the consequences involved?

Power Plant Siting

For another example, take the siting of new electric power plants.

It is all too familiar to many of you, I am sure. If anything, it is even more difficult than siting new refineries.

The nation's need for more electric power is rapidly outrunning our capacity to generate it. The answer would seem to be simply to build more power plants.

But in many areas of the country it has become almost impossible to do so. As many as 40 approvals may be necessary, many of them involving environmental grounds, and even the last one can be reversed as easily as the first.

We all know that New York City has had these troubles for years.

Houston is another case in point. It has all the ingredients of growth except enough electric power. But it can't start to build a new generating plant it urgently needs because the effluents, even after costly cooling, would raise the temperature of the waters that receive it some two degrees above the temperature that would support present marine life.

Isn't it time someone said: "Wait a Minute"?

If we fix the right priorities—if we integrate our environmental, technological and economic interests—*all* of them can be served without one dominating the other.

The President has urged the Congress to enact legislation to resolve the power plant siting problem and wants public agencies designated to assure public discussion of plans, proper resolution of environmental issues and timely construction of the facilities.

DDT

Another case at point is insecticides.

We all know there are valid arguments against some of them, but in the rush away from them, we can create massive new problems.

For example, in New Jersey, without DDT, more than one million oak trees have been blighted and face destruction by the gypsy moth.

Without DDT, forest insects are running rampant in Sweden, eating away the raw material of that country's biggest industry.

In Ceylon, without DDT, malaria cases have become far more prevalent, involving 10 percent of the population. Without DDT in India there would be 100 million cases of malaria each year instead of a few hundred thousand.

In parts of the United States, without DDT, insects have made it increasingly difficult to grow lettuce, lima beans, sweet corn, and so on.

Now, in time, perhaps, substitutes for present insecticides can be developed and proved out. But in the meantime, most of the substitutes are uncertain or don't even exist.

The whole question is whether by precipitous action we will create an expensive gap between the present means and the later solutions.

Again, this is not a brief for DDT. This is just a way of saying:

Wait a Minute. Before we act precipitously and ban products for one reason, shouldn't we at least be certain that the cure is not worse than the disease?

One-Industry Towns

What about one-industry towns? Today a growing number of small communities across the country are fearful that they will lose their economic life if their single sustaining industry is forced to close, either because of rigid environmental protection controls or because they can't cope with the economic cost of complying.

Isn't it time for someone to say "Wait a Minute"?

Are the environmental dangers so imminent, so critical, that we have to throw thousands of productive people out of work? Are the dangers so great, so immediate, that whole communities must be run through the economic wringer?

Isn't it time that we first measure all the evidence, recognizing legitimate concerns on the one hand, weighing them fairly against valid considerations on the other, then act reasonably and carefully to protect both the environment and the jobs? It may take a bit longer but the end result would be far more satisfactory.

SST

For another example, Congress killed the SST.

But shouldn't we as a nation have said "Wait a Minute"? Are we so afraid to build just two experimental airplanes that we would willingly sacrifice thousands of jobs, jeopardize the economic health of an entire city, forgo the technological advantage of an entire industry, and deny major benefits to our balance of payments?

Isn't it time we weigh our potential against the risk in every reasonable case?

Pipeline

What about the Trans-Alaska Pipeline? Some of you have an interest in that.

Again, people have said, "Let's not build it because of the possible adverse consequences to the environment."

No one suggests that we ignore these possible dangers. Everyone agrees that we must take every known precaution to protect the environment.

But there is another side of the coin: the nation's need for the oil and the benefits to Alaska.

Isn't it time somebody says on things like this, "Wait a Minute"?

We already have the technological means to provide reasonable protection against dangers to the Alaskan environment. Are we so afraid of what might happen that we will sacrifice the enormous new sources of oil we need for our homes, our cars, our jobs, our country? Will we sacrifice potential jobs for thousands of people who would be employed in the shipping industries, in Alaska and elsewhere? Will we turn our backs on all the economic benefits to that state and to the country?

The risks are recognized, but isn't it time we recognize that other considerations also must be taken in the national interest?

Emission Standards

And what about the tougher emission standards for transportation? Certainly they should be sought and should be achieved.

But—Wait a Minute—in the past decade the amount of hydrocarbons given off by an automobile has already been reduced by 80 percent, carbon monoxide emissions by 70 percent. And with existing capabilities, these improvements can continue.

But a mandatory standard of the Clean Air Act demands a 90 percent reduction below the remaining emission levels by 1975.

For hydrocarbons, that level is as much as foliage gives off in the average yard of the average American home in the average suburb.

One person has estimated that every car would have to be parked for two days after getting its tank filled—literally—because gasoline going from the pump to the car gives off at least twice the daily allowable hydrocarbons for that car.

Spreading one ounce of house paint uses the same daily quota of hydrocarbons.

Burning up two logs on the fire in the fireplace likewise uses the daily quota.

The list of examples could go on.

The Environmental Protection Agency report to Congress last week said that we do not have the technology to comply with some of the standards that have been set in accordance with law.

To try to achieve these standards will result in millions of dollars of added costs, which inevitably have to go into higher consumer prices.

If we try to solve our environmental problems more quickly than our technology permits, not only will we raise costs sharply and suddenly, but we will also increase the number of false steps that we take along the way. The incomplete state of our knowledge leads directly to pitfalls that can't be foreseen.

So isn't it time to say: "Wait a Minute"? Let's weigh each need against the technological realities and let's not impose any more arbitrary deadlines that can't be met with the technology in sight.

Let's do the things we can do first, while making orderly progress against the others.

Offshore Drilling

What about offshore drilling? Certainly we should take every possible practical step to stop polluting the oceans.

But—Wait a Minute.

Before we make offshore drilling too difficult, let's recognize that by the end of this decade, offshore wells will have to provide 30 percent of our fuel. And it will also provide much of the low-sulphur fuel that is urgently needed for clean air.

Proposals

As all of you know so well, there are many other matters which we could cite and say "Wait a Minute." These examples make the point.

Let me give you some specifics as to guidelines in dealing with these matters in the future.

First, a determination of the economic impact should be required before environmental acts are mandated.

The public must know what the costs will be, what the alternatives are, and whether it will get its money's worth.

Second, a technological determination should be prepared in connection with any governmental action, indicating the time required to carry it out.

Third, we must avoid panicky, ad hoc approaches to the problems of air, land and water pollution, and develop feasible long-range plans to deal with them on a balanced basis of regular, gradual improvements, always with consideration of the public interest and of the economic and technological factors involved.

Fourth, government should study whether companies and industries can finance the improvements they are being required to make without prejudice to their financial security or their normal capital improvements, and consider whether assistance might be required.

Fifth, the Congress should be urged to support all of the President's environmental plans relating to other than the business areas, so that industry's progress will be matched by progress in municipal disposal and other nonindustrial pollution problems.

Observations

Let me add this set of simple observations before I finish.

First, none of the major problems we face can be resolved instantly. All of them are too complex. They call for long-range programs and careful consideration of priorities and financing.

Second, business alone cannot be held responsible for all of our pollution. The burdens of responsibility and cost must be shared by all levels of government, by agriculture and by the public.

And third, the technology we need in order to solve our problems must still be developed in many fields. We have a tremendous flow of uncoordinated, uncertain, imprecise data about the environment, and industry faces a severe shortage of environmental engineering specialists.

Fourth, we have to achieve greater conformity of state and local actions dealing with pollution control before we bog down the whole country in conflicting regulations and deadlines.

Mankind

Finally, we have to recognize that even our manmade problems, in some instances, are essential to satisfying human existence on this planet. After all, every new birth brings us instantly a new polluter. But even the most ardent of the environmentalists have yet to call for "no new starts" there.

Here again I suppose we could say, "Wait a Minute."

But what I am talking about is the necessity to recognize that the pollution problem exists in a real world, and it calls for balance and objectivity.

I can reduce it all to absurdity:

If we had no cars on the street, there would be no automobile pollution.

If we built no power plants, we would have no pollution from utilities. If we had no phosphate detergents, we would have no pollution of our waterways, and so on.

But what kind of country would we have left?

The line between that kind of nonsense and the kind of sense we need to resolve the problem requires a sense of reality in dealing with the economic and technological factors, and with the impatience of those who would like to clean up the country overnight.

Conclusion

The time has come to bring these things into focus and stop overheating the view that we are killing ourselves today.

Without pause or equivocation, we must continue to halt pollution of the world, but we must do it realistically, soundly.

I have support for this point of view from people like Dr. Philip Handler, President of the National Academy of Sciences, who just a few weeks ago said this: "My special plea is that we do not, out of a combination of emotional zeal and ecological ignorance, romanticizing about the 'good old days' that never were, hastily substitute environmental tragedy for existing environmental deterioration. Let's not replace known devils by insufficiently understood unknown devils."

So all we seek fundamentally in all these considerations is a balancing of values, a weighing of proper priorities, a measuring of the costs against benefits.

And, gentlemen, if we approach our problems in that spirit of balance and fairness, we can meet our ecological needs, clean up the country, and do so without undue economic risks for anyone, all within the framework of continued technological progress.

That is the way I think we ought to do it.

"*I keep hoping this is only a dream.*"

Superfru-ity*

J. M. SCOTT

Adam and Eve by God were deeded,
With all His creations that grew and seeded,
But the banishing apple with warning unheeded
Was simply one thing more than they needed.

* Used by permission.

Backswing Slows U.S. Cleanup*

PETER C. STUART

Economic feasibility (*e-ka-nóm-ik fe-ze-bíl-e-ti*) *n. Practicability as measured by the production, distribution, and consumption of wealth.*

This harmless-looking little phrase is fast invading the vocabularies of Washington environmental policymakers—as well as the laws and regulations they write for the United States.

Its little-noticed appearance could signal a not-so-subtle shift in the thrust of the federal antipollution drive: greater heed to economic repercussions, especially jobs and industrial costs.

Industrialists hail the new concept as a victory over "environmental extremism." But many environmentalists deplore it as "backlash."

Whatever the merits, congressional observers expect "economic feasibility" to leave a bold imprint on the environmental legislation of the soon-to-open 1972 session of Congress.

"The tone of Congress is changing," reports one of Capitol Hill's most savvy environmental aides. "It's swinging back toward the middle ground—from looking strictly at environmental aspects, to looking at economic aspects."

This backswing of the pendulum already seems visible:

• The sweeping clean-water bill which the House of Representatives will be asked to approve next month hedges on two major industrial cleanup goals, citing economic reasons.

The 1976 goal for installing "best practicable" control equipment would permit two-year postponements for hard-pressed polluters, and the 1981 goal for "best available" equipment would await a study by the National Academy of Sciences on economic (as well as technological and social) effects.

The House Public Works Committee added these qualifiers last month after the Senate enacted an undiluted version in November, 86 to 0, provoking anguished disapproval from the Nixon administration.

• The equally tough Clean Air Act of 1970 is being softened, on economic grounds, by federal regulators. Final guidelines caution states against cleanup plans that fail to promote, among other things, "productive capacity." They also require states to weigh "economic implications of, and alternatives to, emissions limitations."

Both provisions reportedly were added to the Environmental Protection Agency's original guidelines by other executive agencies sympathetic to White House efforts in Congress to weaken the legislation.

• The EPA—enforcer of antipollution rules which increasingly create economic hardship—is joining with the Labor Department in an "early warning system" to cushion environment-related factory shutdowns. The new program will identify trouble spots, then offer job training, relocation, and other assistance.

• The "changing tone" in Congress already has dimmed the future of a once-glowing environmental proposal: legislation granting citizens an almost unlimited right to press environmental lawsuits in the federal courts.

Committees in both houses held hearings last year. And Rep. John D. Dingell (D) of Michigan—chief advocate with Sen. Philip A. Hart (D) of Michigan and George McGovern (D) of South Dakota—heralded the proposal as "an idea whose time is here."

But today its moment may have passed, admit pessimistic supporters in both the Senate and House. "It may be a victim of the times," said one. "Our chances would have been better a year ago."

President Nixon, who opposes the citizen-suit legislation, argued the case for economic feasibility last August in submitting to Congress the second annual report of his Council on Environmental Quality:

"It is simplistic to seek ecological perfection at the cost of bankrupting the very taxpaying enterprises which must pay for the social advances the nation seeks."

The council then elaborated in a 54-page chapter on "the Economy and the Environment."

But this approach invites—and gets—charges of placing private economic protection above public environmental protection. Sen. Edmund S. Muskie (D) of Maine, chief author of both the clean-air and clean-water legislation, . . . seized the opportunity late last year:

"Special interests have been defeating the common interest in the decisions of the Nixon administration—and the first casualty of defeat is our environment."

Observers here, however, generally attribute the rise of economic feasibility to more than politics:

1. National economic doldrums—just punctuated by the announced shutdown of a 1,020-employee General Motors Corporation automobile tooling plant in Detroit, partially because of "emission standards as dictated by federal law."

2. Traditional ties between the business community and a Republican administration.

3. Natural readjustment after a spurt of ambitious environmental programs.

Marlette from *The Charlotte Observer*. © 1972. Reprinted by permission.

The Idiot King*

L. CLARK STEVENS

As linear organizations, giant corporations congeal like icebergs in the flow of America's energies. Their ability to harden the laws in their favor, much like an ice-jam, makes them the most serious of all impedances which obstruct the natural currents of change which ought to flow with freedom through the broad channels of the U.S. Constitution. These enormous bodies are not individuals, not citizens, and yet, with the advice and consent of their controlling stockholders (that tiny minority known as the "financial community"), these power structures control the jobs and control the laws and control the country. Their power is financial. And that power is unbridled. Moreover, there is no particular clique or cabal guiding this ponderous bulk. There is no leader or group of leaders with intelligent plans (other than to make more money). In supreme charge, there is a profit-and-loss sheet. Like an idiot king, this fiscal report is surrounded by clever advisors who prolong his power and keep their jobs by finding ways to fatten him until he is swollen. In the eyes of a skillful money-manager, military contracts, in general, provide profits, so war is not to be ruled out. Those who are financially astute well understand that the business which dares take the lead in cleaning up pollution commits fiscal suicide. Therefore, the realistic and

* Reprinted from *EST*. L. Clark Stevens. © The Capricorn Press. Used by permission.

skillful money-manager hides pollution as best he can and blames everyone else while being careful not to rock the financial boat as it sinks in a sea of waste. The Movement, with childlike awareness, has discovered that the idiot king is actually destroying the world and has begun to challenge his rule.

End of an Ideology*

<hr />

ANTHONY LEWIS

London, Feb. 13—There is very little panic in Britain as the coal strike gradually darkens the streets and stops industry for want of electric power. The well-known British phlegm in the face of crisis is admirable. But it cannot conceal the troubling questions that this strike poses for established political and economic ideas.

It is the first national coal strike since 1926—an ominous date. The miners then began what turned into the General Strike. That terrible struggle was a symptom of breakdown in the system: trade wars abroad and ignorant economic policies at home that led to depression and mass unemployment.

We believe that we have come a long way since 1926 in economic sophistication and in the diffusion of political power. We have, but the new coal strike in Britain may be a sign that again changes in the forces shaping society have outrun our thinking.

The first thing to recognize is that this is not a strike in the old sense at all—a test of strength between capital and labor. It is a struggle by one group in the community, the miners, for a larger share of the community pie.

The phenomenon is not new. We have realized in recent years that monopolistic industry simply passes on to the customer the price it pays to end a labor dispute. A fight between the automobile workers and General Motors is not about who gets what share of the industry's profits but about how much inflation will be exported to the community. The real interest at stake is the public's.

But the coal strike puts the issue with dramatic clarity. The industry is nationalized, and the governing board will give the miners whatever the Government allows. Everyone knows that the cost will immediately be passed on to the public, in higher prices for coal. That is why Prime Minister Heath spoke of the potential damage to the "silent pickets in our society"—the poor, the old and others on fixed incomes who would have to pay more for coal.

So far there has been remarkably little public resentment directed at the miners. Britons on the whole must sympathize with the miners, must feel that their unpleasant work and historical place in the wage structure entitle them to a big increase now.

The Government has resisted because it knows that the inflationary cost to the whole economy could be deadly. It is easy to say that the miners are a special case. But if they get the 25 per cent wage increase that they demand—and that they have refused even to negotiate—then the engineering and electric and transport workers will want the same. And they have lots of muscle, too.

The question is whether muscle is the right way to solve what are now so plainly seen to be issues of public policy, not isolated industrial disputes. If the problem is how to share the wealth of the community, then would it not be desirable for the community to decide in a deliberate way, by a political and administrative process?

The implications of the miners' strike are especially acute if we think of a future without the idea of economic growth. Until now we have told ourselves that we can keep on giving everyone larger slices of the economic pie because the pie as a whole will grow. That has allowed us to avoid the really hard questions of social justice.

But that illusion is coming to an early end. Politicians do not admit it yet, but someday soon people will be aware that the upward curve of production will have to be stopped if we want to avoid a natural calamity on earth. Human beings will still be able to yearn for more education, more leisure, more beauty—but not rationally for more things.

Seen in that light, the British coal strike is a foretaste of the difficult decisions required of a society without growth. How is it possible to determine whether a miner should earn more, in justice, than an electrician or a journalist? And who is to decide: a legislature, a court, an administrative czar?

If one makes the assumption of a growthless society, it is impossible to avoid the hard questions. For it would be intolerable then to let economic justice be based on the accident of a particular group's key place or willingness to use violent tactics. But the questions are here right now. In Britain, for example, there has not been and will not be enough economic growth to meet demands like the miners'.

Mr. Heath came to office in 1970 with a deep belief that economies worked better if as much as possible were left to individual decision. In a situation without limits, that would undoubtedly be more efficient. But there are limits—and more ahead—and they require social decisions.

The brief experience with President Nixon's attempt at public regulation of prices and wages shows how awkward the questions are. But it is better to try to develop techniques of handling them than to pretend they do not exist. And so this coal strike may be seen in history as a last example of the myth of private battle on public issues.

A Union View*

≈≈≈≈≈≈≈≈≈≈≈≈≈≈≈≈≈≈≈≈≈≈≈≈≈≈≈≈≈≈≈≈≈≈

An interview with HARRY BRIDGES

The ecology movement is obviously antiworker. First of all because it is a product of the ruling class. It recognizes no obligation to the worker, whose sole means of providing food and shelter for his family is his job. What is so wrong with wanting to keep a job?

But don't you recognize that there is a threat to an environment which will support human life—a threat posed by the processes of production?

All right. There are problems with the environment, but most are inevitably a by-product of civilization. Smog, for instance, might be detrimental to health; the way to eliminate smog is to stop burning. If we do that, then what is left?

What about the emission of poisons and noxious wastes into streams and lakes? Isn't this something that concerns your membership when they want to take a vacation?

OK. Certain ordinary sanitary precautions should be required—I don't see that it is such a big deal.

There are simply more pressing problems in this world and in the trade union movement. There is war, racism and poverty. The possibility of some future environmental catastrophe is a very puny consideration to a man who is hungry—who is out of work, or being shot at in Vietnam.

* Taken from *Clear Creek,* May 1971. Reprinted by permission.

For the trade unions, the present immediate problem is fighting to keep jobs which pay enough for a man to feed his family, pay the rent and send his kids to school. And to achieve this, there is the problem of in some way uniting the American trade union movement.

Do you see any grounds for the trade unions to participate in the ecology movement?

It may or may not be part of my duty as a trade union officer to analyze what the environmentalists are saying and to try to come up with a program. Right now, I don't feel compelled to do so because of the enormity of what I see as more immediate problems.

Are Ecologists Antiworker?*

BYRON E. CALAME

Fishing on Wisconsin's scenic Flambeau River has become more than a pastime for members of Local 119 of the Pulp, Sulphite and Paper Mill Workers Union in Park Falls, Wis.

They're fishing to help save their jobs.

The state is pressing their employer, the Flambeau Paper Co., to clean up wastes the mill dumps into the river. The local's 170 members, aiming to show that the wastes aren't hurting fish life, are reeling in some handsome catches. Then local President Lawrence Drexler, armed with pictures of their hauls and with signed reports on fishing conditions, goes before state officials to seek more time for the mill to comply with waste-treatment standards. Thus the local hopes to avoid a partial shutdown that would wipe out about 100 jobs.

"The fishing is excellent," insists the 48-year-old Mr. Drexler, who has been fishing on the river since he was eight years old. "It's just never been better."

While Local 119's efforts have failed so far to win any additional time, its campaign is a prime example of an "environmental backlash" that's spreading through organized labor, particularly at the grass-

* Original title: "Changing Times—Fearing Loss of Jobs, Unions Battle Efforts to Clean Environment." Reprinted from *Wall Street Journal*, November 19, 1971. Used by permission.

roots level. Notwithstanding most national unions' official calls for
protecting both the environment and employment, more and more
local leaders across the counry are teaming up with corporate management against conservationists and pollution-control authorities.
The labor leaders' aim: to preserve union members' jobs.

Some examples:

A United Steelworkers local in El Paso lobbied hard and successfully in the city council recently to help an American Smelting & Refining Co. plant obtain more time in which to bring its air-cleanup
equipment up to par; many of the plant's 1,000 employees faced possible layoffs.

Representatives of the Teamsters Union, Glass Bottle Blowers
Association and Steelworkers helped in September to stymie efforts
by New Jersey legislators to impose restrictions on nonreturnable
containers; there were warnings that up to 30,000 jobs were threatened.

Local 1 of the United Papermakers and Paperworkers in Holyoke,
Mass., has replaced its customary fall job-safety campaign with a
drive "to save jobs by halting the ecology steamroller." Union officials contend a local paper company had to abolish more than 150
jobs this year because of the "excessive cost of a pollution-control
system."

And building-trades union officials seeking a resumption of work
on the cross-Florida barge canal hope to make President Nixon's
decision to halt the construction an issue in next year's elections; more
than 300 hardhats have been thrown out of work.

"Sir, This Must Be Avoided!"

"Why pick on the poor workingman?" demands Robert Dalton, a
Baltimore Steelworkers member and Maryland state senator who
opposes restrictions on throwaway beverage containers. A regional
steel-union official toiling for the same cause declares, "Hysteria is
no substitute for bread and butter." A Maine labor representative
arguing for a new oil refinery along the state's picturesque coast
maintains, "We can't trade off the welfare of human beings for the
sake of scenery."

Union leaders at upper levels are also becoming more keenly aware
of the environment-vs.-jobs dilemma facing labor. Though American
workers are exposed even more than most citizens to industrial pollution, United Auto Workers President Leonard Woodcock recently
told a congressional subcommittee that "their economic circum-

stances require them to think first of jobs, paychecks and bread on the table."

In a recent letter to President Nixon, Joseph Tonelli, national head of the pulp and paper union, urged the government to avoid imposing "do-it-now demands" on the paper industry because "the cost . . . will be too heavy a burden for management to bear." If mills have to close, he added, "I predict there will be poverty, sick men and women, mentally and physically. Sir, this must be avoided! This is not good for America! This is not good for our organization!"

Environmental-cleanup advocates concede they're worried about the union backlash. "It will be a real tragedy if labor falls for this line that controlling pollution destroys jobs," frets a Washington official of Friends of the Earth, a conservation organization. "The union people have got to realize it's their world, too."

"A Gut Issue"

But even A. F. Grospiron, president of the Oil, Chemical and Atomic Workers, which has taken a tougher antipollution stand than most unions, warns: "We will oppose those theoretical environmentalists who would make air and water pure without regard to whether or not people have food on their tables." The ecology movement is "obviously antiworker," says Harry Bridges, the leader of the International Longshoremen's and Warehousemen's Union, because it "is a product of the ruling class."

Management is clearly aware of the advantages of nurturing ties with labor on the environmental issue. At Flambeau Paper, a division of the Kansas City Star Co., Vice President Walter Sherman has warm praise for the "very beneficial" support of Local 119. "One of the things industry and labor have to do is get together to protect ourselves from these ecology groups that have one-track minds," asserts Mr. Sherman. "If we really get together, we can back these people down a little bit. This is the only hope: to have [union members'] votes on our side."

A company warning that a pollution-control edict may cause layoffs is frequently all it takes to stir rank-and-filers into action. When American Smelting & Refining appealed to the Texas Air Control Board this summer for more time to comply with a 1969 abatement order affecting its El Paso plant, company officials indicated layoffs might be necessary if the extension weren't granted. For the 760 members of Local 509 of the United Steelworkers, the board's order quickly became a "gut issue," says Alfredo Montoya, an international staff representative. "I'll be darned if we were going to permit a plant with 1,000 workers to be shut down," he declares.

At an August hearing, an estimated 400 members of Local 509 jammed into an auditorium along with 200 other citizens to hear Mr. Montoya support the company's request for an extension. His message: "You have to have a reasonable, rational approach to stopping pollution; you can't just wave a wand." And since the state board gives considerable weight to the views of city officials, explains Mr. Montoya, Local 509 "used whatever bit of influence we had in the community . . . to convince all four El Paso aldermen to vote in favor of the variance." The result: American Smelting got the extension late in September.

Among the many environmental measures now being pushed, efforts to discourage use of disposable cans and bottles have sparked especially bitter union opposition—at both national and local levels. On this issue, AFL-CIO President George Meany himself has spoken out. "It's easy to point the finger—to call for banning returnable bottles," he told a labor-management group in the beverage industry earlier this year. "It's easy, but not right. It is not right because that's a program for banning jobs, not eliminating litter."

Sharing these sentiments, the New Jersey AFL-CIO joined with the Teamsters, Glass Bottle Blowers and Steelworkers in September to block a proposed bill in the state legislature that would have required stores to collect a five-cent deposit on all beverage containers. After labor lobbyists complained that such a bill could wipe out up to 30,000 Jersey jobs by discouraging sale of nonreturnables, two of the measure's 12 sponsors withdrew their support. Union officials claim the bill now is dead.

And in the Maryland legislature last spring, Steelworkers officials led the lobbying drive that defeated a bill requiring a nickel deposit on all beverage containers. With rank-and-file Steelworkers filling almost half the gallery as the Senate debated the bill, Sen. Dalton drew their applause as he declaimed: "I'm going to stand up today not as a Senator but as a Steelworker. Don't let anybody kid you; this will affect jobs."

But the unions aren't winning every skirmish. Despite union petitions and testimony opposing the measure, the Oregon legislature last June enacted a law requiring five-cent deposits on nonreturnable beverage containers. Labor leaders, who claim the law will wipe out 300 to 500 jobs after it takes effect in October 1972, vow that the defeat will spur union members' activity in next year's state elections.

Says Gordon Bronk, president of Local 112 of the Glass Bottle Blowers in Portland: "We know who voted which way, and we'll remember next fall."

In Florida, building-trades leaders are looking for ways to make Mr. Nixon's canal-halting order an issue in the Democratic presidential primary next March. They hope to get some of the contenders to take their side and support resumption of construction. In any event, Florida labor plans to hammer on the canal issue in state races next year. "We are certainly going to make clear who our friends are," a union strategist says.

Environmental groups' resistance to new industrial plants that are potential sources of pollution has spurred angry reaction from labor in some areas. Thus the Maine State Federated Labor Council has struggled, so far unsuccessfully, to overcome ecologists' objections to proposals for new coastal oil refinery complexes that it says would provide hundreds of jobs.

"We must protect our environment, but we must also provide for the well-being of our people," an official of the labor council told a visiting U.S. Senate subcommittee last fall.

But most union men are more concerned with possible job losses at existing plants. Even the UAW, traditionally tough-minded on pollution issues, has sought to soften the effects on auto makers of government efforts to clean up exhaust emissions. In a letter to Attorney General John Mitchell last May, Mr. Woodcock suggested a waiver of antitrust laws to let manufacturers share their technology related to both pollution and auto safety.

The ultimate solution to the jobs-vs.-environment problem, labor contends, is financial protection for workers. Testifying before a Senate subcommittee last May, Mr. Woodcock and other labor leaders called for special aid by employers and the government to workers who lose their jobs because of pollution-cleanup orders.

Some environmentalists suggest that a coordinated drive for such legislation could be the starting point for a rapprochement between ecology and labor groups. Efforts are under way, says an official of Friends of the Earth, to open a joint drive for new laws that, as he puts it, would "help call the bluff on business."

This reflects a view that many company threats about layoffs and plant closings amount to "environmental blackmail." An oft-cited example involves a Marietta, Ohio, plant of Union Carbide Corp. Last January, the company announced it could comply with federal air-pollution standards only by laying off 625 workers. But the Oil,

Chemical and Atomic Workers Union, which represents the plant's workers, refused to join the company in pressuring the government to relax its order. Several ecology groups blasted the company's position.

The upshot: Union Carbide retreated and announced it was exploring ways to avoid any significant layoffs while complying with the order. "The company wouldn't have backed down," concludes Anthony Mazzocchi, the union's legislative director, "if labor and the environmental groups hadn't been united."

GENTLEMEN, IT'S TIME WE AT **CONSOLIDATED POLLUTION** GOT OFF THE DEFENSIVE AND GAVE THE PUBLIC THE **POSITIVE** SIDE OF THE AIR AND WATER POLLUTION STORY.

CLAP CLAP CLAP CLAP CLAP CLAP

THE TRUE FACT, GENTLEMEN, IS THAT **MORE POLLUTION** EQUALS **MORE INDUSTRY** AND **MORE INDUSTRY** EQUALS **GREATER GROWTH!** IT'S ALL DOWN HERE IN BLACK AND GRAY IN OUR PUBLIC SERVICE BOOKLET, "POLLUTION: HAND MAIDEN TO AFFLUENCE."

CLAP CLAP CLAP CLAPCOUGH

GENTLEMEN, YOU SHOW ME A COUNTRY THAT DOESN'T POISON ITS RESOURCES AND I'LL SHOW YOU A **HAVE-NOT NATION!** THE **AMERICAN** ANSWER TO POLLUTION IS NOT TO **RUN AWAY** FROM IT, BUT TO **INVEST** IN IT! MAY I HAVE THE MODEL, PLEASE —

10-3   © 1965 JULES FEIFFER

GENTLEMEN, ON MY HEAD IS THE LIGHT-WEIGHT, EFFICIENT "**CLEAN BREATHER**" FROM OUR NEW LINE OF **PERSONALIZED** AIR AND **WATER** CONDITIONERS!

WOW! CLAP CLAP CLAP CLAP COUGH COUGH

FROM THE WAY THINGS ARE GOING WE AT **CON POL** HAVE **HIGH** HOPES OF THIS ITEM SOON BECOMING A **MUST** FOR EVERY MAN, WOMAN AND CHILD IN THE COUNTRY!!

HOORAY! COUGH CLAP COUGH CLAP COUGH COUGH

"POLLUTE WE MUST FOR A BETTER AMERICA."

The Hall Syndicate, Inc.

COUGH COUGH COUGH COUGH COUGH COUGH COUGH COUGH COUGH COUGH

Utilities Throughout Nation Grapple
with "Siting Problem"*

"Don't put it here!"

That cry is being heard in many parts of the nation today. It is directed at many types of industries, including the utility industry.

Included in the sweeping admonition are overhead power lines, electrical substations and, of course, power plants.

There was a time when the public was unconcerned about where a utility company put its facilities. In fact, a parade of power towers meant progress and improved living standards. And taxpayers and taxing agencies welcomed with real enthusiasm the added tax base to schools and local government which the facilities represented.

But now things are vastly different. Americans now realize that geographic frontiers are gone and that they must live with what they see, smell, breathe and drink—wherever they are. They are worried about their environment—recalling how things were in "the good old days"—and appear to be resentful about physical reminders of their dependence on industrial productivity.

Running parallel to these concerns is the assumption that they can be cured—instantaneously—while at the sime time preserving all of the conveniences that the Electrical Age has made possible.

* Reprinted courtesy of Southern California Edison Company.

"If we can land a man on the moon," so goes the argument, "why can't we cure the earthly ills of so-called eyesores and pollution?"

The question seems reasonable enough. But the answer is far from simple.

California Congressman Chet Holifield (D, 19th District) recently put the situation into perspective with a statement from the Joint Committee on Atomic Energy, which he serves as chairman. One portion of the statement says:

". . . It seems that what should be a genuine, legitimate, and quite understandable concern about the effects on the environment of large power plants has been transformed in many instances into an insistence on pristine purity that will brook no balancing of the worthwhile but somewhat competing values; namely, the goal of clean air and water and natural beauty, on the one hand, and the objective of abundant, economical, and reliable electric power on the other. Neither of these goals can be achieved without some impact on the other. The task confronting the responsible and the informed is to harmonize these contending goals. . . ."

The committee report also sounded this warning:

". . . Unless the demands for clean air and clean water are kept in perspective—that is, unless there is a reasonable and fruitful union between industry and the environment—the antitechnologists and single-minded environmentalists may find themselves conducting their work by the light of a flickering candle. . . ."

Southern California Edison Company joins Congressman Holifield in hoping this extreme never will be reached. But the California utility is uneasily aware that something akin to this has been occurring elsewhere in the nation.

T. M. McDaniel, Jr., Edison's president, points out that several power "brownouts" were experienced in the East this past summer. Because of power shortages, customers of one utility company were asked to turn off their air conditioners. They were urged to use as little electricity as possible.

"To a large degree, these 'brownouts' occurred because the local electric company in that region has been hampered and delayed from building needed electrical facilities," say McDaniel. "Different groups of citizens have succeeded in blocking first one, then another of the power projects proposed by this utility."

SCE is currently suffering the same type of back-and-forth buffeting, the company president reveals. Groups of people in a coastal region close to the utility's growing load center say, in effect: "We don't want your plant here; why don't you put it out in the desert?" Desert dwellers, on the other hand, complain that much of the power from the new plant is not really needed where they live and is destined, instead, for people in the urban centers. So why, they ask, should they put up with the threatened air pollution?

The company taps remote power sources as much as possible, but runs into opposition not only from some people at these distant points, but also from many living along the routes of the transmission lines required to bring the remotely produced power to Southern California.

The same is true with substations. These are the facilities where transformers and switching equipment reduce or increase voltages and route the power toward the eventual consumer. Hardly anyone wants one in his neighborhood.

And so it goes. . . .

This is all part of what has become known as "the plant siting problem." Certainly, it is the most challenging—and frustrating— problem electric utility people have had to face for decades.

The problem has grim overtones because, even though these different types of facilities have become increasingly unpopular to the public, more and more of them are needed to meet the mounting requirements for electric power. Southern California's energy requirements are growing at a faster rate than those of most other regions of the United States. Electrical peak demand on the Edison system is doubling about every eight years, as contrasted to about every 10 years for the nation as a whole. The average family served by Edison is using twice as much electricity today as it did 10 years ago.

So, what are utilities, such as Edison, doing about this dilemma?

Many things, according to McDaniel. For instance, he says, special care is now taken to design every new substation to blend in with its surroundings. One of the company's ultra-modern substations in Orange County reflects the new "low-profile" look and won praise from the City Beautification Committee where it is located. Edison also is taking steps to improve the appearance of some of its older substations, he reports.

On another esthetics front, Edison is making significant progress in the undergrounding of distribution power lines. More than 850 circuit miles of lower-voltage distribution lines were either installed underground or converted from overhead during 1968, the company president points out. And approximately $40 million is being spent on undergrounding this year.

Burying higher-voltage transmission lines is another story, however, he cautions. Despite extensive research being conducted by the company and the industry, it is still considered economically and technically infeasible to place big transmission lines below ground-level, except for extremely short distances

But the Edison Company is doing a lot to beautify certain transmission facilities which must necessarily remain visible to the public. Power poles featuring the more attractive "Sunburst" design have been installed at a number of locations in Southern California, and in some areas the new award-winning Dreyfuss-designed transmission structure is now being premiered.

While generating stations rarely win beauty contests, the principal public criticism of them relates to fears about air pollution. McDaniel feels these concerns are largely based on misunderstandings, because Edison power plants contribute less than one percent of the total pollutants in the Los Angeles Basin.

Although this low percentage of all contaminants is documented by air pollution control authorities, some people are openly skeptical of it. They have been led to believe that the over-all role of power plants in air pollution is considerably larger.

This misconception stems, according to McDaniel, from the current furore over oxides of nitrogen emissions. It is but one of the contaminants that make up the "less than one percent" figure chargeable to power plants, he notes.

While this particular pollutant has just recently been "discovered" by many people, it is one which the Edison Company has been making substantial progress in controlling for more than a decade, McDaniel points out. The company's early pioneering work in the NO_x field dates back to 1957 and led to the development of the "two-stage" combustion technique which substantially reduced nitrogen oxide emissions.

Edison's research efforts have been redoubled in the past year, and it is estimated that the present figure of approximately 14 percent of NO_x emissions chargeable to all Edison power plants in the basin will soon be reduced by one-third or even a half, the company executive predicts.

At Huntington Beach, for example, the new units—although nearly tripling the plant's existing capacity—will be designed and operated in a manner which will reduce over-all NO_x emissions by 40 percent over the lifetime of the plant, he says.

There have been many other aspects to Edison's air pollution control program, and direct research costs to date exceed $7 million, McDaniel says. However, this figure does not include many other costs, such as consulting fees and the price of more expensive fuels, which are keyed to the company's over-all air quality program. The utility waged a 10-year campaign to secure more supplies of natural gas, for example, and recently made modifications at many of its generating plants to accommodate the new low-sulfur, low-ash Indonesian fuel oil. Use of this imported oil, incidentally, has virtually eliminated the problems of particulate matter and oxides of sulfur from power plant operations, he notes, adding that Edison was the first utility in the state and one of the first in the nation to use the smog-fighting fuel.

To a lesser degree, some people have expressed concern about the ocean water which is used to cool the condensers at coastal generating stations. A rather scary term—"thermal pollution"—has been used to dramatize this concern, although temporarily warming a relatively tiny bit of the vast ocean by a few degrees in the immediate area of the plant outflow pipes can hardly be compared with industrially ravaged Lake Erie, McDaniel says.

Actually, the brief temperature rise is dissipated rapidly, he says, and the only effect that Edison people have ever been able to discern from "borrowing" the sea water is that it appears to improve fishing. Recreational anglers and commercial fishing boats often flock around Edison plant outflows to round out their catches.

All of Edison's esthetics and environmental quality efforts add up to a sincere desire by the company to be a good corporate citizen in the many communities it serves, according to McDaniel.

He warns, however, that all of these efforts also have an impact on costs, and these additional costs have to be passed along to the company's customers.

McDaniel looks for the day when people, mindful of their insatiable appetites for electric power and aware of Edison's beautification and control programs, will cooperate with the company in working out acceptable solutions to the plant siting dilemma and the utility's obligation to provide dependable electric service.

The Walrus and the Carpenter*

LEWIS CARROLL

"The sun was shining on the sea,
    Shining with all his might:
He did his very best to make
    The billows smooth and bright—
And this was odd, because it was
    The middle of the night.

"The moon was shining sulkily,
    Because she thought the sun
Had got no business to be there
    After the day was done—
'It's very rude of him,' she said,
    'To come and spoil the fun!'

"The sea was wet as wet could be,
    The sands were dry as dry.
You could not see a cloud because
    No cloud was in the sky:
No birds were flying overhead—
    There were no birds to fly.

"The Walrus and the Carpenter
    Were walking close at hand:

* Reprinted from *Through the Looking-Glass.*

They wept like anything to see
    Such quantities of sand:
'If this were only cleared away,'
    They said, 'it *would* be grand!'

" 'If seven maids with seven mops
    Swept it for half a year,
  Do you suppose,' the Walrus said,
    'That they could get it clear?'
'I doubt it,' said the Carpenter,
    And shed a bitter tear.

" 'O Oysters, come and walk with us!'
    The Walrus did beseech.
'A pleasant walk, a pleasant talk,
    Along the briny beach:
We cannot do with more than four,
    To give a hand to each.'

"The eldest Oyster looked at him,
    But never a word he said:
The eldest Oyster winked his eye,
    And shook his heavy head—
Meaning to say he did not choose
    To leave the oyster-bed.

"But four young Oysters hurried up,
    All eager for the treat:
Their coats were brushed, their faces washed,
    Their shoes were clean and neat—
And this was odd, because, you know,
    They hadn't any feet.

"Four other Oysters followed them,
    And yet another four;
And thick and fast they came at last,
    And more, and more, and more—
All hopping through the frothy waves,
    And scrambling to the shore.

"The Walrus and the Carpenter
    Walked on a mile or so,
And then they rested on a rock
    Conveniently low:

And all the little Oysters stood
   And waited in a row.

" 'The time has come,' the Walrus said,
   'To talk of many things:
Of shoes—and ships—and sealing-wax—
   Of cabbages—and kings—
And why the sea is boiling hot—
   And whether pigs have wings.'

" 'But wait a bit,' the Oysters cried,
   'Before we have our chat;
For some of us are out of breath,
   And all of us are fat!'
'No hurry!' said the Carpenter.
   They thanked him much for that.

" 'A loaf of bread,' the Walrus said,
   'Is what we chiefly need:
Pepper and vinegar besides
   Are very good indeed—
Now, if you're ready, Oysters dear,
   We can begin to feed.'

" 'But not on us!' the Oysters cried,
   Turning a little blue.
'After such kindness, that would be
   A dismal thing to do!'
'The night is fine,' the Walrus said.
   'Do you admire the view?

" 'It was so kind of you to come!
   And you are very nice!'
The Carpenter said nothing but
   'Cut us another slice.
I wish you were not quite so deaf—
   I've had to ask you twice!'

" 'It seems a shame,' the Walrus said,
   'To play them such a trick.
After we've brought them out so far,
   And made them trot so quick!'
The Carpenter said nothing but
   'The butter's spread too thick!'

" 'I weep for you,' the Walrus said:
    'I deeply sympathize.'
With sobs and tears he sorted out
    Those of the largest size,
Holding his pocket-handkerchief
    Before his streaming eyes.

" 'O Oysters,' said the Carpenter,
    'You've had a pleasant run!
Shall we be trotting home again?'
    But answer came there none —
And this was scarcely odd, because
    They'd eaten every one."

The next piece is taken from a volume which is assumed to be written in 1994. It reflects the experience of a young girl, Teg, who goes round the world in this year to discover the events which developed between the mid-sixties and the year 1994. In this selection, Yvonne invites D, her teacher, to "lecture" on the process by which we moved out of an emphasis on economics to an understanding of ecological relationships.

Economics and Ecology in 1994*

ROBERT THEOBALD AND J. M. SCOTT

I'm delighted you could all come this evening for my third rites-de-passage. As you can already see, this evening's celebration will start with something you have not experienced before. D is going to give a "lecture" in the style and manner he would have used in 1966, the year I was born.

He has asked that you keep several things in mind as he speaks. First, he gave his last lecture in 1975: this was the final time he was unable to insist on a more useful framework for interaction. Second, he will be speaking as an "economist" because economist/ecologists did not exist in 1966. There were then two main schools of economy: Neo-Keynesian economists who believed in the perennial necessity for economic growth, and classical economists who also wanted economic growth, but who believed that fiscal balance was even more important. Third, D will talk as though he were in front of a North American audience because he spent most of his time there during the sixties. Fourth, he will give his lecture as if he were looking forward from the mid-sixties and forecasting future events.

D: Good evening, ladies and gentlemen. I have chosen to address you this evening on the subject of the change in economic thinking

* Reprinted from *Teg's 1994*. © 1972. Swallow Press. Used by permission.

49

and economic trends which I believe will take place over the next ten years. Predictions are, of course, dangerous, but it is necessary that we take risks occasionally if we are to get any view of the future.

My analysis starts from the assumption of John Maynard Keynes, the great British economist whose work has been adapted by the "growth" school. He stated that the condition in which his grand-children (my children) will live must necessarily be profoundly different from those which existed in the 1930's, at the time he was writing. I fear that the predictions I shall make will seem unbeliev-able to many of you, for they suggest that conditions will change fundamentally before the end of the century. I am aware that this contradicts the views of most of those who are now coming to be called "Futurists"; they normally seem to assume that, while there will be very significant increases in technical competence, socio-economic conditions will not be profoundly affected.

I could spend all my allotted twenty minutes stating the reasons why I am convinced that we must expect basic change in socio-economic conditions. Time pressure forces me to move on as rap-idly as possible and I shall therefore begin my analysis with the views of the British physicist, Dennis Gabor:

> In today's world all curves are exponential. It is only in mathe-matics that curves grow to infinity. In the real world, they either saturate gently or they break down catastrophically. It is our duty as thinking men to strive toward a gentle saturation, although this poses new and very distasteful problems.

This insight of Gabor's has been confirmed by Irving Kaplan, an American consulting psychologist, who has stated that, given the accelerating rate of change, there are only three alternatives for the future:

> First, that the rate of progress in the technological world of the near future is beyond the comprehension of minds using the con-temporary frame of reference. . . . second, a deceleration of technological progress, which could be due either to the exhaus-tion of technological potential or to the attainment of such a high level of technology that the culture would be saturated with the technological product and the society would shift its values. . . . the third alternative would be for the curve of progress to end or to fall precipitously. This could only indicate a catastrophic event such as a disease epidemic of tremendous proportions, a rain of

meteorites, or a war of sufficient destructive force to destroy the nation's or the world's industry and technology.

I support Kaplan's view that we are limited to these three alternatives. I believe that we can already perceive that neither the first nor the third alternative can be a possible route into the future. I would hope that we all agree that we must avoid the third alternative, for it would destroy all the potentials we have so arduously built. The first must also be avoided because it is clear that the human psyche cannot keep up with the present rate of progress in the technological world, let alone the rate inevitable in the future, if trends continue to develop.

Problems

Societies will only perceive the need for a slowing-down of technological change if their value systems have already changed fundamentally. The arguments of the neo-Keynesians, who assume that wants can never be satiated and that continuous "growth" in production, achieved through increasing productive efficiency, is therefore always valuable, can already be shown to be ill-founded. Psychologists are now telling us that sensory overload is as damaging to the human psyche as privation. People will therefore inevitably come to see consumption as a *means* to the good life and not as the *good life itself*. The result will be a consumers' revolt in the seventies; people will come to limit their possessions to what they really need. The consumers' revolt will be paralleled by changes in production techniques resulting from the cybernation revolution whose real implications were stated so clearly in the 1964 document of the Ad Hoc Committee on the Triple Revolution. With the implementation of these techniques, cybernated machine systems could take over large parts of production.

But the effects of cybernation are still being masked today. There is a continuing *decline* in unemployment rates at the present time. However, this is due to four temporary effects: first, the Vietnam war; second, the continuing extraordinary inefficiency with which new computer techniques are being used; third, the willingness to retain and hire people who are not truly necessary to the functioning of organizations. The fourth factor, which will become of increasing importance, is associated with the third. More and more people will prevent the effective functioning of machinery and machine-systems in order to try to preserve their jobs. By the beginning of the seventies, this movement will have grown to the point where it will be seen as a neo-Luddite revolt.

In the early seventies, there will be a general atmosphere of pressure tactics, disruption, and destruction. Neo-Luddite sabotage will reach epidemic proportions. It will take the form of direct destruction, the calling of strikes to prevent full utilization of equipment, etc. For a considerable period of years, the technological infrastructure of the society will function extremely inefficiently; in fact, there will be several periods when it will seem as though even minimal services cannot be maintained. (The beginnings of this development will be obvious in the big cities even before the end of the sixties: the productivity of the most creative members of the society will be drastically reduced as they try to obtain security and minimal comfort for themselves and their families.)

Neo-Keynesian economists will, of course, fail to understand the significance of these developments and will respond by attempting to keep the economy "growing" as rapidly as possible, thus overstraining the already malfunctioning infrastructure still further. They will point to their successes, however limited, in absorbing the unemployed as evidence that there is no need for real change. Their "growth" policies will prevent the bankruptcy of marketives and other organizations which no longer have real value to the socioeconomy; these will continue to employ those types of people, and to use those resources, most needed elsewhere to strengthen the infrastructure.

Neo-Keynesian economists will fortunately be increasingly kept in check in the early seventies by conservative economists who are more concerned with "fiscal balance" than with "growth." By the mid-seventies, the neo-Keynesian preoccupation with "growth" will be modified by public concern over the resulting pollution and a growing understanding of the meaning of ecological systems. This latter development will result, in particular, from the fact that we will understand that all production *necessarily* results in a larger amount of final waste and that growth in production systems must be accompanied by growth in recycling systems. In effect, the traditional economist's shorthand for the function of the economic system— PRODUCTION/DISTRIBUTION/CONSUMPTION—will have a fourth term added, RESOURCE RECONSTRUCTION. Thus, economists will become economist/ecologists.

The events of the late sixties and seventies which I have just described from the economist's point of view can also be summarized in socio-political terms: First, the continued, deliberate policy of overstraining both national economies and international exchange systems will cause growing instability, with constant devaluations and an emerging trend toward protectionism in international trade policies and consequent international tensions. Second, public indignation at the attempt to preserve artificial scarcity by restrictive and disruptive practices in education, communication, transportation, construction, medicine, etc., will be reflected at the polls. Politicians will be forced to respond. Third, there will be a challenge to existing patterns of income distribution. This will start with complaints about the injustice of the relative tax load. However, as an understanding of the principle of artificial scarcity spreads, there will be governmental attempts to limit the wages, salaries, and incomes of those in the medical profession, the construction unions, and others who appear to the public to have taken unfair advantage of their power.

It also seems very possible that a fourth element may develop: legislation abolishing common stocks will be passed following the recognition that stock speculation is merely a *respectable* form of gambling.

In order to emerge from this multi-crisis, triggered by piecemeal governmental intervention, we shall have to change completely our understanding of the way the economic system works. We shall have to perceive that so long as the preservation of artificial scarcity is permitted, patterns of income distribution do not depend on the value of contributions to production but rather on the power each group has been given or has seized.

When we come to understand that, given the changes in the socio-economic system over the past half-century, the value of a person's contribution is not presently measured by his wages or salary, the first practical results will be the introduction of new forms of income distribution.

I foresee the need for two steps. The first is to provide everybody with a constitutionally guaranteed, basic income regardless of the activity he engages in. It has been proposed that this should be called Basic Economic Security. I also see a transitional need to provide new forms of income maintenance for those who presently have higher levels of income, but who will inevitably lose their jobs to machines and machine-systems in the seventies; this proposal is usually called Committed Spending. This is necessary so that the individual can meet the financial obligations to which he is already committed. It is also necessary because the totality of these payments has been anticipated in long-term economic planning, and a sudden cessation of payments would disturb national and even international economics.

Yvonne, ladies and gentlemen, I must end here, for my crystal ball would have seen no further. Indeed, I may already have shown more prescience than was available to me in 1966. Perhaps I should remind you that you may "clap" at this point, if you want this speech to have the proper period flavor. I should add that even by 1966 I'd got rid of *that* particular pattern, which aimed, in part, to permit the audience to feel that it had made its contribution and therefore had a "right" to forget what had been said and also to reassure the lecturer that his audience had not been totally asleep.

Certainly, none of D's audience had been asleep. When Yvonne announced a question period, explaining that this was the normal custom of the time, the only question was why didn't D continue: the lecture had been all too brief. D explained that in 1966 he wasn't anticipating beyond the mid-seventies, and he felt his lecture should not do so either. He said that he'd give us a very brief description of the events which actually followed the introduction of Basic Economic Security and Committed Spending and then describe the roles which economist/ecologists tried to fulfill at the present time, if we were really interested, but that he'd have to continue from the point of view of 1994. Everybody wanted to hear more, so D continued.

D: New forms of income distribution did, in fact, develop during the seventies. They were not what I had ideally hoped to see, because a constitutional guarantee of rights to Basic Economic Security and Committed Spending was never passed. But the degree of flexibility introduced into the socio-economy was sufficient to ensure two significant changes: one synergetic and the other entropic.

The synergy occurred because, although most people still performed their work as structured jobs in marketives, others joined together in consentives in order to create a more supportive environment for their work (which was useful to the society but which was not "profitable" for marketives). At the same time, a limited entropic change took place as consentives were also founded by creative and imaginative people who left key jobs in marketives and other organizations which were without real value to the socio-economy. Their departure destroyed the viability of many of these organizations. The fact that these organizations had ceased to produce was not detrimental to society, as some of their activities did not meet any real needs, but their bankruptcy contributed to the socio-economic and political collapse of the mid-seventies. This was the time of the "entropic-seventies," of the Republican and Democratic realignments, of the creation of the Planning Party, and also the time when the ABC was putting its strongest pressure on bureaucracies.

It was precisely those bureaucratically-structured organizations, which had been used to convince the population that they should buy products that they did not need and should enjoy situations which were actually intolerable, which collapsed. After their collapse, the reality of the seventies entropy became manifest to a growing part of the population. I personally believe that this factor played a larger role in the replacement of the concept of *anomie* by the concept of *amondie* than is generally agreed. People really became aware that their society was in breakdown, and that socio-economic and cultural confusion was worldwide. Nevertheless, the limited entropy of superfluous marketive and organization collapse was, of course, necessary and permitted the larger synergy of the seventies to take place.

I must add a parenthesis here. We are still not clear about the methods we can use to determine which local entropies are essential to larger synergies and which can be avoided without damaging larger synergies. This is probably the most critical theoretical issue confronting the Ecology/Economy P/P Institute at the present time.

By the beginning of the eighties, the economic situation was changing rapidly. The 1979 Scientists Synergy had reinforced concerns about limiting waste of materials and the time of creative people with vital skills and had also led to the end of the neo-Luddite revolt. The consumers' revolt of the seventies had helped people to perceive that the good life could not be achieved on the basis of an "ever-higher standard of living." The abolition of common stocks in 1980 made managers of marketives responsible to the society and not the stockholder.

Many personal and societal needs were being satisfied by the development of consentives. The goods and services produced by the consentives came to be known as sociofacts. As superfluous marketives had disappeared, those marketives which continued their activities were necessary to the socio-economy. Their level of activity was increasingly regulated by demand, according to "classical" economic principles. The goods and services produced by marketives came to be called ecofacts because they were sold on the open market with the price rising and falling according to the relation of demand to supply.

At the beginning of the eighties, economist/ecologists were acting as ecology facilitators. They were using a new shorthand to describe the systems with which they were concerned: RESOURCE CONSTRUCTION/PRODUCTION/USE. It was partly the clarity which resulted from this new analytical framework which helped us to understand that by 1985 ecofact-production in North America was already fully sufficient to meet auto-estimated needs for ecofacts. Continuance of money as a rationing (or priority) mechanism was therefore no longer necessary. Today, as you know, North America, Australia, Japan, and almost all of Europe are abundance-regions and are committed to providing as many ecofacts to the scarcity-regions as can be absorbed without damage to their culture. This does not strain current productive potential in the abundance regions.

The main roles of the economist/ecologist in the abundance-regions presently are:

First, to ensure that auto-estimated personal needs for ecofacts and community ecofact needs throughout abundance-regions are available in the necessary quantities *without* forcing people into activities which they do not enjoy.

Second, to minimize use of materials which are in limited supply and which cannot presently be reconstructed by recycling or other measures. Despite the progress we've made in resource reconstruction and the very real possibility that a universal matter converter may be technically feasible, the interaction facilitators in the Ecology/Economy Institute agree that we have to be extremely prudent.

Third, to try to develop a conceptual framework within which we could create total, terran patterns of land use. Of course, even after we've established the framework, we'll still have to deal with the reality that most communities are unwilling to cooperate in this area.

Scarcity-region economist/ecologists also strive toward the goals I've just stated, but, in order to attain them fully, they will have to create abundance. This requires, as in the abundance-regions in the past, that the amount of ecofacts available be increased until it balances auto-estimated personal needs and community needs. The task would be far easier if the original definition of satisfaction in many scarcity-regions had not been destroyed in post World-War II years. Most non-Western countries traditionally perceived satisfaction in terms of absolute amounts of consumption. This culturally limited consumption pattern was destroyed in the postwar drive for economic development, which was accompanied by the introduction of the goal of maximum consumption.

Today the problem of increasing production in the scarcity-regions is no longer a shortage of machinery and machine systems: abundance-regions have the techniques to produce and provide fully cybernated production marketives which require little or no manpower. The difficulty is to introduce these marketives into functioning cultures without disrupting land-use or imposing distribution and consumption patterns. During the fifties and sixties, economists undermined the cultures of many scarcity-regions which were unfortunate enough to be considered suitable recipients for aid. At least we've learned enough to avoid *this* mistake.

So long as the division of the world into abundance- and scarcity-regions persists, the threat of a total breakdown in transnational understanding is possible. It is generally agreed that abundance-regions bear the responsibility for the continued existence of scarcity-regions. It is difficult for the many in scarcity-regions who are poorly educated to comprehend why higher levels of ecofact transfer from the abundance-regions to the scarcity-regions and higher levels of emigration from the scarcity-regions to the abundance-regions would be entropic. In fact, understanding of this point requires considerable sophistication in the use of system theory.

Thus high levels of tension are inevitable in scarcity-regions, particularly in non-functioning conglomerates such as Shanghai, Calcutta, Rio de Janeiro, and Lagos. In general, these tensions have so far been prevented from causing breakdown because there has been a rapid rise in ecofact availability throughout most of the scarcity-regions. It is only in the non-functioning conglomerates that socio-economic progress is not matching population pressure. I must add, however, that there is some evidence that the rate of improvement has not been as rapid recently.

I often wish that societies could have perceived the realities of the cybernation era a few years earlier than 1980. The scarcity-regions needed to move directly from the agricultural era to the cybernation era. By the time we had perceived this reality it was already too late, and most of the scarcity-regions have been forced to move through the cultural patterns associated with the industrial era before they can reach the cybernation era.

And now I intend to enjoy the remainder of the evening. What next, Yvonne?

Yvonne: The dolphins want to do an aquatic display to celebrate with us. Can we have the room-lights out? They will start as soon as it's dark in here.

PART II.

What Do We Mean by
Development?

WHAT does the clash between our economic and ecological views imply for appropriate policies? America has, up to now, looked primarily at the implications for her own behavior. We have made little effort to clarify the issues which face the poor countries of the world. It is high time that we focussed on some hard questions which we have so far tried to avoid.

This section of the book will examine questions of development from this new viewpoint. It will challenge, as a consequence, the theory created by W. W. Rostow. He argued that the poor countries could only be successful if they followed the route which had previously been pioneered by the rich countries of the world.

This theory has enabled us to screen out all sorts of unattractive realities. Just a few of them will be stated here:

—The disparity in incomes per head between the rich and the poor countries of the world is now so great that the poor countries cannot possibly catch up economically with the rich so long as we perpetuate the industrial era. In many cases, growth in income per *head* in the rich countries is now greater than the *total* income per head in the poor countries.

—The ability of the poor countries to follow the same pattern of development as the rich countries depends on the possibility of ensuring jobs for all. This argument was developed in the introduction to the previous part. It is impossible to achieve full employment in the rich countries—it is inconceivable in the poor countries.

—The key reality now taking place is the shift between eras as development takes place. We are presently asking the poor countries to move from the agricultural era through the industrial era and on to the communications era in one generation. This cannot be done. The only realistic hope is that the poor countries find ways to move from the agricultural era directly into the communications era. It seems quite probable that it will be easier for the poor countries to move from the agricultural era to the communications era than it will be for the rich countries to move from the industrial era to the communications era.

The concept of development as a straight line process is obsolete: it makes failure of the poor countries *inevitable*. The policies we have followed in the attempt to create an industrial era pattern destroy the lifestyles and values of the agricultural era. Western experts have justified this destruction of family and tribal ties by arguing that this process is necessary to create committed work

61

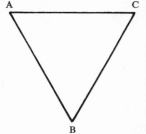

forces. Such a policy may have been necessary in the nineteenth century. Today it is deeply immoral, because there is no chance of jobs for those whose cultural ties are being deliberately destroyed.

What are the alternatives? In effect, the poor countries must discover how to move directly from the agricultural era to the communications era. Such a possibility can be perceived once we cease to think of the development process as a straight line and envisage it, instead, as a triangle. The rich countries have moved from the agricultural era (point A) to the industrial era (point B) and must now make a sharp turn in order to reach the communications era (point C). The poor countries can move directly from the agricultural era (point A) to the communications era (point C).

In discussing such a possibility there are twin dangers. The first of these is to exaggerate the ease with which a culture could move from the agricultural era to the communications era. Such a task will inevitably be difficult because each poor country must discover its own route to make an extraordinarily complex transition in a relatively limited period of time. The other danger—which is probably more critical given our present perceptions—is that we shall fail to recognize that the poor countries may be able to make the transition more easily than the rich countries.

Both the agricultural era and the communications era necessarily involve immediate feedback. Both are based to a substantial extent on cooperation between nature and man and on a process orientation. The industrial era, on the contrary, has replaced cooperation with competition and a process orientation with a goal orientation. The value shifts which the rich countries must make if they are to enter the communications era are larger than those which are necessary if the poor countries are to enter the communications era.

We have almost always thought of development as a process of replacing less with more. Such a definition is deeply misleading. Development is the process of moving from one value set to another value set. Both rich countries and poor countries now face an immediate need for such a shift in values—all of us must seek together for the guidelines we shall need in order to be able to determine effective directions.

The rich countries have technological capacities which must be shared if the process of development is to be achieved. The poor countries possess value sets which the rich countries must learn to appreciate if their own values are to change sufficiently rapidly. Above all, ideas about development must cease to flow solely in one direction, from the rich countries to the poor. We need an imaginative interchange where each individual, group and cultural area contributes what it can to discovering the diverse new success criteria for the communications era.

I do not wish to seem overdramatic, but I can only conclude from the information that is available to me as Secretary-General that the Members of the United Nations have perhaps ten years left in which to subordinate their ancient quarrels and launch a global partnership to curb the arms race, to improve the human environment, to defuse the population explosion and to supply the required momentum to development efforts. If such a global partnership is not forged within the next decade, then I very much fear that the problems I have mentioned will have reached such staggering proportions that they will be beyond our capacity to control.

U THANT
May 1969

Mankind must decide during the seventies whether it is willing to change in order to take advantage of its new potentials. Continuation of present patterns of behavior for a further decade will create a situation in which our very survival will be uncertain.

We must rid ourselves of the poisons which result from continued colonialism and racism. These divisive factors limit co-operation. They also prevent us from creating the true global partnership required for success in the process of development.

Three immediate steps are essential. We must commit ourselves to using our rapidly increasing technological knowledge to feed, clothe and shelter every human being on this earth. We must commit ourselves to eliminating war as a method of settling international disputes, thus freeing the resources required for the development process. We must commit ourselves to maintaining the viability of this planet whose very survival is now threatened by pollution.

If we are to succeed, we must recognize that not only are these three commitments necessary but that their priorities are seen differently by the rich and the poor. The poor are naturally primarily concerned with their immediate needs for food, clothing and shelter. The rich, on the other hand, have achieved their immediate physical needs and they are therefore freed to be concerned about the impact of environmental pollution.

U THANT
October 1970

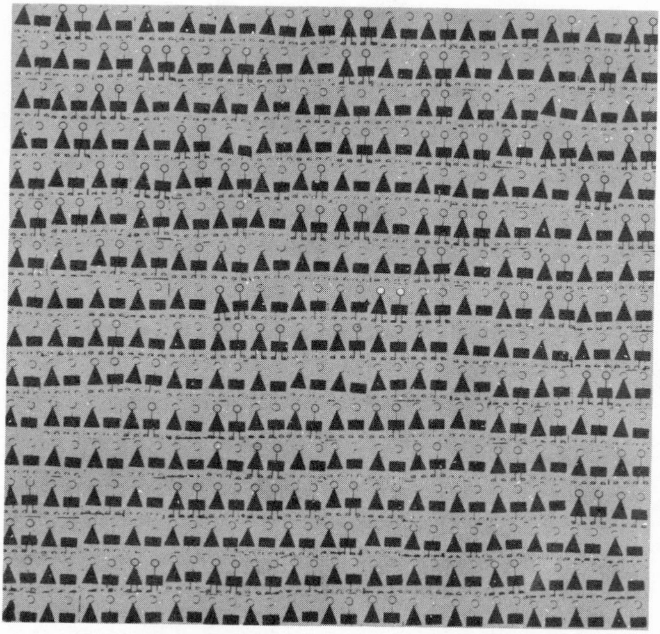

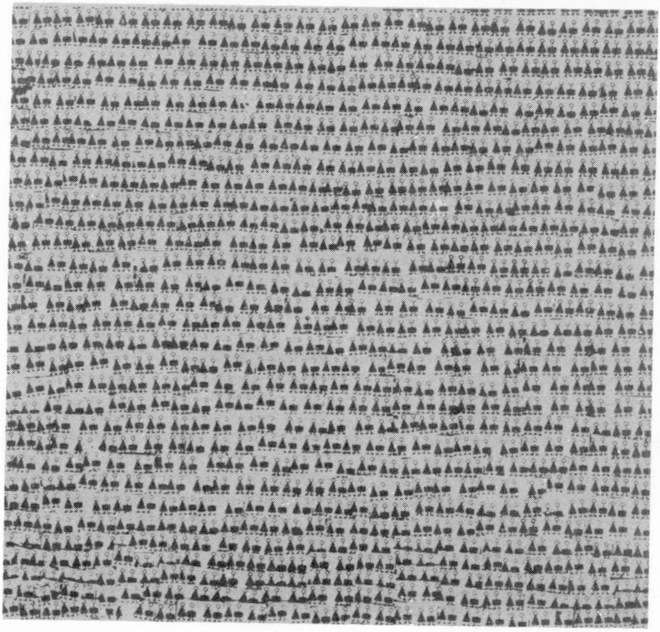

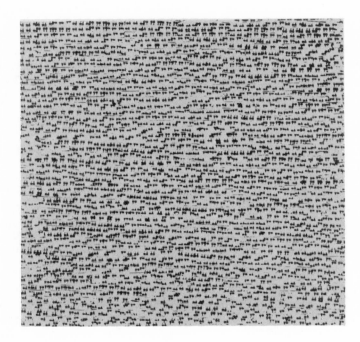

Reprinted courtesy of Robin Nuse and the Population Institute.

The Helping Hand*

POUL ANDERSON

A mellow bell tone was followed by the flat voice of the roboreceptionist: "His Excellency Valka Vahino, Special Envoy from the League of Cundaloa to the Commonwealth of Sol."

The Earthlings rose politely as he entered. Despite the heavy gravity and dry chill air of terrestrial conditions, he moved with the flowing grace of his species, and many of the humans were struck anew by what a handsome people his race was.

People—yes, the folk of Cundaloa were humanoid enough, mentally and physically, to justify the term. Their differences were not important; they added a certain charm, the romance of alienness, to the comforting reassurance that there was no really basic strangeness.

Ralph Dalton let his eyes sweep over the ambassador. Valka Vahino was typical of his race—humanoid mammal, biped, with a face that was very manlike, differing only in its beauty of finely chiseled features, high cheekbones, great dark eyes. A little smaller, more slender than the Earthlings, with a noiseless, feline ease of movement. Long shining blue hair swept back from his high forehead to his slim shoulders, a sharp and pleasing contrast to the rich golden skin color. He was dressed in the ancient ceremonial garb of Luai on Cundaloa—shining silvery tunic, deep-purple cloak from which

* Reprinted by permission of the author and his agents: Scott Meredith Literary Agency, Inc., 580 Fifth Avenue, New York, N.Y. 10036.

little sparks of glittering metal swirled like fugitive stars, gold-worked boots of soft leather. One slender six-fingered hand held the elaborately carved staff of office which was all the credentials his planet had given him.

He bowed, a single rippling movement which had nothing of servility in it, and said in excellent Terrestrial, which still retained some of the lilting, singing accent of his native tongue: "Peace on your houses! The Great House of Cundaloa sends greetings and many well-wishings to his brothers of Sol. His unworthy member Valka Vahino speaks for him in friendship."

Some of the Earthlings shifted stance, a little embarrassed. It did sound awkward in translation, thought Dalton. But the language of Cundaloa was one of the most beautiful sounds in the Galaxy.

He replied with an attempt at the same grave formality. "Greetings and welcome. The Commonwealth of Sol receives the representative of the League of Cundaloa in all friendship. Ralph Dalton, Premier of the Commonwealth, speaking for the people of the Solar System."

He introduced the others then—Cabinet ministers, technical advisers, military staff members. It was an important assembly. Most of the power and influence in the Solar System was gathered here.

He finished: "This is an informal preliminary conference on the economic proposals recently made to your gov . . . to the Great House of Cundaloa. It has no legal standing. But it is being televised, and I daresay the Solar Assembly will act on a basis of what is learned at these and similar hearings."

"I understand. It is a good idea." Vahino waited until the rest were seated before taking a chair.

There was a pause. Eyes kept going to the clock on the wall. Vahino had arrived punctually at the time set, but Skorrogan of Skontar was late, thought Dalton. Tactless, but then the manners of the Skontarans were notoriously bad. Not at all like the gentle deference of Cundaloa, which in no way indicated weakness.

There was aimless conversation, of the "How do you like it here?" variety. Vahino, it developed, had visited the Solar System quite a few times in the past decade. Not surprising, in view of the increasingly close economic ties between his planet and the Commonwealth. There were a great many Cundaloan students in Earthian universities, and before the war there had been a growing tourist traffic from Sol to Avaiki. It would probably revive soon—especially if the devastation were repaired and—

"Oh, yes," smiled Vahino. "It is the ambition of all young *anamai,* men on Cundaloa, to come to Earth, if only for a visit. It is not mere flattery to say that our admiration for you and your achievements is boundless."

"It's mutual," said Dalton. "Your culture, your art and music, your literature—all have a large following in the Solar System. Why, many men, and not just scholars, learn Luaian simply to read the *Dvanagoa-Epai* in the original. Cundaloan singers, from concert artists to nightclub entertainers, get more applause than any others." He grinned. "Your young men here have some difficulty keeping our terrestrial coeds off their necks. And your few young women here are besieged by invitations. I suppose only the fact that there cannot be issue has kept the number of marriages as small as it has been."

"But seriously," persisted Vahino, "we realize at home that your civilization sets the tone for the known Galaxy. It is not just that Solarian civilization is the most advanced technically, though that has, of course, much to do with it. *You* came to *us,* with your space-ships and atomic energy and medical science and all else—but, after all, we can learn that and go on with you from there. It is, however, such acts as . . . well, as your present offer of help: to rebuild ruined worlds light-years away, pouring your own skill and treasure into our homes, when we can offer you so little in return—it is that which makes you the leading race in the Galaxy."

"We have selfish motives, as you well know," said Dalton a little uncomfortably. "Many of them. There is, of course, simple humani-tarianism. We could not let races very like our own know want when the Solar System and its colonies have more wealth than they know what to do with. But our own bloody history has taught us that such programs as this economic-aid plan redound to the benefit of the initiator. When we have built up Cundaloa and Skontar, got them producing again, modernized their backward industry, taught them our science—they will be able to trade with us. And our economy is still, after all these centuries, primarily mercantile. Then, too, we will have knitted them too closely together for a repetition of the disastrous war just ended. And they will be allies for us against some of the really alien and menacing cultures in the Galaxy, planets and systems and empires against which we may one day have to stand."

"Pray the High One that that day never comes," said Vahino soberly. "We have seen enough of war."

The bell sounded again, and the robot announced in its clear in-human tones: "His Excellency Skorrogan Valthak's son, Duke of

Kraakahaym, Special Envoy from the Empire of Skontar to the Commonwealth of Sol."

They got up again, a little more slowly this time, and Dalton saw the expressions of dislike on several faces, expressions which smoothed into noncommittal blankness as the newcomer entered. There was no denying that the Skontarans were not very popular in the Solar System just now, and partly it was their own fault. But most of it they couldn't help.

The prevailing impression was that Skontar had been at fault in the war with Cundaloa. That was plainly an error. The misfortune was that the suns Skang and Avaiki, forming a system about half a light-year apart, had a third companion which humans usually called Allan, after the captain of the first expedition to the system. And the planets of Allan were uninhabited.

When terrestrial technology came to Skontar and Cundaloa, its first result had been to unify both planets—ultimately both systems— into rival states which turned desirous eyes on the green new planets of Allan. Both had had colonies there, clashes had followed, ultimately the hideous five years' war which had wasted both systems and ended in a peace negotiated with terrestrial help. It had been simply another conflict of rival imperialisms, such as had been common enough in human history before the Great Peace and the formation of the Commonwealth. The terms of the treaty were as fair as possible, and both systems were exhausted. They would keep the peace now, especially when both were eagerly looking for Solarian help to rebuild.

Still—the average human liked the Cundaloans. It was almost a corollary that he should dislike the Skontarans and blame them for the trouble. But even before the war they had not been greatly admired. Their isolationism, their clinging to outmoded traditions, their harsh accent, their domineering manner, even their appearance told against them.

Dalton had had trouble persuading the Assembly to let him include Skontar in the invitation to economic-aid conferences. He had finally persuaded them that it was essential—not only would the resources of Skang be a material help in restoration, particularly their minerals, but the friendship of a potentially powerful and hitherto aloof empire could be gained.

The aid program was still no more than a proposal. The Assembly would have to make a law detailing who should be helped, and how much, and then the law would have to be embodied in treaties with the planets concerned. The initial informal meeting here was only the first step. But—crucial.

Dalton bowed formally as the Skontaran entered. The envoy responded by stamping the butt of his huge spear against the floor, leaning the archaic weapon against the wall, and extending his holstered blaster handle first. Dalton took it gingerly and laid it on the desk. "Greeting and welcome," he began, since Skorrogan wasn't saying anything. "The Commonwealth—"

"Thank you." The voice was a hoarse bass, somehow metallic, and strongly accented. "The Valtam of the Empire of Skontar sends greetings to the Premier of Sol by Skorrogan Valthak's son, Duke of Kraakahaym."

He stood out in the room, seeming to fill it with his strong, forbidding presence. In spite of coming from a world of higher gravity and lower temperature, the Skontarans were a huge race, over two meters tall and so broad that they seemed stocky. They could be classed as humanoid, in that they were bipedal mammals, but there was not much resemblance beyond that. Under a wide, low forehead and looming eyebrow ridges, the eyes of Skorrogan were fierce and golden, hawk's eyes. His face was blunt-snouted, with a mouthful of fangs in the terrific jaws; his ears were blunt and set high on the massive skull. Short brown fur covered his muscular body to the end of the long restless tail, and a ruddy mane flared from his head and throat. In spite of the, to him, tropical temperature, he wore the furs and skins of state occasions at home, and the acrid reek of his sweat hung about him.

"You are late," said one of the ministers with thin politeness. "I trust you were not detained by any difficulties."

"No, I underestimated the time needed to get here," answered Skorrogan. "Please to excuse me." He did not sound at all sorry, but lowered his great bulk into the nearest chair and opened his portfolio. "We have business now, my sirs?"

"Well . . . I suppose so." Dalton sat down at the head of the long conference table. "Though we are not too concerned with facts and figures at this preliminary discussion. We want simply to agree on general aims, matters of basic policy."

"Naturally, you will wish a full account of the available resources of Avaiki and Skang, as well as the Allanian colonies," said Vahino in his soft voice. "The agriculture of Cundaloa, the mines of Skontar, will contribute much even at this early date, and, of course, in the end there must be economic self-sufficiency."

"It is a question of education, too," said Dalton. "We will send many experts, technical advisers, teachers—"

"And, of course, some question of military resources will arise—" began the Chief of Staff.

"Skontar have own army," snapped Skorrogan. "No need of talk there yet."

"Perhaps not," agreed the Minister of Finance mildly. He took out a cigarette and lit it.

"Please, sir!" For a moment Skorrogan's voice rose to a bull roar. "No smoke. You know Skontarans allergic to tobacco—"

"Sorry!" The Minister of Finance stubbed out the cylinder. His hand shook a little and he glared at the envoy. There had been little need for concern: the air-conditioning system swept the smoke away at once. And in any case—you don't shout at a cabinet minister. Especially when you come to ask him for help—

"There will be other systems involved," said Dalton hastily, trying with a sudden feeling of desperation to smooth over the unease and tension. "Not only the colonies of Sol. I imagine your two races will be expanding beyond your own triple system, and the resources made available by such colonization—"

"We will have to," said Skorrogan sourly. "After treaty rob us of all fourth planet— No matter. Please to excuse. Is bad enough to sit at same table with enemy without being reminded of how short time ago he *was* enemy."

This time the silence lasted a long while. And Dalton realized, with a sudden feeling almost of physical illness, that Skorrogan had damaged his own position beyond repair. Even if he suddenly woke up to what he was doing and tried to make amends—and who ever heard of a Skontaran noble apologizing for anything—it was too late. Too many millions of people, watching their telescreens, had seen his unpardonable arrogance. Too many important men, the leaders of Sol, were sitting in the same room with him, looking into his contemptuous eyes and smelling the sharp stink of unhuman sweat.

There would be no aid to Skontar.

With sunset, clouds piled up behind the dark line of cliffs which lay to the east of Geyrhaym, and a thin, chill wind blew down over the valley with whispers of winter. The first few snowflakes were borne on it, whirling across the deepening purplish sky, tinted pink by the last bloody light. There would be a blizzard before midnight.

The spaceship came down out of darkness and settled into her cradle. Beyond the little spaceport, the old town of Geyrhaym lay wrapped in twilight, huddling together against the wind. Firelight glowed ruddily from the old peak-roofed houses, but the winding cobbled streets were like empty canyons, twisting up the hill on whose crest frowned the great castle of the old barons. The Valtam had taken it for his own use, and little Geyrhaym was now the capital of the Empire. For proud Skirnor and stately Thruvang were radioactive pits, and wild beasts howled in the burned ruins of the old palace.

Skorrogan Valthak's son shivered as he came out of the airlock and down the gangway. Skontar was a cold planet. Even for its own people it was cold. He wrapped his heavy fur cloak more tightly about him.

They were waiting near the bottom of the gangway, the high chiefs of Skontar. Under an impassive exterior, Skorrogan's belly muscles tightened. There might be death waiting in that silent, sullen group of men. Surely disgrace—and he couldn't answer—

The Valtam himself stood there, his white mane blowing in the bitter wind. His golden eyes seemed luminous in the twilight, hard and fierce, a deep sullen hate smoldering behind them. His oldest son, the heir apparent, Thordin, stood beside him. The last sunlight gleamed crimson on the head of his spear; it seemed to drip blood against the sky. And there were the other mighty men of Skang, counts of the provinces on Skontar and the other planets, and they all stood waiting for him. Behind them was a line of imperial household guards, helmets and corselets shining in the dusk, faces in shadow, but hate and contempt like a living force radiating from them.

Skorrogan strode up to the Valtam, grounded his spear butt in salute, and inclined his head at just the proper degree. There was silence then, save for the whimpering wind. Drifting snow streamed across the field.

The Valtam spoke at last, without ceremonial greeting. It was like a deliberate slap in the face: "So you are back again."

"Yes, sire." Skorrogan tried to keep his voice stiff. It was difficult to do. He had no fear of death, but it was cruelly hard to bear this weight of failure. "As you know, I must regretfully report my mission unsuccessful."

"Indeed. We receive telecasts here," said the Valtam acidly.

"Sire, the Solarians are giving virtually unlimited aid to Cundaloa. But they refused any help at all to Skontar. No credits, no technical advisers—nothing. And we can expect little trade and almost no visitors."

"I know," said Thordin. "And *you* were sent to get their help."

"I tried, sire." Skorrogan kept his voice expressionless. He had to say something—*but be forever damned if I'll plead!* "But the Solarians have an unreasonable prejudice against us, partly related to their wholly emotional bias toward Cundaloa and partly, I suppose, due to our being unlike them in so many ways."

"So they do," said the Valtam coldly. "But it was not great before. Surely the Mingonians, who are far less human than we, have received much good at Solarian hands. They got the same sort of help that Cundaloa will be getting and that we might have had.

"We desire nothing but good relations with the mightiest power in the Galaxy. We might have had more than that. I know, from firsthand reports, what the temper of the Commonwealth was. They were ready to help us, had we shown any cooperativeness at all. We could have rebuilt, and gone farther than that—" His voice trailed off into the keening wind.

After a moment he went on, and the fury that quivered in his voice was like a living force: "I sent you as my special delegate to get that generously offered help. You, whom I trusted, who I thought was aware of our cruel plight— Arrrgh!" He spat. "And you spent your whole time there being insulting, arrogant, boorish. You, on whom all the eyes of Sol were turned, made yourself the perfect embodiment of all the humans think worst in us. No wonder our request was refused! You're lucky Sol didn't declare war!"

"It may not be too late," said Thordin. "We could send another—"

"No." The Valtam lifted his head with the inbred iron pride of his race, the haughtiness of a culture where for all history face had been more important than life. "Skorrogan went as our accredited representative. If we repudiated him, apologized for—not for any overt act but for bad manners!—if we crawled before the Galaxy— no! It isn't worth that. We'll just have to do without Sol."

The snow was blowing thicker now, and the clouds were covering the sky. A few bright stars winked forth in the clear portions. But it was cold, cold.

"And what a price to pay for honor!" said Thordin wearily. "Our folk are starving—food from Sol could keep them alive. They have only rags to wear—Sol would send clothes. Our factories are devastated, are obsolete, our young men grow up in ignorance of Galactic civilization and technology—Sol would send us machines and engineers, help us rebuild. Sol would send teachers, and we could become great— Well, too late, too late." His eyes searched through the gloom, puzzled, hurt. Skorrogan had been his friend. "But why did you do it? Why did you do it?"

"I did my best," said Skorrogan stiffly. "If I was not fitted for the task, you should not have sent me."

"But you were," said Valtam. "You were our best diplomat. Your wiliness, your understanding of extra-Skontaran psychology, your personality—all were invaluable to our foreign relations. And then, on this simple and most tremendous mission— No more!" His voice rose to a shout against the rising wind. "No more will I trust you. Skontar will know you failed."

"Sire—" Skorrogan's voice shook suddenly. "Sire, I have taken words from you which from anyone else would have meant a death duel. If you have more to say, say it. Otherwise let me go."

"I cannot strip you of your hereditary titles and holdings," said the Valtam. "But your position in the imperial government is ended, and you are no longer to come to court or to any official function. Nor do I think you will have many friends left."

"Perhaps not," said Skorrogan. "I did what I did, and even if I could explain further, I would not after these insults. But if you ask my advice for the future of Skontar—"

"I don't," said the Valtam. "You have done enough harm already."

" . . . then consider three things." Skorrogan lifted his spear and pointed toward the remote glittering stars. "First, those suns out there. Second, certain new scientific and technological developments here at home—such as Dyrin's work on semantics. And last —look about you. Look at the houses your fathers built, look at the clothes you wear, listen, perhaps, to the language you speak. And then come back in fifty years or so and beg my pardon!"

He swirled his cloak about him, saluted the Valtam again, and went with long steps across the field and into the town. They looked after him with incomprehension and bitterness in their eyes.

There was hunger in the town. He could almost feel it behind the dark walls, the hunger of ragged and desperate folk crouched over their fires, and wondered whether they could survive the winter. Briefly he wondered how many would die—but he didn't dare follow the thought out.

He heard someone singing and paused. A wandering bard, begging his way from town to town, came down the street, his tattered cloak blowing fantastically about him. He plucked his harp with thin fingers, and his voice rose in an old ballad that held all the harsh ringing music, the great iron clamor of the old tongue, the language of Naarhaym on Skontar. Mentally, for a moment of wry amusement, Skorrogan rendered a few lines into Terrestrial:

> *Wildly the winging*
> *War birds, flying*
> *wake the winter-dead*
> *wish for the sea-road.*
> *Sweetheart, they summon me,*
> *singing of flowers*
> *fair for the faring.*
> *Farewell, I love you.*

It didn't work. It wasn't only that the metallic rhythm and hard barking syllables were lost, the intricate rhyme and alliteration, though that was part of it—but it just didn't make sense in Terrestrial. The concepts were lacking. How could you render, well, such a word as *vorkansraavin* as "faring" and hope to get more than a mutilated fragment of meaning? Psychologies were simply too different.

And there, perhaps, lay his answer to the high chiefs. But they wouldn't know. They couldn't. And he was alone, and winter was coming again.

Valka Vahino sat in his garden and let sunlight wash over his bare skin. It was not often, these days, that he got a chance to *aliacaui*—What was that old Terrestrial word? "Siesta"? But that was wrong. A resting Cundaloan didn't sleep in the afternoon. He sat or lay outdoors, with the sun soaking into his bones or a warm rain like a benediction over him, and he let his thoughts run free. Solarians called that daydreaming, but it wasn't; it was, well—they had no real word for it. Psychic recreation was a clumsy term, and the Solarians never understood.

Sometimes it seemed to Vahino that he had never rested, not in an eternity of years. The grinding urgencies of wartime duty, and then his hectic journeys to Sol—and since then, in the past three years, the Great House had appointed him official liaison man at the highest level, assuming that he understood the Solarians better than anyone else in the League.

Maybe he did. He'd spent a lot of time with them and liked them as a race and as individuals. But—by all the spirits, how they worked! How they drove themselves! As if demons were after them.

Well, there was no other way to rebuild, to reform the old obsolete methods and grasp the dazzling new wealth which only lay waiting to be created. But right now it was wonderfully soothing to lie in his garden, with the great golden flowers nodding about him and filling the summer air with their drowsy scent, with a few honey insects buzzing past and a new poem growing in his head.

The Solarians seemed to have some difficulty in understanding a whole race of poets. When even the meanest and stupidest Cundaloan could stretch out in the sun and make lyrics—well, every race has its own peculiar talents. Who could equal the gadgeteering genius which the humans possessed?

The great soaring, singing lines thundered in his head. He turned them over, fashioning them, shaping every syllable, and fitting the pattern together with a dawning delight. This one would be—good! It would be remembered, it would be sung a century hence, and they wouldn't forget Valka Vahino. He might even be remembered as a masterversemaker—*Alia Amaui cauianriho, valana, valana, vro!*

"Pardon, sir." The flat metal voice shook in his brain; he felt the delicate fabric of the poem tear and go swirling off into darkness and forgetfulness. For a moment there was only the pang of his loss; he realized dully that the interruption had broken a sequence which he would never quite recapture.

"Pardon, sir, but Mr. Lombard wishes to see you."

It was a sonic beam from the roboreceptionist which Lombard himself had given Vahino. The Cundaloan had felt the incongruity of installing its shining metal among the carved wood and old tapestries of his house, but he had not wanted to offend the donor—and the thing was useful.

Lombard, head of the Solarian reconstruction commission, the most important human in the Avaikian System. Just now Vahino appreciated the courtesy of the man's coming to him rather than simply sending for him. Only—why did he have to come exactly at this moment?

"Tell Mr. Lombard I'll be there in a minute."

Vahino went in the back way and put on some clothes. Humans didn't have the completely casual attitude toward nakedness of Cundaloa. Then he went into the forehall. He had installed some chairs there for the benefit of Earthlings, who didn't like to squat on a woven mat—another incongruity. Lombard got up as Vahino entered.

The human was short and stocky, with a thick bush of gray hair above a seamed face. He had worked his way up from laborer through engineer to High Commissioner, and the marks of his struggle were still on him. He attacked work with what seemed almost a personal fury, and he could be harder than tool steel. But most of the time he was pleasant, he had an astonishing range of interests and knowledge, and, of course, he had done miracles for the Avaikian System.

"Peace on your house, brother," said Vahino.

"How do you do," clipped the Solarian. As his host began to signal for servants, he went on hastily: "Please, none of your ritual hospitality. I appreciate it, but there just isn't time to sit and have a meal and talk cultural topics for three hours before getting down to business. I wish . . . well, you're a native here and I'm not, so I wish you'd personally pass the word around—tactfully, of course—to discontinue this sort of thing."

"But . . . they are among our oldest customs—"

"That's just it! Old—backward—delaying progress. I don't mean to be disparaging, Mr. Vahino. I wish we Solarians had some customs as charming as yours. But—not during working hours. Please."

"Well . . . I dare say you're right. It doesn't fit into the pattern of a modern industrial civilization. And that is what we are trying to build, of course." Vahino took a chair and offered his guest a cigarette. Smoking was one of Sol's characteristic vices, perhaps the most easily transmitted and certainly the most easily defensible. Vahino lit up with the enjoyment of the neophyte.

"Quite. Exactly. And that is really what I came here about, Mr. Vahino. I have no specific complaints, but there has accumulated a whole host of minor difficulties which only you Cundaloans can handle for yourselves. We Solarians can't and won't meddle in your internal affairs. But you must change some things, or we won't be able to help you at all."

Vahino had a general idea of what was coming. He'd been expecting it for some time, he thought grayly, and there was really nothing to be done about it. But he took another puff of smoke, let it trickle slowly out, and raised his eyebrows in polite inquiry. Then he remembered that Solarians weren't used to interpreting nuances of expression as part of a language, and said aloud, "Please say what you like. I realize no offense is meant, and none will be taken."

"Good." Lombard leaned forward, nervously clasping and unclasping his big work-scarred hands. "The plain fact is that your

whole culture, your whole psychology, is unfitted to modern civilization. It can be changed, but the change will have to be drastic. You
can do it—pass laws, put on propaganda campaigns, change the
educational system, and so on. But it *must* be done.

"For instance, just this matter of the siesta. Right now, all through
this time zone on the planet, hardly a wheel is turning, hardly a
machine is tended, hardly a man is at his work. They're all lying in
the sun making poems or humming songs or just drowsing. There's
a whole civilization to be built, Vahino! There are plantations, mines,
factories, cities abuilding—you just can't do it on a four-hour working day."

"No. But perhaps we haven't the energy of your race. You are a
hyperthyroid species, you know."

"You'll just have to learn. Work doesn't have to be backbreak-
ing. The whole aim of mechanizing your culture is to release you
from physical labor and the uncertainty of dependence on the land.
And a mechanical civilization can't be cluttered with as many old
beliefs and rituals and customs and traditions as yours is. There just
isn't time. Life is too short. And it's too incongruous. You're still
like the Skontarans, lugging their silly spears around after they've
lost all practical value."

"Tradition *makes* life—the meaning of life—"

"The machine culture has its own tradition. You'll learn. It has its
own meaning, and I think that is the meaning of the future. If you
insist on clinging to outworn habits, you'll never catch up with history. Why, your currency system—"

"It's practical."

"In its own field. But how can you trade with Sol if you base your
credits on silver and Sol's are an abstract actuarial quantity? You'll
have to convert to our system for purpose of trade—and you might
as well change over at home, too. Similarly, you'll have to learn the
metric system if you expect to use our machines or make sense to
our scientists. You'll have to adopt . . . oh, everything!

"Why, your very society— No wonder you haven't exploited even
the planets of your own system when every man insists on being
buried at his birthplace. It's a pretty sentiment, but it's no more than
that, and you'll have to get rid of it if you're going to reach the stars.

"Even your religion . . . excuse me . . . but you must realize
that it has many elements which modern science has flatly disproved."

"I'm an agnostic," said Vahino quietly. "But the religion of
Mauiroa means a lot to many people."

"If the Great House will let us bring in some missionaries, we can convert them to, say, Neopantheism. Which I, for one, think has a lot more personal comfort and certainly more scientific truth than your mythology. If your people are to have faith at all, it must not conflict with facts which experience in a modern technology will soon make self-evident."

"Perhaps. And I suppose the system of familial bonds is too complex and rigid for modern industrial society. . . . Yes, yes—there is more than a simple conversion of equipment involved."

"To be sure. There's a complete conversion of minds," said Lombard. And then, gently, "After all, you'll do it eventually. You were building spaceships and atomic-power plants right after Allan left. I'm simply suggesting that you speed up the process a little."

"And language—"

"Well, without indulging in chauvinism, I think all Cundaloans should be taught Solarian. They'll use it at some time or other in their lives. Certainly all your scientists and technicians will have to use it professionally. The languages of Laui and Muara and the rest are beautiful, but they just aren't suitable for scientific concepts. Why, the agglutination alone— Frankly, your philosophical books read to me like so much gibberish. Beautiful, but almost devoid of meaning. Your language lacks—*precision.*"

"Aracles and Vranamaui were always regarded as models of crystal thought," said Vahino wearily. "And I confess to not quite grasping your Kant and Russell and even Korzybski—but then, I lack training in such lines of thought. No doubt you are right. The younger generation will certainly agree with you.

"I'll speak to the Great House and may be able to get something done now. But in any case you won't have to wait many years. All our young men are striving to make themselves what you wish. It is the way to success."

"It is," said Lombard; and then, softly, "Sometimes I wish success didn't have so high a price. But you need only look at Skontar to see how necessary it is."

"Why—they've done wonders in the last three years. After the great famine they got back on their feet, they're rebuilding by themselves, they've even sent explorers looking for colonies out among the stars." Vahino smiled wryly. "I don't love our late enemies, but I must admire them."

"They have courage," admitted Lombard. "But what good is courage alone? They're struggling in a tangle of obsolescence. Al-

ready the overall production of Cundaloa is three times theirs. Their
interstellar colonizing is no more than a feeble gesture of a few hundred individuals. Skontar can live, but it will always be a tenth-rate
power. Before long it'll be a Cundaloan satellite state.

"And it's not that they lack resources, natural or otherwise. It's
that, having virtually flung our offer of help back in our faces, they've
taken themselves out of the main stream of Galactic civilization.
Why, they're even trying to develop scientific concepts and devices
we knew a hundred years ago, and are getting so far off the track
that I'd laugh if it weren't so pathetic. Their language, like yours,
just isn't adapted to scientific thought, and they're carrying chains
of rusty tradition around. I've seen some of the spaceships they've
designed themselves, for instance, instead of copying Solarian models, and they're ridiculous. Half a hundred different lines of approach,
trying desperately to find the main line we took long ago. Spheres,
ovoids, cubes—I hear someone even thinks he can build a tetrahedral spaceship!"

"It might just barely be possible," mused Vahino. "The Rie-
mannian geometry on which the interstellar drive itself is based
would permit—"

"No, no! Earth tried that sort of thing and found it didn't work.
Only a crank—and, isolated, the scientists of Skontar are becoming
a race of cranks—would think so.

"We humans were just fortunate, that's all. Even we had a long
history before a culture arose with the mentality appropriate to a
scientific civilization. Before that, technological progress was almost
at a standstill. Afterward, we reached the stars. Other races can do
it, but first they'll have to adopt the proper civilization, the proper
mentality—and without our guidance, Skontar or any other planet
isn't likely to evolve that mentality for many centuries to come.

"Which reminds me—" Lombard fumbled in a pocket. "I have a
journal here, from one of the Skontaran philosophical societies. A
certain amount of communication still does take place, you know;
there's no official embargo on either side. It's just that Sol has given
Skang up as a bad job. Anyway"—he fished out a magazine—"there's
one of their philosophers, Dyrin, who's doing some new work on
general semantics which seems to be arousing quite a furor. You read
Skontaran, don't you?"

"Yes," said Vahino. "I was in military intelligence during the war.
Let me see—" He leafed through the journal to the article and began
translating aloud:

"The writer's previous papers show that the principle of non-elementalism is not itself altogether a universal, but must be subject to certain psychomathematical reservations arising from consideration of the *broganar*—that's a word I don't understand—field, which couples to electronic wave-nuclei and—"

"What is that jabberwocky?" exploded Lombard.

"I don't know," said Vahino helplessly. "The Skontaran mind is as alien to me as to you."

"Gibberish," said Lombard. "With the good old Skontaran to-hell-with-you dogmatism thrown in." He threw the magazine on the little bronze brazier, and fire licked at its thin pages. "Utter nonsense, as anyone with any knowledge of general semantics, or even an atom of common sense, can see." He smiled crookedly, a little sorrowfully, and shook his head. "A race of cranks!"

"I wish you could spare me a few hours tomorrow," said Skorrogan.

"Well—I suppose so." Thordin XI, Valtam of the Empire of Skontar, nodded his thinly maned head. "Though next week would be a little more convenient."

"Tomorrow—please."

The note of urgency could not be denied. "All right," said Thordin. "But what will be going on?"

"I'd like to take you on a little jaunt over to Cundaloa."

"Why there, of all places? And why must it be tomorrow, of all times?"

"I'll tell you—then." Skorrogan inclined his head, still thickly maned though it was quite white now, and switched off his end of the telescreen.

Thordin smiled in some puzzlement. Skorrogan was an odd fellow in many ways. But . . . well . . . we old men have to stick together. There is a new generation, and one after that, pressing on our heels.

No doubt thirty-odd years of living in virtual ostracism had changed the old joyously confident Skorrogan. But it had, at least, not embittered him. When the slow success of Skontar had become so plain that his own failure could be forgotten, the circle of his friends had very gradually included him again. He still lived much alone, but he was no longer unwelcome wherever he went. Thordin, in particular, had discovered that their old friendship could be as alive as ever before, and he was often over to the Citadel of Kraaka-

haym, or Skorrogan to the palace. He had even offered the old noble
a position back in the High Council, but it had been refused, and
another ten years—or was it twenty?—had gone by with Skorrogan
fulfilling no more than his hereditary duties as duke. Until now, for
the first time, something like a favor was being asked. . . . Yes, he
thought, I'll go tomorrow. To blazes with work. Monarchs deserve
holidays, too.

Thordin got up from his chair and limped over to the broad win-
dow. The new endocrine treatments were doing wonders for his
rheumatism, but their effect wasn't quite complete yet. He shivered
a little as he looked at the wind-driven snow sweeping down over
the valley. Winter was coming again.

The geologists said that Skontar was entering another glacial
epoch. But it would never get there. In another decade or so the
climate engineers would have perfected their techniques and the gla-
ciers would be driven back into the north. But meanwhile it was
cold and white outside, and a bitter wind hooted around the palace
towers.

It would be summer in the southern hemisphere now, fields would
be green, and smoke would rise from freeholders' cottages into a
warm blue sky. Who had headed that scientific team?—Yes, Aes-
gayr Haasting's son. His work on agronomics and genetics had made
it possible for a population of independent smallholders to produce
enough food for the new scientific civilization. The old freeman, the
backbone of Skontar in all her history, had not died out.

Other things had changed, of course. Thordin smiled wryly as he
reflected just how much the Valtamate had changed in the last fifty
years. It had been Dyrin's work in general semantics, so fundamental
to all the sciences, which had led to the new psychosymbological
techniques of government. Skontar was an empire in name only now.
It had resolved the paradox of a libertarian state with a nonelective
and efficient government. All to the good, of course, and really it was
what past Skontaran history had been slowly and painfully evolving
toward. But the new science had speeded up the process, compressed
centuries of evolution into two brief generations. As physical and
biological science had accelerated beyond belief— But it was odd
that the arts, music, literature had hardly changed, that handicraft
survived, that the old High Naarhaym was still spoken.

Well, so it went. Thordin turned back toward his desk. There was
work to be done. Like that matter of the colony on Aesric's Planet—

you couldn't expect to run several hundred thriving interstellar colonies without some trouble. But it was minor. The empire was safe. And it was growing.

They'd come a long way from that day of despair fifty years ago, and from the famine and pestilence and desolation which followed. A long way— Thordin wondered if even he realized just how far.

He picked up the microreader and glanced over the pages. His mind training came back to him and he arrished the material. He couldn't handle the new techniques as easily as those of the younger generation, trained in them from birth, but it was a wonderful help to arrish, complete the integration in his subconscious, and indolate the probabilities. He wondered how he had ever survived the old days of reasoning on a purely conscious level.

Thordin came out of the warp just outside Kraakahaym Citadel. Skorrogan had set the point of emergence there, rather than indoors, because he liked the view. It was majestic, thought the Valtam, but dizzying—a wild swoop of gaunt gray crags and wind-riven clouds down to the far green valley below. Above him loomed the old battlements, with the black-winged kraakar which had given the place its name hovering and cawing in the sky. The wind roared and boomed about him, driving dry white snow before it.

The guards raised their spears in salute. They were unarmed otherwise, and the vortex guns on the castle walls were corroding away. No need for weapons in the heart of an empire second only to Sol's dominions. Skorrogan stood waiting in the courtyard. Fifty years had not bent his back much or taken the fierce golden luster from his eyes. It seemed to Thordin today, though, that the old being wore an air of taut and inwardly blazing eagerness: he seemed somehow to be looking toward the end of a journey.

Skorrogan gave conventional greeting and invited him in. "Not now, thanks," said Thordin. "I really am very busy. I'd like to start the trip at once."

The duke murmured the usual formula of polite regret, but it was plain that he could hardly wait, that he could ill have stood an hour's dawdling indoors. "Then please come," he said. "My cruiser is all set to go."

It was cradled behind the looming building, a sleek little roboship with the bewildering outline of all tetrahedral craft. They entered and took their seats at the center, which, of course, looked directly out beyond the hull.

"Now," said Thordin, "perhaps you'll tell me why you want to go to Cundaloa today?"

Skorrogan gave him a sudden look in which an old pain stirred.

"Today," he said slowly, "it is exactly fifty years since I came back from Sol."

"Yes——?" Thordin was puzzled and vaguely uncomfortable. It wasn't like the taciturn old fellow to rake up that forgotten score.

"You probably don't remember," said Skorrogan, "but if you want to vargan it from your subconscious, you'll perceive that I said to them, then, that they could come back in fifty years and beg my pardon."

"So now you want to vindicate yourself." Thordin felt no surprise —it was typically Skontaran psychology—but he still wondered what there was to apologize for.

"I do. At that time I couldn't explain. Nobody would have listened, and in any case I was not perfectly sure myself that I had done right." Skorrogan smiled, and his thin hands set the controls. "Now I am. Time has justified me. And I will redeem what honor I lost then by showing you, today, that I didn't really fail.

"Instead, I succeeded. You see, I alienated the Solarians on purpose."

He pressed the main-drive stud, and the ship flashed through half a light-year of space. The great blue shield of Cundaloa rolled majestically before them, shining softly against a background of a million blazing stars.

Thordin sat quietly, letting the simple and tremendous statement filter through all the levels of his mind. His first emotional reaction was a vaguely surprised realization that, subconsciously, he had been expecting something like this. He hadn't ever really believed, deep down inside himself, that Skorrogan could be an incompetent.

Instead—no, not a traitor. But—what, then? What had he meant? Had he been mad, all these years, or——

"You haven't been to Cundaloa much since the war, have you?" asked Skorrogan.

"No—only three times, on hurried business. It's a prosperous system. Solar help put them on their feet again."

"Prosperous . . . yes, yes, they are." For a moment a smile tugged at the corners of Skorrogan's mouth, but it was a sad little smile: it was as if he were trying to cry but couldn't quite manage it. "A bustling, successful little system, with all of three colonies among the stars."

With a sudden angry gesture he slapped the short-range controls and the ship warped down to the surface. It landed in a corner of the great spaceport at Cundaloa City, and the robots about the cradle went to work, checking it in and throwing a protective force-dome about it.

"What—now?" whispered Thordin. He felt, suddenly, dimly afraid; he knew vaguely that he wouldn't like what he was going to see.

"Just a little stroll through the capital," said Skorrogan. "With perhaps a few side trips around the planet. I wanted us to come here unofficially, incognito, because that's the only way we'll ever see the real world, the day-to-day life of living beings which is so much more important and fundamental than any number of statistics and economic charts. I want to show you what I saved Skontar from." He smiled again, wryly. "I gave my life for my planet, Thordin. Fifty years of it, anyway—fifty years of loneliness and disgrace."

They emerged into the clamor of the great steel and concrete plain and crossed over the gates. There was a steady flow of beings in and out, a never-ending flux, the huge restless energy of Solarian civilization. A large proportion of the crowd was human, come to Avaiki on business or pleasure, and there were some representatives of other races. But the bulk of the throng was, naturally, native Cundaloans. Sometimes one had a little trouble telling them from the humans. After all, the two species looked much alike, and with the Cundaloans all wearing Solarian dress—

Thordin shook his head in some bewilderment at the roar of voices. "I can't understand," he shouted to Skorrogan. "I know Cundaloan, both Laui and Muara tongues, but—"

"Of course not," answered Skorrogan. "Most of them here are speaking Solarian. The native languages are dying out fast."

A plump Solarian in shrieking sports clothes was yelling at an impassive native storekeeper who stood outside his shop. "Hey, you boy, gimme him fella souvenir chop-chop—"

"Pidgin Solarian," grimaced Skorrogan. "It's on its way out, too, what with all young Cundaloans being taught the proper speech from the ground up. But tourists never learn." He scowled, and for a moment his hand shifted to his blaster.

But no—times changed. You did not wipe out someone who simply happened to be personally objectionable, not even on Skontar. Not any more.

The tourist turned and bumped him. "Oh, so sorry," he exclaimed, urbanely enough. "I should have looked where I was going."

"Is no matter," shrugged Skorrogan.

The Solarian dropped into a struggling and heavily accented High Naarhaym: "I really must apologize, though. May I buy you a drink?"

"No matter," said Skorrogan, with a touch of grimness.

"What a Planet! Backward as . . . as Pluto! I'm going on to Skontar from here. I hope to get a business contract—you know how to do business, you Skontarans!"

Skorrogan snarled and swung away, fairly dragging Thordin with him. They had gone half a block down the motilator before the Valtam asked, "What happened to your manners? He was trying hard to be civil to us. Or do you just naturally hate humans?"

"I like most of them," said Skorrogan. "But not their tourists. Praise the Fate, we don't get many of that breed on Skontar. Their engineers and businessmen and students are all right. I'm glad that relations between Sol and Skang are close, so we can get many of that sort. But keep out the tourists!"

"Why?"

Skorrogan gestured violently at a flashing neon poster. "That's why." He translated the Solarian:

SEE THE ANCIENT MAUIROA
CEREMONIES!

COLORFUL! AUTHENTIC! THE
MAGIC OF OLD CUNDALOA!

AT THE TEMPLE OF THE HIGH ONE
ADMISSION REASONABLE

"The religion of Mauiroa meant something, once," said Skorrogan quietly. "It was a noble creed, even if it did have certain unscientific elements. Those could have been changed— But it's too late now. Most of the natives are either Neopantheists or unbelievers, and they perform the old ceremonies for money. For a show."

He grimaced. "Cundaloa hasn't lost all its picturesque old buildings and folkways and music and the rest of its culture. But it's become conscious that they are picturesque, which is worse."

"I don't quite see what you're so angry about," said Thordin. "Times have changed. But they have on Skontar, too."

"Not in this way. Look around you, man! You've never been in the Solar System, but you must have seen pictures from it. Surely you realize that this is a typical Solarian city—a little backward, maybe, but typical. You won't find a city in the Avaikian System which isn't essentially—*human*.

"You won't find significant art, literature, music here any more— just cheap imitations of Solarian products, or else archaistic cling- ing to outmoded native traditions, romantic counterfeiting of the past. You won't find science that isn't essentially Solarian, you won't find machines basically different from Solarian, you'll find fewer homes every year which can be told from human houses. The old society is dead; only a few fragments remain now. The familial bond, the very basis of native culture, is gone, and marriage relations are as casual as on Earth itself. The old feeling for the land is gone. There are hardly any tribal farms left; the young men are all coming to the cities to earn a million credits. They eat the products of Solarian-type food factories, and you can only get native cuisine in a few expensive restaurants.

"There are no more handmade pots, no more handwoven cloths. They wear what the factories put out. There are no more bards chanting the old lays and making new ones. They look at the tele- screen now. There are no more philosophers of the Araclean or Vranamauian schools; there are just second-rate commentaries on Aristotle versus Korzybski or the Russell theory of knowledge—"

Skorrogan's voice trailed off. Thordin said softly, after a moment, "I see what you're getting at. Cundaloa has made itself over into the Solarian pattern."

"Just so. It was inevitable from the moment they accepted help from Sol. They'd *have* to adopt Solar science, Solar economics, ulti- mately the whole Solar culture. Because that would be the only pat- tern which would make sense to the humans who were taking the lead in reconstruction. And, since that culture was obviously success- ful, Cundaloa adopted it. Now it's too late. They can never go back. They don't even want to go back.

"It's happened before, you know. I've studied the history of Sol. Back before the human race even reached the other planets of its system, there were many cultures, often radically different. But ulti- mately one of them, the so-called Western society, became so over- whelmingly superior technologically that . . . well, no others could coexist with it. To compete, they had to adopt the very approach of the West. And when the West helped them from their backward- ness, it necessarily helped them into a Western pattern. With the best intentions in the world, the West annihilated all other ways of life."

"And you wanted to save us from that?" asked Thordin. "I see your point, in a way. Yet I wonder if the sentimental value of old institutions was equal to some millions of lives lost, to a decade of sacrifice and suffering."

"It was more than sentiment!" said Skorrogan tensely. "Can't you see? Science is the future. To amount to anything, we *had* to become scientific. But was Solarian science the only way? Did we have to become second-rate humans to survive—or could we strike out on a new path, unhampered by the overwhelming helpfulness of a highly developed but essentially alien way of life? I thought we could. I thought we would have to.

"You see, no nonhuman race will ever make a really successful human. The basic psychologies—metabolic rates, instincts, logical patterns, *everything*—are too different. One race *can* think in terms of another's mentality, but never too well. You know how much trouble there's been in translating from one language to another. And all thought is in language, and language reflects the basic patterns of thought. The most precise, rigorous, highly thought out philosophy and science of one species will never quite make sense to another race. Because they are making somewhat different abstractions from the same great basic reality.

"I wanted to save us from becoming Sol's spiritual dependents. Skang was backward. It *had* to change its ways. But—why change them into a wholly alien pattern? Why not, instead, force them rapidly along the natural path of evolution—our own path?"

Skorrogan shrugged. "I did," he finished quietly. "It was a tremendous gamble, but it worked. We saved our own culture. It's *ours*. Forced by necessity to become scientific on our own, we developed our own approach.

"You know the result. Dyrin's semantics was developed—Solarian scientists would have laughed it to abortion. We developed the tetrahedral ship, which human engineers said was impossible, and now we can cross the Galaxy while an old-style craft goes from Sol to Alpha Centauri. We perfected the spacewarp, the psychosymbology of our own race—not valid for any other—the new agronomic system which preserved the freeholder who is basic to our culture— everything! In fifty years Cundaloa has been revolutionized, Skontar has revolutionized itself. There's a universe of difference.

"And we've therefore saved the intangibles which are our own, the arts and handicrafts and essential folkways, music, language, literature, religion. The *élan* of our success is not only taking us to the stars, making us one of the great powers in the Galaxy, but it is producing a renaissance in those intangibles equaling any Golden Age in history.

"And all because we remained ourselves."

He fell into silence, and Thordin said nothing for a while. They had come into a quieter side street, an old quarter where most of the buildings antedated the coming of the Solarians, and many ancient-style native clothes were still to be seen. A party of human tourists was being guided through the district and had clustered about an open pottery booth.

"Well?" said Skorrogan after a while. "Well?"

"I don't know." Thordin rubbed his eyes, a gesture of confusion. "This is all so new to me. Maybe you're right. Maybe not. I'll have to think a while about it."

"I've had fifty years to think about it," said Skorrogan bleakly. "I suppose you're entitled to a few minutes."

They drifted up to the booth. An old Cundaloan sat in it among a clutter of goods, brightly painted vases and bowls and cups. Native work. A woman was haggling over one of the items.

"Look at it," said Skorrogan to Thordin. "Have you ever seen the old work? This is cheap stuff made by the thousands for the tourist trade. The designs are corrupt, the workmanship's shoddy. But every loop and line in those designs had meaning once."

Their eyes fell on one vase standing beside the old boothkeeper, and even the unimpressionable Valtam drew a shaky breath. It glowed, that vase. It seemed almost alive; in a simple shining perfection of clean lines and long smooth curves, someone had poured all his love and longing into it. Perhaps he had thought: This will live when I am gone.

Skorrogan whistled. "That's an authentic old vase," he said. "At least a century old—a museum piece! How'd it get in this junk shop?"

The clustered humans edged a little away from the two giant Skontarans, and Skorrogan read their expressions with a wry inner amusement: They stand in some awe of us. Sol no longer hates Skontar; it admires us. It sends its young men to learn our science and language. But who cares about Cundaloa any more?

But the woman followed his eyes and saw the vase glowing beside the old vendor. She turned back to him: "How much?"

"No sell," said the Cundaloan. His voice was a dusty whisper, and he hugged his shabby mantle closer about him.

"You sell." She gave him a bright artificial smile. "I give you much money. I give you ten credits."

"No sell."

"I give you hundred credits. Sell!"

"This mine. Fambly have it since old days. No sell."

"Five hundred credits!" She waved the money before him.

He clutched the vase to his thin chest and looked up with dark liquid eyes in which the easy tears of the old were starting forth. "No sell. Go 'way. No sell *oamaui*."

"Come on," mumbled Thordin. He grabbed Skorrogan's arm and pulled him away. "Let's go. Let's get back to Skontar."

"So soon?"

"Yes. Yes. You were right, Skorrogan. You were right, and I am going to make public apology, and you are the greatest savior of history. But let's get home!"

They hurried down the street. Thordin was trying hard to forget the old Cundaloan's eyes. But he wondered if he ever would.

The world is a curious theatre, full of contrasts and full of unity at the same time. In astronomic terms Earth is a single sphere, in environmental terms there is one planetary ecosystem, in transportation terms Earth is small, in communication terms it is close, in commercial terms it is interdependent, in population terms it is a crowd if not crowded, in danger terms it has the capacity to destroy itself, in knowledge terms it has the capacity to prosper. All these forces pull toward a single state, a global village, a world community . . .

Thus the world theatre has become a maze of interlocking, interconnected, interdependent systems which continue to reinforce each other and exert powerful, growing, unitary pressures. But the age-old centrifugal forces of human existence have not abated to any significant degree; the social, economic, political, ideological and individual ambitions and competitions are as pronounced as ever. . . .

The one global system which is not functioning is the human system; rather it is in catastrophic disarray of such magnitude that the theatre of the world cannot be expected to endure, unless modified and made beneficial to the entire audience, rather than just to the dress circle . . .

WILMER H. KINGSFORD

Bum Steer in India*

MICHAEL PERELMAN

The warp and woof of societies are made up of a complex array of customs and beliefs as well as social and political institutions. The economist must be wary of tampering with them, for he may unwittingly cause the unraveling of the entire fabric of society. The sacred cow of India has long been a target for western economists who are concerned with India's underfed masses. The western eye sees the sacred cow as an animal that competes, unmolested, with humans for food and, since Hindus do not eat meat, never returns its protein to the human community. But it is dangerous to consider any institution such as the sacred cow outside the context of the society which formed it.

The sacred cow of India is Mata, the great mother. Worshipped as a god, it is believed to be central to the well-being of the whole society and the concept of it as a motherly, all-encompassing source of life is found throughout the society. A cow is never killed, and the mere rumor that Moslems have slaughtered a cow for its meat is often enough to start a riot. To a Hindu, eating a cow would seem like eating the flesh of your mother.

The burden of cultural conditioning which the western economist brings to any consideration of India's problems is reflected in the English phrase "sacred cow" which we use to mean anything use-

* Published by *Clear Creek*. © March 1972. Reprinted by permission.

less and hollow which people worship without reason. Unfortunately, some basic concepts of western economics become "sacred cows" themselves when they are applied outside of the societies which produced them.

The economist who wants to abolish the sacred cow would do well to consider the results of the end of serfdom in England which Karl Polanyi describes in *The Great Transformation*. Strict legal restrictions on physical mobility bound laborers to their parishes until the late eighteenth century. Just after the serfs were freed, a welfare system was instituted to shelter the common man from the tempest of the market. Many people, conditioned by servitude and unused to an open market, preferred poor relief to wages. Then the Reform Bill of 1832 and the Poor Law Amendment of 1834 put an end to this last humiliating protection, with the result that society saw "an almost miraculous increase in production accompanied by near starvation of the masses."

The lesson we can learn from the freeing of the serfs is most important for today's economists who are intent on "developing" the Third World. They give little indication that they have given any consideration to the complex roles played by local institutions. These institutions often play important roles which are necessary to maintain the stability of the economy. Their abrupt abolition can create infinitely more hardships than those imposed on the English serfs when they were cut loose from the moorings of traditional paternalism.

Almost all contemporary economists seem united in condemning the sacred cow. S. N. Mishra expressed the typical economist's view when he said, "Legislation of cattle slaughter will leave every sector of the society better and no sector worse off. The measure is self propelling in that it distributes the welfare gains by itself. The measure, apart from the cost of adoption, does not involve any cost."

Gandhi disagreed: "Why the cow was selected for apotheosis is obvious to me. The cow was in India the best companion. Not only did she give milk, but she also made agriculture possible."

Both Gandhi and the economists are right from their own point of view. The economists argue that reducing the number of uneconomic animals would make it easier to improve the quality of those that remain. On the other hand, it may be rational for the Indians to maintain a large number of scrawny, aged cattle.

No one can know when any particular cow will begin to lactate or conceive again, so it is difficult to know which cattle should be culled. The farmer rations his feed among his animals according to their productivity. Since the cost involved in maintaining the oldest cattle is almost nil, if one comes back into productivity, it is a windfall; and if one dies, it is a windfall for the untouchables for whom carrion is a major source of protein.

The untouchables form a caste of Indian society that is so low on the social scale, they are considered subhuman. Despite government attempts to eradicate the stigma of "untouchable," the system persists, and untouchables remain most numerous in irrigated areas where they form the bulk of landless laborers. Kusim Nair says that in one survey of the district of Basti in Eastern Uttar Pradesh, the National Council of Economic Research found that "Eating carrion is common. Almost a fifth of the population of the district is compelled to resort to these abnormal practices."

Cattle are most likely to die during times of stress or famine, just when the malnourished most need protein. The habit of many primitive people of eating protein during times of stress—funerals, war parties—may be related to an adaptation in which antibody production is mobilized during the greatest need and strain. Perhaps we can think of the marginal cattle as "protein banks." Society invests a portion of its meager surplus of vegetable matter in these cattle during good times so that it can make withdrawals in times of need. If slaughter became commonplace, unproductive cattle would be sent to the butcher, and their protein would nourish the rich instead of those who need it most. The slaughter taboo has a subtle income distributing effect built into it.

Suppose the economists *are* correct that India would be better off if some of its cattle were culled. Alan Heston estimates that if India slaughtered 30 million female cattle, those remaining would be able to convert the same feed supply into more milk, meat, and dung, and the hides would be of superior quality. Which cattle would be slaughtered? This question is important since many of the dry, marginal cattle are owned by poor peasants. The reason so many of them are underfed and neglected is that the resources for feeding them are unevenly distributed. If the poor peasants' cattle are slaughtered, are they going to be able to buy or rent the services which their cattle now give them for almost no cost?

Aside from the socio-economic effects of the sacred cow, it has qualities which enable it to play a unique ecological role. It is able to manufacture protein in the form of milk and meat. Its dung provides an excellent source of fertilizer which is also used for fuel—the annual amount of dung used as fuel in India is estimated to be equivalent to over 35 million tons of coal—and the bullock pulls the peasants' plows and carts. Remarkably, the cow can do all this without consuming any protein at all. The cow can live on non-edible organic waste such as stalks of rice and wheat; it can even consume large amounts of paper in its diet. Paul Meinhardt says that as much as 50 per cent of Holstein diets have been successfully replaced by paper, and in some cases paper diets have resulted in higher beef to fat ratios and 20 per cent faster gain. In short, the cow need not compete with humans for food.

If the taboo on cattle slaughter were lifted, economists argue, the peasant would, of course, still have the option to use traditional methods; just let the market determine who does what. But if we accept that point of view, we must face up to certain external economies. Changing the ancient custom would undoubtedly have a profound effect on the whole society, and there are some questions to be answered. If slaughter becomes profitable, how will the untouchables get their protein? What will this mean for the rural population as a whole if, once slaughter is permitted, tractors replace bullocks? What sort of employment will the rural population find? Unless we find, or already have, a form of safe atomic technology, we are facing an energy crisis, and our fossil fuels represent a fixed stock of capital. Replacing the rice-stalk-eating bullock with a tractor means a more rapid drain on fossil fuels. . . .

Because of the expense of transportation, modernized Indian cattlemen might find it cheaper to feed their stock more concentrated foodstuffs like grain or fish protein. In 1968, Peru and Chile shipped about 700,000 tons of high protein fish products which were mostly fed to animals. Moreover, in the U.S. from 1954 to 1956, more than 72 per cent of the tonnage of all our harvested crops was used for feeding livestock. U.S. cattle certainly do compete for food with humans.

Because cattle are no longer raised on farms in the United States, the nutrient exchange between land and livestock is no longer direct. For the most part, it still seems more "economical" to most of the livestock industry to leave both dung and organic refuse to build up as solid waste disposal problems. Even if these wastes were fed to the cattle, the dung would still remain in the city since it is too bulky to ship back to the farms as fertilizer. With the cattle separated from the farms, farmers often find it cheaper to burn "waste" products like rice and wheat stalks so that the useful materials are converted into air pollution. Then since the soil loses its fertility as its nutrients are shipped to the city, the farmer must buy fertilizers from factories.

Howard Odum said in *Environment, Power and Society,* "the living forests and reefs have an economy, but instead of money, the currency is made up of materials like phosphorus, carbon, water and the exchange of work services. Plants use the minerals to make food and the consumer sends the wastes back to the plant." The sacred cow probably evolved to maintain this mineral economy, and it has its functional counterpart in parts of Africa and in the Yakut culture where cattle or reindeer are killed only in religious ceremonies or in the times of need.

Long ago when India had fewer people, she could be less careful of the delicate ecological balance. In those days Indians ate meat. Today, the traditional economy and ecology is strained, possibly near the breaking point. India has too many people and a heritage of centuries of colonialism. It's a simple matter to point to the sacred cattle and say that poverty is the fault of the impoverished peasant who should simply sell his cow for slaughter. It is much more difficult, and much more important, to consider the institution of the sacred cow in the social and ecological context of India and to really determine whether anyone would profit by the acceptance of slaughter.

There are many people who consider slum dwellers marginal, intrinsically wicked and inferior. To such people we recommend the profitable experience of discussing the slum situation with slum dwellers themselves. As some of these critics are often simply mistaken, it is possible that they may rectify their mythical clichés and assume a more scientific attitude. . . . They may . . . end up realizing that if intrinsic evil exists it is part of the structures, and that it is the structures which need to be transformed.

It should be pointed out that the Third World as a whole . . . suffers from the same misunderstanding from certain sectors of the so-called metropolitan societies. They see the Third World as the incarnation of evil, the primitive, the devil, sin, and sloth—in sum, as historically unviable without the director societies. Such a manichean attitude is at the source of the impulse to "save" the "demon-possessed" Third World, "educating it" and "correcting its thinking" according to the director societies' own criteria . . .

Thus, "salvation" of the Third World by the director societies can only mean its domination, whereas in its legitimate aspiration to independence lies its utopian vision: to save the director societies in the very act of freeing itself.

PAOLO FREIRE

The Meaning of Limits*

JERRY MANDER

Everyone talks about the Earth being round, but does anyone actually believe it? Maybe the problem in really getting the idea across has to do with understanding the nature of roundness, which is that you eventually get back to the same place. That is, there's nowhere else to go. There is no infinity.

People who live on islands understand the phenomenon very well. I have some friends who about three years ago moved to Hawaii after living most of their lives on the mainland, and who recently wrote me that they are suffering from island sickness (a common syndrome of expatriate mainlanders). They spend weekends driving clear around the island, maybe more than once, thinking that eventually some new direction will appear, but it never does.

The *natives* of Hawaii don't have this problem, I am told. As I've just returned from the tiny islands in Micronesia, I can tell you that most of the natives there don't have the problem either. They know perfectly well what *finiteness* means and, still undazzled by what we westerners "know" is true—that technology can accomplish anything—simply don't think about getting off the island. Well, in history there have been some brave souls in outrigger canoes who attempt to cross the seas to see if they can make it, or to see what's

* An informal speech given before the John Muir Institute Seminar, Aspen, Colorado, September 20, 1969. Reprinted by permission.

on the other side. You might think of them as the astronauts of the islands, but the difference between the islanders and us is that they don't put much faith in those canoes ever getting back in time to feed anybody next year, or at all. I think we are all so technology crazed that some of us actually believe *our* astronauts will lift us all off of here the day before we all starve to death. Or we believe that farming the oceans will feed an infinitely growing population, as though the oceans were infinite.

Micronesian "out-islanders" in particular—that is, those who live across a hundred miles or more of sea from any neighboring islands, and whose contact with the rest of the world is limited to the few souls who arrive on the eighty-foot government boat every six months —simply don't think about infinity, or to put it more accurately, the idea that everything is possible. In order to survive out there by themselves, they've had to gain a pretty good feeling for pacing the breadfruit production and the coconut eating. In some of those places the highest crime is cutting down a coconut tree without communal permission. And on the islands surrounding Yap—where a culture thrives that is as nearly untouched by non-island ideas as any in the world—there is a very rigid birth control which works this way. Everyone gets married very late—late twenties or early thirties. While there is no particular emphasis on virginity until then, there is plenty of emphasis and sanction against illegitimate children. No man will ever marry a woman who has given birth first, and consequently the ladies have devised an intrauterine device made of hibiscus bark which works as well as the plastic ones and I'll bet doesn't cause cancer.

What I'm talking about, of course, is balance between man and environment. In some places it still exists and in other places it doesn't. I'm suggesting that perhaps it's time to take as a model for our future survival-thinking the way islanders have managed to do things, because the world we're on is round.

C. P. Snow alludes to all this in *State of Siege* where he describes the generalized anxiety that everyone, *but everyone,* seems to be feeling these days. He says that it is caused by "condensation," that is, the Earth is getting smaller, and there's no place to hide. People are therefore getting panicky, forming communes on mountain-tops, becoming ever more isolationist, not leaving their neighborhoods, not leaving their homes at night (with good cause), and so on.

Of course it isn't really condensation, it's just condensation of the mind. We are all living through one of our most terrifying dream/

horror fantasies: we're locked in a room, and the walls and ceiling are closing in on us.

All the things we've been raised to worship—Man's limitless power, the ever-giving nature of Mother Earth—all those infinite possibilities, are beginning to seem less infinite. In fact, the infinite horizon is heading this way fast. We should have known all that the minute Columbus did his thing.

The major struggle in conservation is obviously what the black studies demonstrators called "the need for reeducation." In other words, it is a propaganda problem. And, I believe, the propaganda goal might very effectively be defined as this: develop an island psychology in everyone on Earth. Maybe we should start by giving a few professorships to the out-islanders of Yap.

But the trouble with that is, as soon as the Yapese arrive (as some, of course, already have, as students in our colleges) they are dazzled by such things as roads and cars and most especially, by the way, canned fish. It's reverse culture shock . . . they are prepared to give up their house by the sea, their leisure economy, their abundant fruit and relaxed loving life—in other words, everything all us businessmen have been working for—for a Yamaha motorcycle. They will be (and are being) dazzled by technology because they have never articulated a value judgment about which way of life is better. They have only known one lifestyle and are stunned by the other, much as a fish is stunned when he sees your face mask shining under the water. He doesn't notice the spear. The Yapese are really in need of, let's call them, island appreciation courses . . . so if they do opt for plastic culture they'll at least know there's no getting the other back. I'm not kidding about this. The educational problem is as serious for islanders who already know how to survive on islands and who can teach us what we need to know, as it is for the rest of us.

All of us should start agitating for Departments of Humilities. The Humilities curriculum would be the opposite of the sort of curricula black studies departments have lately been introducing, whose goals are to help some people feel their potency for the first time. The Humilities courses would strive to develop a little more feeling of impotence, respecting the limits of things, most especially our technological toys.

If all of us recognized our quite limited place in the order of things, we might relax a little, getting-ahead-wise, and find there is time for some other joys we've only barely heard about. I didn't meet

any Yapese that I could describe as unhappy, and they seemed to
fill their day quite satisfactorily without any of the accoutrements
we find necessary. I'm not advocating any return to nature philosophy, though that's not a bad idea, but I am saying that we don't
have to wait for the computer-operated robot men we will soon create to turn on us and enslave us like the movies say they will. Their
technological parents already have.

But let's get back to Humilities. Dave Brower has begun the fight
beautifully, I think. I have heard him speak more than once about
the nonsense of our current economic and political rhetoric, ex-
horting towards "a vigorous expanding economy." That has to be
the first infinite idea to go.

And I like the implications of Dr. Hardin's Pregnant Pause very
much. However, the problem is so basic to Western thinking that
we must face the fact that re-education means everything, starting
in grade schools with some kind of environmental studies . . .
maybe even nature walks, depending on who's doing the leading.

It's the schools that, in the long run, are most important. However, what about meanwhile? Can we really wait for all those children—educated better than we are—to grow up and save us?

Of course we cannot, and I for one am committed to the use of
media to get across the message, which, as an ad writer, let me put
this way:

WE ARE STRANDED ON AN ISLAND IN SPACE: WE ARE RUNNING
LOW ON FOOD AND WATER: AND [with due credit to Dr. Snow]
WE SEEM TO BE GOING CRAZY.

It's the island part that, I think, is most important. If we can con-
vey somehow, in a mass way, the islandness of things, we may have
to live through some mass hysteria while people drive around (or
fly, perhaps) aimlessly. However, once they get the idea that it's all
a big circle, the race may survive. (Nature will survive in any event,
of course, since it is everything. If we all go under, that won't stop
the regenerative process, so let's be clear that it's people that are
the endangered species.)

I never thought I'd be glad about the flight to the Moon, but in
spite of its absurdity, in my view, considering the other needs of the
day, it may yet turn out to be the critically important thing from a
conservationist's viewpoint, because *it* may accelerate the idea of
Earth as an island.

It seems to me that if we can get enough pictures of Earth taken from space, and the farther away the better, the more the context will sink in. We are isolated in all that blackness. We can never, as a race, make it across that sea. This is the only place we have and these people on this globe are our only possible friends and lovers.

We proposed once before in a Sierra Club ad the idea of an Earth National Park, a wildlife island in space, where *we* are the wildlife. It is our only possible home, and perhaps we should practice thinking about it in those terms and thinking of more ways to pass it along.

Who's for DDT?*

Dr. Norman E. Borlaug is a onetime Iowa farm boy who probably knows as much about growing food as anyone else in the world. He won the 1970 Nobel Peace Prize for his contribution to the development of "miracle" high-yield strains of wheat, which produced up to four bushels where only one bushel had grown before, and which have helped make India, West Pakistan and Mexico nearly self-sufficient for their cereal supply.

Last week Dr. Borlaug gave the keynote speech at a meeting of the U.N.'s Food and Agricultural Organization in Rome. To the bemusement of the assembled notables, he violently attacked "the current vicious, hysterical campaign against the use of agricultural chemicals being promoted today by fear-provoking, irresponsible environmentalists." Today's greatest danger, Borlaug pointed out, is the pressure put on food supplies by the world's rapidly growing population. Fully 50% of mankind is undernourished, perhaps another 15% is malnourished. To make matters worse, the soil in many developing nations is worn out, and crops are ravaged by ravenous insects. The need for chemical fertilizers and pesticides is not only clear, Borlaug said, but imperative.

In stark contrast, he continued, "the so-called environmentalist

* Reprinted by permission from *Time,* the Weekly Newsmagazine; © Time, Inc., 1971.

movement" is endemic to rich nations, where the most rabid crusaders tend to be well-fed urbanites who sample the delights of nature on weekend outings. Borlaug feels that campaigns to ban agricultural chemicals—starting with DDT—reveal a callous misordering of social priorities. If such bans become law, he warned, "then the world will be doomed not by chemical poisoning but by starvation."

Borlaug has a point. The probable hazards of DDT poisoning are a proper matter of concern for a society like the U.S., which is so well fed that many of its people spend much of their time dieting. But peoples on the borderline of starvation are more interested in simply getting enough to eat, and the possibility of getting poisoned by accumulated DDT is the least of their worries.

Nonetheless, many U.S. environmentalists remain skeptical about the Green Revolution precisely because it depends so heavily on agricultural chemicals. Those chemicals boost harvests, but they also have unpredictable side effects that may not show up for years. In recent Philippine experience with new strains of rice, for example, farmers were delighted to reap bumper crops. But so many chemicals were needed that the fish in the paddyfields and nearby waterways died. Result: more rice but less protein in the local diet—a net loss in food values.

DDT on My Brain*

I don't need your L S D,
Can't think like I used to do,

Head to toe I'm D D T, D D T on my
Still I know it's not good for you,

brain, on my brain.   brain, on my brain.

2. They spray the wheat the chickens eat,
   It's in my eggs, it's in my meat . . .
   It kills the bugs in the apple tree,
   I eat the pie and it's killing me . . .

3. All the farms they get that spray,
   It washes down into my Bay . . .
   It kills the crabs, it kills the fish,
   It shines up from my supper dish . . .

4. Falcon's flying wild and free,
   His babies die of the DDT . . .
   Chemical stocks are riding high,
   Farm field workers spray and die . . .

5. Bring back the bugs in my apple tree,
   Don't lay that poison spray on me . . .
   I don't need your LSD,
   DDT is killing me,
           DDT on my brain,
           On my brain.

*Words and music by Malvina Reynolds. © 1969, Schroder Music Co. (ASCAP), Berkeley, California 94704. Used by permission.

. . . Societies with lineal concepts of time tend to stress ends, results, or goals [while] those with a cyclical perspective will emphasize process, means or the experience. Our society believes in setting up what are called targets which we struggle to reach. Traditional societies usually prefer gradual evolution. That the newest or the latest is necessarily the best, whether in seeds, ideas, or institutions, has not often been the experience of the oldest of these civilizations. Generally, they respect the age which we scorn. They revere the aged whom we put in nursing homes. Their long established customs give them a continuum in the stream of life beginning many centuries before our own civilization. If they do not discard those time-honored ways, perhaps it is because they feel that they have been well-served by them. The anti-age perspective which is reflected in the pejorative connotations of English words such as "obsolete," "archaic," "old-fashioned," "out-of-date," "reactionary," or very simply "old" is not necessarily shared by many of the peoples of Asia.

J. W. SPELLMAN

EDITOR'S NOTE

It is difficult to be aware of the levels of anger which many of those in the poor countries feel about the policies of the rich countries. We are perceived by more and more people as being unwilling to consider the real needs in the poor countries of the world. A growing number of the world's population are willing to write us off as non-human.

The essay by Robin Way which follows represents a modest statement of this view. In addition, some of the flavor of Third World thinkers is conveyed by the quotations scattered through this part of the book.

World Conservation: The United States and the Third World*

ROBIN E. WAY

A few months ago I visited that most dreadful of American cities, New York. While I was there I dropped by the United Nations. I had two reasons to go there. First of all, I needed some research material for a book I am working on. And secondly, in my typical idealistic naïveté, I wished to inquire about the possibility of participating in the United Nations Conference on the Human Environment to be held in Stockholm this June.

To my surprise I was told not only that was it too late for me to participate in the conference but that the papers to be delivered there were already being prepared, discussed in meetings, and analyzed within the UN bureaucracy. It seems that the Stockholm conference will be little more than a glorified press conference, intended to avoid intellectual confrontation.

I believed then, as I do now, that the UN has far more important things to worry about than the environmental problems commonly associated with the environmental and ecology movement in the United States today. Both of these issues—on a world level and without adequate attention to the major issue of world conservation of natural resources—are irrelevant and pedantic. Don't get me

* Taken from a speech given before a citizen's preparatory meeting to the UN Conference on the Human Environment, February 4, 1972. Reprinted by permission.

wrong. Each of these issues is important, but not as an end in itself. If the UN instead were to organize a conference on world conservation, these two issues—ecology and human environment—could be considered in their proper perspective.

We will never beat our swords into plowshares without focusing attention on the essential differences in the general condition of mankind. I refer to the terribly inequitable distribution of resources among and between the people of the Earth. Millions of people live in slums and hovels. Two-thirds of the world's people go to bed undernourished. Medical and sanitation facilities are often nonexistent in many parts of the world. Illiteracy and substandard education are widespread. In most parts of the world industry is embryonic, productivity and consumption of essentials are low. And, most tragic of all in the broad view, many countries have populations that consistently grow faster than their economies. But at the same time, a dozen or so countries, comprising some 20 percent of the world population, consume well in excess of 80 percent of the world's resources every year. No wonder so many *other* people are poor and wretched.

The press releases being prepared for delivery in Stockholm are arrogantly concerned with human environment and human ecology. Instead, they should be concerned with the conservation of man, the means and policies of lifting the Third World from its wretchedness through the wise use of natural resources, and the causes and prevention of war.

In official preparatory meetings to the UN conference, most representatives of the Third World agreed that ". . . the relationship between development and environment varied according to different levels of economic and social development and that solutions to environmental problems . . . could only be found within a dynamic process of economic and social development." And that "Policies for the protection and improvement of the environment must be considered within the context of national strategies for economic and social development." Furthermore, they rightly feel that they are not responsible for present global environmental problems such as marine and air pollution.[1] In short, the Third World countries basically feel that most of the items to be considered at the UN conference do not confront the issues of major concern to them.

The United States, in particular, is hardly concerned with the eco-

[1] Preparatory Committee for the United Nations Conference on the Human Environment, Third Session, New York, September 13–24, 1971, pp. 12, 13.

nomic and social development of the Third World, and does not plan to participate in the conference dialogues that will evaluate the environment with economic development and natural resource management. To understand our official lack of concern with emerging Third World countries requires an investigation of the natural resource policies of our nation.

To gain this understanding, we must first recognize the international distribution patterns of deposits of natural resources: i.e., those naturally occurring products of the Earth which man can use to his advantage. Natural resources include copper, nickel, tin, petroleum, rubber, iron and aluminum ores, and many others, in addition to forests, natural ports and harbors, soil, wilderness and parks, wildlife and fisheries. All of them are distributed unevenly around the world, and most of what is left is found in abundance only in the Third World.

For instance, South East Asia possesses 40 percent of the world's tin, 25 percent of the world's nickel, oil reserves that may be the world's largest, and huge reserves of iron, tungsten, and columbium (niobium), in addition to rubber and rice. South America is rich in petroleum, copper, tin, aluminum, quartz, and mica, in addition to the Pacific Coast yellow fin tuna. Africa has most of the world's diamonds, chromium, manganese and asbestos, plus huge reserves of petroleum, gold, titanium, silver, cobalt, and rubber.[2] And throughout the Third World are tremendous forests, hydroelectric potential, and rich agricultural lands, as well as abundant, cheap labor.

In contrast, what are the natural resources found in the United States and the other developed countries of the world—of western Europe, the Soviet Union, Japan, Australia-New Zealand, Canada, and South Africa? With few exceptions, the fully industrialized nations are deficient in the natural resources essential to their industrialization. Each nation, or group of nations, may have one or two minerals in surplus quantities, but all are dependent upon imports for the bulk of their consumption. The exceptions are Canada, the USSR, South Africa, and Australia, which are relatively wealthy, at least more so than the other developed countries. To remedy such deficiencies, and to maintain economic growth, the U.S. and the others are busily and systematically exploiting the riches of the underdeveloped nations for their own benefit.

Consider these facts: The U.S. has less than 6 percent of the

[2] Commodity Data Summaries, Bureau of Mines, U.S. Department of the Interior, January 1970.

world's population but consumes in excess of 50 percent of the world's resources every year.

The U.S. produces only three metals (molybdenum, sulfur, and uranium) in large enough quantities so as not to require imports. For many other resources, like lead, zinc, iron, copper, and petroleum, we depend upon imports for considerable portions of our annual consumption, although we produce large amounts of them.

Furthermore, for many other essential resources the U.S. produces insignificant amounts or none at all. For instance, we produce insignificant amounts of aluminum ores, nickel, gold, fluorspar, and asbestos. We produce no chromium, tin, rubber, quartz, mica, or manganese, and no titanium metal ores. And of these two categories of resources we consume up to two-thirds of the annual world production, all through imports.[3]

It is obvious that the United States is deficient in most essential raw materials. We are a resource-poor country, a have-not nation in the most important and critical sense, relative to our consumption demands. Yet our 6 percent of the world consumes over half of the world's resources every year.

How is it that we alone are able to control for our own use such tremendous amounts of world natural resources, almost to the exclusion of the rest of the world? It is the answer to this question that reveals the world-wide conservation ethics and policies of the U.S.

Our resource policies are a direct reflection of the necessity and essentiality of natural resources to the American economic system and to the intimately related American military system. Our economy is predicated on the principle of inexorable growth of profits, of productivity and of consumption. To nurture it, to make possible our continued economic growth, we import huge amounts of Third World resources. Every increase in our productivity and consumption necessarily and automatically requires a greater share of the wealth of the Third World. Consumer goods, industrial goods, and military goods require exotic resources from around the world. . . .

We must define world conservation in terms of the needs of all the people of the world. We must understand the role resources play in the quality and dignity of life and in man's confidence in his future. We must confront these problems in the context of the one-world nature of natural resources, that no one area of the world has all the resources required to fulfill its needs and that all areas must share what they have for the good of all. We must understand that it is the

[3] Ibid.

Third World, comprising two-thirds of the world population, that produces and contributes the bulk of the resources, and that it is the Third World that participates least in the benefits and advantages of their own wealth. This situation must be changed. It is the imperative of this decade and the essential responsibility of the United Nations.

If we don't confront these issues squarely and immediately, the scarcity of world resources will leave the world's exploding population with very little to prevent mass starvation, disease, and inevitable internecine warfare. And we then will be faced with the suggestion endorsed by Paul Ehrlich in *The Population Bomb* (1968), namely, that *we* let the most unfortunate of the world's people die.

Dr. Ehrlich recommends, basically, that the Earth be divided into areas along political, economic, agricultural, and demographic lines. Of these areas, only those whose populations may be supported by adequate supplies of basic resources will be permitted to live. Tragically, the others must die.[4]

Such an idea was first suggested by the Paddock brothers in *Famine—1975!* They borrowed the idea from the system of military medical treatment during time of war in which the wounded are divided into three classifications: those with minor problems who will survive without immediate treatment, those whose injuries require immediate care in order to survive, and those whose situations are so severe that they will die regardless of medical care. The Paddocks insist that those who fit this third classification—relative to certain parts of the world population—be abandoned to die. Paul Ehrlich concurs, and endorses the Paddocks for their courage and foresight to publish *Famine—1975!*

I reject Dr. Ehrlich's suggestion. First of all, the U.S. is one of the resource-poor nations of the world, with the exception of agricultural resources and a few others. Looking at the statistics of U.S. import consumption rates of all resources leads me to believe that if we applied Dr. Ehrlich's suggestion, Americans then deserve to be some of the first people to die. More to the point, however, I reject the idea that there is enough wealth in the world for our economy to prosper but not enough wealth to lift the Third World from its wretchedness.

Instead, we must develop a new concept of world conservation, one that meets face to face the needs of mankind. We must end the squandering of wealth by the favored few. The new world conserva-

---

[4] *The Population Bomb,* Dr. Paul Ehrlich, 1968, pp. 158–165.

tion ethic must be the essence of wise use, so that all men may share the wealth and the life support of our Earth. I believe that we must define conservation of natural resources to mean from each according to his ability, and to each according to his need.

The concept of from each according to his ability, relative to the use of natural resources, means, simply, that those areas capable of contributing essential materials for the common good will do so. Those unable to contribute materials or resources may contribute instead the knowledge, technology or manpower to utilize them most efficiently.

The world's resources can be mobilized to serve man, to fulfill the concept of to each according to his need. And what are his needs? What do the masses of mankind need most? Without a doubt, they need better housing and clothing, and adequate food supplies. Men need education, medical and sanitation facilities, and the means of transportation and communication. Translated to terms of natural resources, the need is for steel and aluminum, copper and tin, lead, mica, and chromium. The need is for alloys, for petrochemicals and rubber products, and for timber and construction materials. Most of these things the Third World already has in raw form, and in great abundance.

To work these resources, to make the things they need most, requires basic industrial facilities. According to Buckminster Fuller the most efficient uses of essential resources are the very forms of capital required by the Third World. Fuller estimates that ships and railroad equipment, agricultural machinery, industrial and metal working equipment, construction, mining and lumbering machinery, and air conditioning and refrigeration equipment have the longest service lives of all capital goods. They represent the wisest use of natural resources.

Furthermore, these are exactly the capital goods needed to build houses, schools and hospitals, to improve agricultural productivity and food storage and processing, and to provide for transportation and communication—all of these being essential to the future of the Third World.

From each according to his ability and to each according to his need is a realizable goal. The Third World already possesses the natural wealth and the obvious need to use it. What they lack is the very commodity that we as Americans are uniquely qualified to offer them—that is, our technological sophistication. It should be our responsibility in this decade and the one following, to contribute our technological abilities, primarily as teachers, instructors and technicians in the context of the emerging utilization patterns of world resources.

How exactly will we as a nation contribute our abilities to the emerging Third World? And what changes must be made in the American way of life to accomplish our new global task? Make no mistake about it, basic changes will have to be made in the U.S. to fulfill our new world-wide responsibilities.

In the economic sphere, we must stop growing. This is essential. As long as every increase in our Gross National Product, our national income and our consumption is dependent upon the exploitation of Third World wealth, then our expanding prosperity is no longer justifiable.

The American economic system is undoubtedly the most successful in the history of the world. In purely economic terms, and strictly from the standpoint of the United States, it is a great achievement that we consume half of the world's resources every year. But the success of our economy has been achieved only with the unwilling involvement of the rest of the world. Our success certainly has not brought success to the Third World. There can be no doubt about that. And as long as this continues to be true, our economy and the institutions and corporations responsible for its growth and for the exploitation of the Third World must be stopped where they are. The continued success of our economy is no longer enough justification for its future growth and prosperity at the expense of others.

At the same time, the military must be stopped. Waging war against humans and destroying the life support system of the Earth, as any observer of the Vietnam war knows all too well, is only part of the anti-life mentality of the masters of war. War preparations— whether they are employed or not—require tremendous amounts of materials from around the world. Think of the good these materials could bring if instead they were employed to keep people alive.

It is not mere coincidence that the U.S. and Europe too have military facilities deployed around the world. Military strategy entails more than containment and encirclement. In the industrial age, strategy obviously includes the imperative of ready and secure access to sources of raw materials wherever in the world they may be found. And it is for this reason, in addition to that of political strategy, that the U.S. eagerly supports the governments of military dictatorships throughout the Third World. Raw materials for war and for profit concern the military equally. The Pentagon and the Natural Resources Mafia, together, must be stopped.

Another characteristic of our economic and military establishment deserves attention. That is the relationship between raw materials and manufactured goods in trade with the Third World. At the present time, U.S. exports consist primarily of manufactured goods and military aid. Foreign aid, channeled primarily through the State Department, is so closely tied to the purchase of manufactured goods and military hardware that it must be counted in the same category. Imports, meanwhile, overwhelmingly are of raw materials from the Third World. What is actually happening, of course, is that U.S. exports are manufactured from previously imported Third World resources which in turn are exported. So the Third World is caught in the classic imperialist-colonialist trap of exporting raw materials and importing high-cost manufactured goods made from their own exports.

This tremendously exploitative economic trap will, of course, be ended as the Third World develops its industry and infrastructure. In the meantime, U.S. exports of engineering and design technology should be expanded significantly, particularly to the underdeveloped nations. As a matter of fact, the Commerce Department reports that engineering services are a rapidly growing segment of U.S. exports. We are increasingly selling abroad our expertise as engineers, chemists, and industrial designers, although most of these services are to the other developed countries of the world. Such exports of our technology must entail, naturally, the incorporation of the most modern and efficient pollution control techniques known. The design and construction of pollution-free industrial facilities, which incorporate the total utilization and recycling of materials, and the capture of noxious and toxic substances are an engineering reality. And no other type of industrial facilities should be permitted.

An example of U.S. technology at work in the Third World is in Algeria. This former French colony is rich, among other things, in petroleum and natural gas. For years, however, Algerian oil resources had been exploited by French oil companies. They extracted the crude oil and gas and transported them to France where they were refined and manufactured to serve the French economy. But a year or two ago Algeria nationalized the French oil holdings and contracted with the Bechtel Corporation, an international engineering company headquartered in San Francisco, to design and supervise the construction of one of the most modern and efficient petrochemical complexes in the world. Very soon, Algeria will be able to sell petrochemicals, rather than crude oil and gas, to the lucrative European markets, in addition to employing them in their own growing economy.

There are many other African countries that are rich in resources but not so fortunate as Algeria. One in particular is Angola, to this day one of fascist Portugal's colonies in black Africa. Angola originally served Portugal in its slave trade. Angola's huge reserves of aluminum, oil and iron ore, and lesser amounts of diamonds and chromium, in addition to its agricultural and forest products, have only recently attracted attention, primarily from Japanese and American corporations.

The way Angola's resources are being exploited, and an investigation of her principal imports and exports, establishes the economic dependence Portugal forces upon its colony. Angola's principal exports are crude petroleum, iron ore, coffee and timber. Her aluminum ore (bauxite) deposits are not yet being developed. Her major imports are mining, petroleum and railroad equipment, the latter necessary to transport iron ore from the mines to the coast, where it is loaded upon foreign ships for export. Obviously, Angola is a typical supplier of raw materials and an importer of manufactured goods, the same manufactured goods necessary to the foreign exploitation of her raw materials. This situation ensures that Angola's prosperity is entirely dependent upon the whims of her masters in Portugal and the U.S., and that her future economic independence is doubtful at best.

Angola should have constructed a modern steel smelter and fabrication plant and a petroleum refining facility. The steel fabricator could easily produce the rails for the railroad and basic mining and petroleum drilling equipment. While Angola may have had to import the diesel railroad engines, certainly the ore cars could be made domestically, as well as diesel fuel by the petroleum refinery. These industrial facilities could serve as indispensable beginnings to the development of Angola's economy. Surplus production, what could not immediately be used or consumed in Angola could be exported, either to other African countries or to Europe.

But in the politics of colonial and imperialist exploitation, this route to African development and independence was not adopted. Being a colony, of course, means that Angola has no representation in the United Nations. So for all intents and purposes, its conservation and environmental problems are irrelevant and non-existent, at least as far as the UN is concerned. Angola will not participate in the Stockholm conference, but will be represented by Portugal.

Some Angolans are actively resisting Portugal's colonialism. For more than a decade now, revolutionary armies have been waging a war for independence. Unfortunately, the Portuguese military is crushing the Angolan rebels. Portugal is receiving tremendous financial and material support from the United States, as well as the use of American military advisors. Most military aid is channeled through NATO and the CIA. Through such aid, Portugal has one of the highest per capita military budgets in the world.

There are other examples, some successful and some not, of the Third World throwing off imperialist domination of their natural resources. Cuba, China, and Chile, for instance, are examples of successful nationalistic recaptures of their wealth. Cuba has one-fourth of the world's nickel, China has most of the world's tungsten, and Chile has huge copper and natural nitrate deposits. Each of these countries had experienced severe foreign exploitation. The world is learning that wherever valuable resources are found, the inherent wealth created by them is more than enough to permit domestic development and exploitation, as well as the establishment of basic industrial facilities for smelting, refining and manufacture.

Let's get back to our responsibilities under the new global conservation ethic. What can we do, as individual citizens, to fulfill our responsibilities as Americans? One of the most important things we can do is to make it safe here in America for the Third World to nationalize or confiscate exploitative American interests abroad. No longer must we tolerate or permit the calling out of the Marines to protect the foreign interests of the Natural Resources Mafia and the other war profiteers.

And secondly, we must adopt a lifestyle consistent with the conservation of world resources and in harmony with our environment. A great deal has already been said about the evils of automobiles, electric can openers, hairdryers and razors, and fancy home appliances. Electro-mechanical gadgetry like this deserves all the criticism it can attract. But so do nuclear weapons, supersonic transports and bombers, ICBMs and ABMs, Polaris submarines, the automated battlefield and the Short Take-Off and Landing aircraft. And so do new freeways, subdivisions, nuclear power generators and new office buildings.

We simply do not need more economic growth, particularly when it is dependent upon, or when its intention is, the continued importation of natural resources. If we cannot make what we want by recycling the tremendous amounts of wealth we already have, then we do not deserve anything else new.

Natural resources are scarce, and they belong to all people. They are the basis of the quality of life of all people. And they must be managed to serve the interests of all people.

Underdevelopment is shocking: the squalor, disease, unnecessary deaths, and hopelessness of it all! No man understands if underdevelopment remains for him a mere statistic reflecting low income, poor housing, premature mortality, or underemployment. The most empathetic observer can speak objectively about underdevelopment only after undergoing, personally or vicariously, the "shock of underdevelopment." This unique culture shock comes to one as he is initiated to the emotions which prevail in the "culture of poverty" . . .

Chronic poverty is a cruel kind of hell; and one cannot understand how cruel that hell is merely by gazing upon poverty as an object. Unless the observer gains entry into the inner sanctum of these emotions and feels them himself, he will not understand the condition he seeks to abolish . . .

This revelation is no mere adventure of the spirit, however . . . , which humbles the sensitive man's soul but bears no consequences for his actions. The very opposite is true: this psychic transformation can revolutionize his technical and political dealings . . .

DENIS GOULET

Outwitting the "Developed" Countries*

IVAN ILLICH

It is now common to demand that the rich nations convert their war machine into a program for the development of the Third World. The poorer four-fifths of humanity multiply unchecked while their per capita consumption actually declines. This population expansion and decrease of consumption threaten the industrialized nations, who may still, as a result, convert their defense budgets to the economic pacification of poor nations. And this in turn could produce irreversible despair, because the plows of the rich can do as much harm as their swords. U.S. trucks can do more lasting damage than U.S. tanks. It is easier to create mass demand for the former than for the latter. Only a minority needs heavy weapons, while a majority can become dependent on unrealistic levels of supply for such productive machines as modern trucks. Once the Third World has become a mass market for the goods, products, and processes which are designed by the rich for themselves, the discrepancy between demand for these Western artifacts and the supply will increase indefinitely. The family car cannot drive the poor into the jet age, nor can a school system provide the poor with education, nor can the family icebox ensure healthy food for them.

It is evident that only one man in a thousand in Latin America

can afford a Cadillac, a heart operation, or a Ph.D. This restriction
on the goals of development does not make us despair of the fate
of the Third World, and the reason is simple. We have not yet come
to conceive of a Cadillac as necessary for good transportation, or
of a heart operation as normal health care, or of a Ph.D. as the
prerequisite of an acceptable education. In fact, we recognize at once
that the importation of Cadillacs should be heavily taxed in Peru,
that an organ transplant clinic is a scandalous plaything to justify
the concentration of more doctors in Bogota, and that a Betatron is
beyond the teaching facilities of the University of Sao Paolo.

Unfortunately, it is not held to be universally evident that the majority of Latin Americans—not only of our generation, but also of
the next and the next again—cannot afford any kind of automobile,
or any kind of hospitalization, or for that matter an elementary
school education. We suppress our consciousness of this obvious
reality because we hate to recognize the corner into which our imagination has been pushed. So persuasive is the power of the institutions we have created that they shape not only our preferences, but
actually our sense of possibilities. We have forgotten how to speak
about modern transportation that does not rely on automobiles and
airplanes. Our conceptions of modern health care emphasize our
ability to prolong the lives of the desperately ill. We have become
unable to think of better education except in terms of more complex
schools and of teachers trained for ever longer periods. Huge institutions producing costly services dominate the horizons of our inven-
tiveness.

We have embodied our world view into our institutions and are
now their prisoners. Factories, news media, hospitals, governments,
and schools produce goods and services packaged to contain our
view of the world. We—the rich—conceive of progress as the expansion of these establishments. We conceive of heightened mobility as
luxury and safety packaged by General Motors or Boeing. We conceive of improving the general well-being as increasing the supply
of doctors and hospitals, which package health along with protracted
suffering. We have come to identify our need for further learning
with the demand for ever longer confinement to classrooms. In other
words, we have packaged education with custodial care, certification
for jobs, and the right to vote, and wrapped them all together with
indoctrination in the Christian, liberal, or communist virtues. . . .

Rich nations now benevolently impose a straightjacket of traffic
jams, hospital confinements, and classrooms on the poor nations,

and by international agreement call this "development." The rich and schooled and old of the world try to share their dubious blessings by foisting their pre-packaged solutions on to the Third World. Traffic jams develop in Sao Paolo, while almost a million northeastern Brazilians flee the drought by walking 500 miles. Latin American doctors get training at the New York Hospital for Special Surgery, which they apply to only a few, while amoebic dysentery remains endemic in slums where 90 per cent of the population live. A tiny minority gets advanced education in basic science in North America—not infrequently paid for by their own governments. If they return at all to Bolivia, they become second-rate teachers of pretentious subjects at La Paz or Cochibamba. The rich export outdated versions of their standard models.

The Alliance for Progress is a good example of benevolent production for underdevelopment. Contrary to its slogans, it did succeed—as an alliance for the progress of the consuming classes, and for the domestication of the Latin American masses. The Alliance has been a major step in modernizing the consumption patterns of the middle classes in South America by integrating them with the dominant culture of the North American metropolis. At the same time, the Alliance has modernized the aspirations of the majority of citizens and fixed their demands on unavailable products.

Each car which Brazil puts on the road denies fifty people good transportation by bus. Each merchandised refrigerator reduces the chance of building a community freezer. Every dollar spent in Latin America on doctors and hospitals costs a hundred lives, to adopt a phrase of Jorge de Ahumada, the brilliant Chilean economist. Had each dollar been spent on providing safe drinking water, a hundred lives could have been saved. Each dollar spent on schooling means more privileges for the few at the cost of the many; at best it increases the number of those who, before dropping out, have been taught that those who stay longer have earned the right to more power, wealth, and prestige. What such schooling does is to teach the schooled the superiority of the better schooled. . . .

In most Third World countries, the population grows, and so does the middle class. Income, consumption, and the well-being of the middle class are all growing while the gap between this class and the mass of people widens. Even where per capita consumption is rising, the majority of men have less food now than in 1945, less actual care in sickness, less meaningful work, less protection. This is partly a consequence of polarized consumption and partly caused by the

breakdown of traditional family and culture. More people suffer from
hunger, pain, and exposure in 1969 than they did at the end of World
War II, not only numerically, but also as a percentage of the world
population.

These concrete consequences of underdevelopment are rampant;
but underdevelopment is also a state of mind, and understanding it
as a state of mind, or as a form of consciousness, is the critical problem. Underdevelopment as a state of mind occurs when mass needs
are converted to the demand for new brands of packaged solutions
which are forever beyond the reach of the majority. Underdevelopment in this sense is rising rapidly even in countries where the supply of classrooms, calories, cars, and clinics is also rising. The ruling groups in these countries build up services which have been designed for an affluent culture; once they have monopolized demand
in this way, they can never satisfy majority needs. . . .

Underdevelopment is the result of rising levels of aspiration
achieved through the intensive marketing of "patent" products. In
this sense, the dynamic underdevelopment that is now taking place
is the exact opposite of what I believe education to be: namely, the
awakening awareness of new levels of human potential and the use
of one's creative powers to foster human life. Underdevelopment,
however, implies the surrender of social consciousness to pre-packaged solutions.

The process by which the marketing of "foreign" products increases underdevelopment is frequently understood in the most super-
ficial ways. The same man who feels indignation at the sight of a
Coca-Cola plant in a Latin American slum often feels pride at the
sight of a new normal school growing up alongside. He resents the
evidence of a foreign "license" attached to a soft drink which he
would like to see replaced by "Cola-Mex." But the same man is willing to impose schooling—at all costs—on his fellow citizens, and is
unaware of the invisible license by which this institution is deeply
enmeshed in the world market.

Some years ago I watched workmen putting up a sixty-foot Coca-
Cola sign on a desert plain in the Mexquital. A serious drought and
famine had just swept over the Mexican highland. My host, a poor
Indian in Ixmiquilpan, had just offered his visitors a tiny tequila glass
of the costly black sugar-water. When I recall this scene I still feel
anger; but I feel much more incensed when I remember UNESCO
meetings at which well-meaning and well-paid bureaucrats seriously

discussed Latin American school curricula, and when I think of the speeches of enthusiastic liberals advocating the need for more schools.

The fraud perpetrated by the salesmen of schools is less obvious but much more fundamental than the self-satisfied salesmanship of the Coca-Cola or Ford representative, because the schoolman hooks his people on a much more demanding drug. Elementary school attendance is not a harmless luxury, but more like the coca chewing of the Andean Indian, which harnesses the worker to the boss.

The higher the dose of schooling an individual has received, the more depressing his experience of withdrawal. The seventh-grade dropout feels his inferiority much more acutely than the dropout from the third grade. The schools of the Third World administer their opium with much more effect than the churches of other epochs. As the mind of a society is progressively schooled, step by step its individuals lose their sense that it might be possible to live without being inferior to others. As the majority shifts from the land into the city, the hereditary inferiority of the peon is replaced by the inferiority of the school dropout who is held personally responsible for his failure. Schools rationalize the divine origin of social stratification with much more rigor than churches have ever done.

Until this day no Latin American country has declared youthful underconsumers of Coca-Cola or cars as lawbreakers, while all Latin American countries have passed laws which define the early dropout as a citizen who has not fulfilled his legal obligations. The Brazilian government recently almost doubled the number of years during which schooling is legally compulsory and free. From now on any Brazilian dropout under the age of sixteen will be faced during his lifetime with the reproach that he did not take advantage of a legally obligatory privilege. This law was passed in a country where not even the most optimistic could foresee the day when such levels of schooling would be provided for only 25 percent of the young. The adoption of international standards of schooling forever condemns most Latin Americans to marginality or exclusion from social life—in a word, underdevelopment. . . .

Underdevelopment is at the point of becoming chronic in many countries. The revolution of which I speak must begin to take place before this happens. Education again offers a good example: chronic educational underdevelopment occurs when the demand for schooling becomes so widespread that the total concentration of educational

resources on the school system becomes a unanimous political demand. At this point the separation of education from schooling becomes impossible.

The only feasible answer to ever-increasing underdevelopment is
a response to basic needs that is planned as a long-range goal for
areas which will always have a different capital structure. It is easier
to speak about alternatives to existing institutions, services, and
products than to define them with precision. It is not my purpose
either to paint a Utopia or to engage in scripting scenarios for an
alternate future. We must be satisfied with examples indicating simple
directions that research should take.

Some such examples have already been given. Buses are alternatives to a multitude of private cars. Vehicles designed for slow transportation on rough terrain are alternatives to standard trucks. Safe
water is an alternative to high-priced surgery. Medical workers are
an alternative to doctors and nurses. Community food storage is an
alternative to expensive kitchen equipment. Other alternatives could
be discussed by the dozen. Why not, for example, consider walking
as a long-range alternative for locomotion by machine, and explore
the demands which this would impose on the city planner? And why
can't the building of shelters be standardized, elements be pre-cast,
and each citizen be obliged to learn in a year of public service how
to construct his own sanitary housing?

It is harder to speak about alternatives in education, partly because schools have recently so completely pre-empted the available
educational resources of good will, imagination, and money. But
even here we can indicate the direction in which research must be
conducted.

At present, schooling is conceived as graded, curricular, class attendance by children, for about 1000 hours yearly during an uninterrupted succession of years. On the average, Latin American
countries can provide each citizen with between eight and thirty
months of this service. Why not, instead, make one or two months a
year obligatory for all citizens below the age of thirty?

Money is now spent largely on children, but an adult can be taught
to read in one-tenth the time and for one-tenth the cost it takes to
teach a child. In the case of the adult there is an immediate return
on the investment, whether the main importance of his learning is
seen in his new insight, political awareness, and willingness to assume
responsibility for his family's size and future, or whether the emphasis
is placed on increased productivity. There is a double return in the

case of the adult, because he can contribute not only to the education of his children, but to that of other adults as well. In spite of
these advantages, basic literacy programs have little or no support
in Latin America, where schools have a first call on all public resources. Worse, these programs are actually ruthlessly suppressed
in Brazil and elsewhere, where military support of the feudal or industrial oligarchy has thrown off its former benevolent disguise.

Another possibility is harder to define, because there is as yet no
example to point to. We must therefore imagine the use of public
resources for education distributed in such a way as to give every
citizen a minimum chance. Education will become a political concern
of the majority of voters only when each individual has a precise
sense of the educational resources that are owing to him—and some
idea of how to sue for them. Something like a universal G.I. Bill of
Rights could be imagined, dividing the public resources assigned to
education by the number of children who are legally of school age,
and making sure that a child who did not take advantage of his credit
at the age of seven, eight, or nine would have the accumulated benefits at his disposal at age ten.

What could the pitiful education credit which a Latin American
republic could offer to its children provide? Almost all of the basic
supply of books, pictures, blocks, games, and toys that are totally
absent from the homes of the really poor, but enable a middle-class
child to learn the alphabet, the colors, shapes, and other classes of
objects and experiences which ensure his educational progress. The
choice between these things and schools is obvious. Unfortunately,
the poor, for whom alone the choice is real, never get to exercise
this choice.

Defining alternatives to the products and institutions which now
pre-empt the field is difficult, not only, as I have been trying to show,
because these products and institutions shape our conception of
reality itself, but also because the construction of new possibilities
requires a concentration of will and intelligence in a higher degree
than ordinarily occurs by chance. This concentration of will and intelligence on the solution of particular problems regardless of their
nature we have become accustomed over the last century to call research.

I must make clear, however, what kind of research I am talking
about. I am not talking about basic research in either physics, engineering, genetics, medicine, or learning. The work of such men as
Crick, Piaget, and Gell-Mann must continue to enlarge our horizons

in other fields of science. The labs and libraries and specially trained collaborators these men need cause them to congregate in the few research capitals of the world. Their research can provide the basis for new work on practically any product.

I am not speaking here of the billions of dollars annually spent on applied research, for this money is largely spent by existing institutions on the perfection and marketing of their own products. Applied research is money spent on making planes faster and airports safer; on making medicines more specific and powerful and doctors capable of handling their deadly side-effects; on packaging more learning into classrooms; on methods to administer large bureaucracies. This is the kind of research for which some kind of counterfoil must somehow be developed if we are to have any chance to come up with basic alternatives to the automobile, the hospital, and the school, and any of the many other so-called "evidently necessary implements for modern life."

I have in mind a different, and peculiarly difficult, kind of research, which has been largely neglected up to now, for obvious reasons. I am calling for research on alternatives to the products which now dominate the market; to hospitals and the profession dedicated to keeping the sick alive; to schools and the packaging process which refuses education to those who are not of the right age, who have not gone through the right curriculum, who have not sat in a classroom a sufficient number of successive hours, who will not pay for their learning with submission to custodial care, screening, and certification or with indoctrination in the values of the dominant elite.

This counter-research on fundamental alternatives to current prepackaged solutions is the element most critically needed if the poor nations are to have a livable future. Such counter-research is distinct from most of the work done in the name of the "year 2000," because most of that work seeks radical changes in social patterns through adjustments in the organization of an already advanced technology. The counter-research of which I speak must take as one of its assumptions the continued lack of capital in the Third World.

The difficulties of such research are obvious. The researcher must first of all doubt what is obvious to every eye. Second, he must persuade those who have the power of decision to act against their own short-run interests or bring pressure on them to do so. And, finally, he must survive as an individual in a world he is attempting to change fundamentally so that his fellows among the privileged minority see him as a destroyer of the very ground on which all of us stand. He knows that if he should succeed in the interest of the poor, technologically advanced societies still might envy the "poor" who adopt this vision.

There is a normal course for those who make development policies, whether they live in North or South America, in Russia or Israel. It is to define development and to set its goals in ways with which they are familiar, which they are accustomed to use in order to satisfy their own needs, and which permit them to work through the institutions over which they have power or control. This formula has failed, and must fail. There is not enough money in the world for development to succeed along these lines, not even in the combined arms and space budgets of the super-powers.

An analogous course is followed by those who are trying to make political revolutions, especially in the Third World. Usually they promise to make the familiar privileges of the present elites, such as schooling, hospital care, etc., accessible to all citizens; and they base this vain promise on the belief that a change in political regime will permit them to sufficiently enlarge the institutions whch produce these privileges. The promise and appeal of the revolutionary are therefore just as threatened by the counter-research I propose as is the market of the now dominant producers.

In Vietnam a people on bicycles and armed with sharpened bamboo sticks have brought to a standstill the most advanced machinery for research and production ever devised. We must seek survival in a Third World in which human ingenuity can peacefully outwit machined might. The only way to reverse the disastrous trend to increasing underdevelopment, hard as it is, is to learn to laugh at accepted solutions in order to change the demands which make them necessary. Only free men can change their minds and be surprised; and while no men are completely free, some are freer than others.

Reprinted courtesy Sawyer Press, Los Angeles, California 90046.

Poverty is not the real problem of the modern world, for we have the knowledge and the resources which will enable us to overcome poverty. The real problem of the modern world, the thing which creates misery, wars, and hatred amongst men, is the division of mankind into rich and poor . . .

The significance about this division between rich and poor is not simply that one man has more food than he can eat, more clothes than he can wear, and more houses than he can live in, while others are hungry, unclad, or homeless. The reality and the depth of the problem arise because the man who is rich has power over the lives of those who are poor, and the rich nation has power over the policies of those who are not rich. And even more important is that a social and economic system, nationally and internationally, supports these divisions, and constantly increases them so that the rich get ever richer and more powerful, while the poor get relatively ever poorer and less able to control their own future. . . .

Both nationally and internationally this division of mankind into a tiny minority of rich and a great majority of poor is rapidly becoming intolerable to the majority, as it should be. The poor nations and the poor peoples of the world are already in rebellion. If they do not succeed in securing a change which leads towards greater justice, then that rebellion will become an explosion.

JULIUS NYERERE

Why We Know Nothing About Development Theory and Practice and What We Should Do to Discover Something*

ROBERT THEOBALD

The basic value systems which lie behind the industrial era must be altered fundamentally and immediately if the survival of planet Earth is to be assured. We must no longer make decisions on the basis that more is *necessarily* better than less, bigger is *necessarily* better than smaller, action is *necessarily* better than inaction. This conclusion emerges clearly from the work of Dennis Meadows and his team in the report sponsored by the Club of Rome, *The Limits of Growth.*

The insight achieved by this report is not new, of course. Dennis Gabor, the recent Nobel Prize winner, stated more than a decade ago: "In today's world all curves are exponential. It is only in mathematics that exponential curves grow to infinity. In real life, they either saturate gently or they decline catastrophically. It is our duty as thinking men to strive toward a gentle saturation."

The activities of the Club of Rome are having a major impact in bringing this reality to the attention of the American and the world public. An increasingly violent debate is now raging around the studies. The question we must now ask is whether we are getting so involved in the debate that we shall once again forget its policy implications. At the moment I consider it possible—even probable— that we shall spend so much time discussing the studies of the Club

* Speech given to the International Development Conference, April 1972.

of Rome and other similar work that we shall forget the immediate implications for development theory and practice.

Such a pattern will not be new. Americans seem peculiarly prone to ignore new ideas and then suddenly, with an extraordinary swing of the pendulum, spend excessive attention on them. For example, during the sixties, development theory was largely based on W. W. Rostow's thesis that the poor countries could easily follow the path already blazed by the rich countries. In a 1961 review of his volume I challenged the conclusion he reached: that "the tricks of growth are not all that difficult; though they may seem so, at moments of frustration and confusion in traditional societies." I argued that "there seems to be a real possibility that Rostow's theory may shift attention away from immediate problems to more theoretical controversies" and referred to a recent meeting of the Society for International Development where a discussion of Rostow's approach to growth took place with hardly a single reference to the everyday problems in the underdeveloped countries or to the pressures on the price level and the balance of payments. I am still convinced that Rostow's work was one of the prime factors which caused us to ignore the realities of a rapidly worsening socio-economic situation in both rich and poor countries and permitted us to concentrate on trying to develop industrial era conditions throughout the world.

The work of the Club of Rome seems only too likely to provide us with another excuse for forgetting the real, immediate crises of the world. Academicians and development theorists could seize upon this set of studies and use them to engage in interminable debates around the exact dates when disaster will strike planet Earth on the basis of various sets of assumptions. Indeed, such studies could well be used as an excuse to move us still further into the current pathology—that of treating human beings as statistics. The danger is that we shall continue to abstract human complexities in terms of birth rates and death rates, juvenile delinquency rates, rates of abortion, number of radios and newspapers per head, etc. We may well continue to ignore the reality that human beings are complex, that excessive frustration all too often causes behavior which is damaging to self, society, and the world.

It seems particularly significant that it took the spurious accuracy of computer studies to draw attention to the obvious. We could not "hear" Gabor—it was only the availability of computer runs that brought the debate about the finiteness of the planet to public attention. This computer approach could reinforce still further another industrial era pathology—the idea that decisions can and should be made without the consent of the governed. In the Meadows study, various computer runs were made on the basis of different assumptions; the patterns chosen were those that appeared most interesting to the investigating team. No attention was paid in these studies to the nature of the process by which changes in values and decisions occur. As a result we may continue to forget that new understandings of data are not *automatically* translated into appropriate decisions. (This lack is doubly unfortunate because we do today possess the skills required to simulate the decision-making process.)

It is often considered unreasonable to criticize writers in terms of the probable response to their work rather than in terms of the stated purpose of their study. I believe, on the contrary, that one must always consider possible responses to communication. I believe that each writer has the responsibility to ensure that the ideas he advances will be as effective as possible in changing dynamics in desirable directions. The fact that the Meadows/Club of Rome study may actually serve to reinforce existing pathologies should have been perceived by those involved and avoided by more appropriate experimental designs and patterns of communications.

Let us now move on to consider what part of the understandings of Meadows are valid. We need to retain his *primary* conclusion—that the drive toward economic growth must be controlled in the near future. We need to remember that there are limits to available resources and that these will certainly be overrun unless we change our policies in the near future.

On the other hand, it is critical that we avoid taking time to argue about the exact date at which a Meadows-style crisis will develop. We are *already* in the middle of a crisis which threatens to be terminal. In the words of U Thant, the recently retired Secretary-General of the United Nations: "I do not wish to seem overdramatic, but I can only conclude from the information available to me as Secretary-General, that the members of the United Nations have perhaps ten years left in which to subordinate their ancient quarrels and launch a global partnership to curb the arms race, to improve the human environment, to defuse the population explosion and to supply the needed momentum to development efforts. If such a global partnership is not forged within the next decade, then I very much fear that the problems that I have mentioned will have reached such staggering proportions that they will be beyond our capacity to control." As this speech was made three years ago, we have perhaps another seven to make significant progress toward a new international order before our situation becomes irreversible.

We face massive, immediate social, economic, and political crises today in the rich countries, in the poor countries, and internationally. These crises emerge from our continued efforts to see development as a linear process, with the rich countries continuing further along the directions of the past two centuries and the poor countries trying to catch up. We now know that this route is infeasible because we dare not aim to achieve the rates of growth which would make full employment in the Western sense a possible goal.

Will we be prepared as a world culture to accept the necessity for fundamental changes in our ways of thinking and acting? We need to recognize immediately that the validity of present theories of development has been irrevocably disproved. We must rethink our models from the beginning.

The quickest way to prove this point is to recognize that any realistic socio-economic theory must necessarily include a viable method of distributing resources and must ensure that the community/country involved accepts the patterns of rights to resources which exist. The agricultural era patterns of the poor countries depend on a complex intermeshing of family/village/tribal mechanisms for determining methods of production and ensuring distribution.

Such complex human-related patterns are not efficient in the industrial era. Community norms of the agricultural type work against a permanent, committed labor force. The success criteria of agricultural era people are related to their village or tribe rather than to the company by which they are employed; they therefore tend to return to their family/village/tribe when they have made "enough" money. Even if the individual becomes committed to the firm, incentives for work are often limited by the fact that relatives and/or people from the tribe/community have the right to demand subsistence from the relatively successful individual; this cuts into the extra money gained as the individual is promoted and receives a higher income.

Our attempts to change patterns of behavior in the poor countries in post-World War II years are similar to the steps we took in the Western world in the nineteenth century. We have tried to create a stable, committed labor force by destroying family, tribal and community ties. At the same time we have tried to convince people that they should measure success in terms of their ability to buy goods and services.

We are, in effect, engaged in destroying the informal mechanisms which ensure the distribution of resources in the poor countries of the world. We have justified this approach on the grounds that we can, and should, achieve Western industrial era economic patterns. We have argued that income should be distributed on the basis of the availability of jobs for all who want them. The fact that we must now recognize the impossibility of continued economic growth makes this point of view obsolete.

Even before we were willing to realize the finiteness of the planet, studies which aimed to prove the possibility of full employment were less than credible. The work of the International Labor Office in this area required heroic assumptions about possible rates of growth and also a willingness to slow down the rate of labor productivity increase. Such assumptions were improbable of realization even in a maximum growth climate—they are utterly impossible now we know that growth must be curtailed. Today we have no development theory, for we have no valid proposals which would permit us to distribute resources fairly in either the rich or the poor countries.

There is another major developmental issue raised by the Meadows/Club of Rome study. We are forced to recognize that our whole theory of foreign aid is also implicitly based on the possibility of continued economic growth. Our success criteria for foreign aid are presently predominantly determined by its success or failure in creating conditions similar to those that exist in the countries already rich. Even those foreign aid experts from the rich countries who are most conscious of the need for different processes of development almost necessarily carry industrial era values with them.

The dangers of foreign aid were dramatically illustrated in a classic science-fiction story [reprinted above: "The Helping Hand"]. Planet Earth defeated the other planets in a space war. Delegates from the two defeated planets were sent to ask for foreign aid. The delegate from one planet turned up on time, was duly humble and got the foreign aid. His planet did very well for two decades, but after fifty years the culture of the planet had been destroyed and its socio-economic viability eliminated. The attempted meshing of the defeated planet's culture with that of Earth failed. The delegate from the other planet deliberately chose to anger the foreign aid negotiators of Earth and was refused foreign aid. The initial result was great hardship, but in fifty years the vitality of the culture had reasserted itself and inventions were being made which were incomprehensible to Earth.

Most of us would probably argue that differences between cultures on Earth could not possibly be as large as those between planets.

Let me suggest that, on the contrary, the parallel is reasonably exact, because there exist four different eras on earth at the present time and each of these necessarily requires the existence of profoundly different value systems.

First, a few people—a very few people—live in hunting and gathering conditions.

Second, the vast majority of the world still lives in the agricultural era.

Third, most of those in the rich countries and those in the cities in the poor countries live in the industrial era.

Fourth, we must all move into the communications era in the immediate future if we are to survive. A few people are living in this era already.

Once we perceive fully that development is actually a process of changing values and myths to make it possible to move from one *era* to another, we necessarily achieve a totally different understanding of the process of development. Both the rich *and* the poor countries need to achieve a transformation in their value systems: the rich need to move from the industrial era to the communications era, the poor need to move from the agricultural era to the communications era.

Given such a changed perspective, it becomes obvious that it is ridiculous to expect the poor countries to move from the agricultural era through the industrial era and then on into the communications era. It is difficult enough to conceive of a single massive shift in values within a restricted period. It is clearly inconceivable to make two major cultural shifts in one generation.

We can no longer assume, therefore, that the rich countries are the teachers and the poor countries should be the learners. Both sets of countries are trying to enter unknown territory, to discover the nature of a new era brought about by man's ever-increasing power. The arrogant superiority of the West must end if we are to have any chance of success.

Indeed, it may well be that those in the agricultural era may find it easier than those now in the industrial era to make the necessary shift. It is already abundantly clear that the keynotes of the culture in the communications era will be an understanding of process and an acceptance of cooperation. Agriculturalists are necessarily aware of the requirement for both process and cooperation in their relations with nature and the environment. Those living in the industrial era have tried, unsuccessfully, to replace these values with force and competition. . . .

Regrettably, we have made little progress in defining the appropriate routes of development in either the rich or the poor countries. Until very recently we have continued to assume that we could work on the straight line theory of development in both the rich and the poor countries.

What *can* we say? We are hampered not only because we have failed to do the necessary thinking but also because it is inevitable that the process of change will be different for each rich and each poor country depending on their past traditions, their present realities and resources and their future dreams. But certain conclusions do seem to be reasonably clear—lack of time forces me to state these baldly with little elaboration.

1. We must break the link between the production of goods and services and the distribution of rights to resources. We must solve the two problems separately. We can no longer afford to make the neo-Keynesian assumption that jobs will be available for all who want them, that these jobs will provide the money to buy the available goods and services, and that the purchase of the goods and services will ensure the availability of additional jobs.

Today, we must aim to discover how to produce the required goods and services with as little human and environmental damage as possible. We must then discover how the rights to the available resources can be provided to the population. The production problem can only be solved by the use of the most modern technologies.

In the rich countries, the distribution of income and resources requires the passage of a true guaranteed income, and also income-maintenance plans for the middle-class. In the poor countries, we shall have to base our thinking on the existing informal systems as well as on government redistribution.

The effect of a commitment to reexamine proper patterns of income distribution would be a massive shift in the distribution of resources. Such a step would be justified because present allocation patterns are grossly distorted by the fact of power. The powerful both within countries and internationally obtain more resources than are morally/socially/economically justified; those without power obtain fewer.[1]

[1] For an elaboration of this point see Problem/Possibility Focuser on the Distribution of Resources, available from Box 1531, Wickenburg, Arizona 85358. For a more extended analysis see Robert Theobald, *The Economics of Abundance.*

2. We shall have to learn what it means to live in a world of enoughness. Each of us will need to discover his own personal goals and use just enough resources to fulfill effectively the purpose he has defined for his life. We must break our present patterns of behavior which are based on the belief that more is necessarily better, that consumption provides satisfaction in and of itself.

It is profoundly dismaying that one of the major efforts of the developed countries in post-World War II years has been to destroy the concepts of enoughness which existed in many religions and philosophies of the non-Western world. Development theorists and businessmen saw correctly that economic growth could not be attained without the achievement of new desires for goods and services. We are only now perceiving that an insatiable desire for additional goods and services is infeasible in ecological terms, and all too often destructive in human terms as well.

3. The communications era will be a world of diversity if we succeed in bringing it into existence. Our sterile monoculture of kids and crops must necessarily give way to synergetic interactions of all living things. We now know that environments are dynamically stable when they contain a large number of organisms, styles and cultures.

The drive toward equality and similarity was necessary to the functioning of the industrial era. If we are to enter successfully the communications era, we *must* break down the uniformity and create a world of profoundly unique individuals grouped together in widely diverse communities.

Teilhard de Chardin has argued that we must move toward an Omega point if we want to survive. John Calhoun has called for a compassionate revolution. I believe that these demands, and those of other thinkers, are necessary to our survival. Man must now grow up; he must achieve the capacity for responsible decision-making. The Whole Earth Catalogue stated: "We are as Gods and we might as well get good at it." I find this idea deeply relevant.

Events that are too large to be perceived in immediate history register in the unconscious in the collective form of myth, and since artists and visionaries possess strongly mythopoeic imaginations, they can express in the microcosm of their works what is going on in the macrocosm of mankind. Because they lack economic power, they are open to other possibilities, and they can cultivate other faculties. The man of power so fills himself with politics, business, and single-step events that he is no longer open to visions of the complete cultural transformation of mankind. Ironically, it is only the man who is free to escape technology who is in position to master it.

What the individual conscious ego does not know, however, does not limit the collective unconscious of mankind, and so one can make some intelligent guesses by paying attention to the seemingly unrelated shifts in human culture at large. As the old civilization of the industrial nation-state is falling apart, it is also falling into new forms of a very old consciousness . . . A new ideology is being created in advance of its social need; what particular institutional form this ideology will take no one can say . . . Perhaps it will take no institutional form at all, for it now seems that social institutions are no longer adequate vehicles of cultural evolution.

WILLIAM IRWIN THOMPSON

Technology and De-Development*

PAUL R. EHRLICH and JOHN P. HOLDREN

It has become increasingly fashionable to view with alarm the purported disaffection of the American people with technology. Those who have called attention to the misuses of technology, and to the fact that technology is incapable in principle of solving certain problems of biological and sociological origin, have been carelessly labeled "anti-technology," "nihilists," and "extremists." And one is being continually reminded that technology is only a tool, of itself neither benevolent nor evil—but neutral.

If technology is indeed neutral (and we believe it is), then one should be able to discuss its potential and limitations openly, without eliciting the defensive and *ad hominem* responses to which we have just referred. To our knowledge, no responsible observer has seriously suggested that technology be abandoned or that mankind return to "hunting and gathering." Those who have rushed to technology's defense should stop grappling with this straw man and deal with the real issues: the focusing of technology on genuine human needs, the minimization of its adverse side effects, and the recognition that some problems do not have purely technological solutions.

A particularly unwarranted attack on those who have questioned the present course of technology has been that they are condemning the poor both at home and abroad to continued poverty. It is beyond dispute that technology is an essential ingredient if the bulk of mankind is to be provided a decent existence. But this does not mean that the answer is simply more of the same kinds of technology that have helped to create today's predicament, and it does not mean that a particular technological scheme is wise simply because it is well-intentioned. We need more transportation, but fewer automobiles. We need more housing, but less suburban sprawl. The world may need more aluminum and steel for communications networks, bridges, and railroads, but the United States certainly does not need more beer cans.

It appears to us that certain spokesmen for technology are attempting to use the legitimate needs of the poor as blanket justification for technological circuses that have no real relevance to those needs. These spokesmen seem to be suggesting that the only route to prosperity for all is the escalation of today's wasteful technologies to ever higher plateaus of profligacy. In other words, we will not be able to give the poor many crumbs until our own loaf, already more than ample, gets even bigger. Implicit in this philosophy is the assumption—perhaps even the desire—that the present inequitable *distribution* of the fruits of technology will endure.

We do not believe this is the only possible scenario, and it is certainly not the most desirable one—both because of the agonizing slowness with which the poor's level of living rises under existing inequities and because of the enormous ecological impact of letting the already affluent get much more so. One of us has therefore set forth in two recent books (*Population/Resources/Environment,* P. R. Ehrlich and A. H. Ehrlich, W. H. Freeman, 1970, and *How To Be a Survivor,* P. R. Ehrlich and R. L. Harriman, Ballantine, 1971) the rudiments of an alternative. It is based on the proposition that what Western society has been calling "development" (epitomized by the United States and held out as a model for the rest of the world to follow) is really "overdevelopment." In other words, we have probably exceeded the levels of consumption of resources and energy that the resource base and the environment can long endure, and to which the less privileged peoples of the world can realistically aspire. The solution would seem to be "de-development" for the United States—and, to a lesser extent, for Europe, the USSR, and Japan—at the same time that "semi-development" is pursued in what today are called underdeveloped countries. In this process, the diversion of resources and energy from frivolous uses in the over-developed countries to necessity-oriented uses in the underdeveloped countries would hasten an adequate standard of living in the underdeveloped countries and an ecologically rational standard in the developed countries.

At least one critic (Dr. Alvin Weinberg, writing in *BioScience*, April 16, 1971 issue) has announced that the foregoing is a proposal to "destroy technology." To any but the most defensive technologist, it should be obvious that this is not the case. De-development and semi-development would involve the abandonment of some technologies, the modification of others, and the invention of some new ones. Few would deny, we suspect, that the sooner we abandon the technologies of war and planned obsolescence, the better. Similarly, the existing technologies of power generation and temperate zone agriculture must be modified to reduce their environmental impact, and we need altogether new technologies for recycling, for ecologically sound farming of tropical rain forest areas, for the direct harnessing of solar energy, and for birth control. The list could be greatly expanded, but the message is clear: on balance, these enterprises will require more science and technology, not less. At the same time, they will surely fail if we are unsuccessful in grappling with the fundamentally nontechnological issues that accompany them: the elimination of discrimination, inequity, and exploitation, and the recognition that both population and consumption must be stabilized.

PART III.

The Search for a New Ethic

THE FACT that our old criteria for selecting success no longer work is increasingly obvious. We must now, therefore, try to discover what does constitute success in the new cooperative communications era. The next three sections examine this issue. This section considers the point of view of the total system, and the next two begin to suggest some of the issues which all of us as individuals face as we try to make the transition from the industrial era to the communications era.

We are trying here to help people perceive that there are some fundamental requirements which must be met if any person—or any system—is to be healthy. We are only just beginning to understand that certain patterns must exist if systems are to survive and flourish. Perhaps the most surprising aspect of our growing understanding is that system thinking and religious thinking lead us to the same conclusions. Not surprisingly, these conclusions turn out to be profoundly different from our present economic, social, and political patterns.

In order to comprehend this reality, we must understand the word "system" as it is being used here. A system is any living phenomenon or set of living and non-living phenomena that it is convenient to analyze together. Thus, an animal is a system and a plant is a system, as is a school, a firm, a church, a ship together with its passengers and crew.

System theorists state the requirements for system survival in the following way:

—any system must provide for the movement of the most accurate possible information to those within the system. If information is inaccurate, people will inevitably make the wrong decisions, for their perception of their self-interest will be inaccurate.

—any system must have decision-making functions built into it so that when there is a need for changes in the system, they will be made. If there are no decision-makers, there will be an ever-wider divergence between desired conditions and actual conditions.

—the control patterns of any system must be appropriate to the size of the system, for otherwise they will be ineffective. The methods which permit effective management of a college of 500 people will not work for a university of 25,000; the techniques which could be used to govern a nation of a few million will not work when the nation is over 200 million. Even more obviously,

149

the techniques are not appropriate for governing a planet of some three and a half billion people.

—the amount of information moving within the system must be neither too much nor too little. If too little information is available, the system will collapse for lack of input. If too much information is available, the system will be unable to discriminate between all the data it is receiving in order to determine which messages are critical and which are unimportant: collapse is inevitable under these circumstances.

—finally, systems must have room for growth and change. This means that they must not be completely defined, for this deprives them of the possibility of developing new patterns and new interconnections. In the absence of such looseness the system will stagnate and will be unable to respond to challenges.

Religious thinkers have defined the necessary values for human beings in the following terms:

—Honesty: the need to tell the other person the truth as fully as he can understand it.
—Responsibility: the need to act when the patterns in which one is involved are not humanly or effectively conducted.
—Humility: the need to be aware of your weaknesses but also your strengths.
—Love: the ability to develop oneself and to help others develop themselves. The Christian biblical text: "Love thy neighbor as thyself" has been consistently misinterpreted. Correctly interpreted, it means that one can only love one's neighbor if one first loves oneself.
—Mystery: the understanding that the world can never be fully controlled, but that one must accept God's help in one's developing life.

How do these two sets of ideas mesh? We feel that it will be better if we let you try to perform the meshing. Let us only say that the ideas are arranged in the same order for both system thinkers and religious thinkers. Thus, the first idea of system thinkers requiring accuracy of information movement corresponds to the religious thinkers' concept of honesty.

Once you have seen how there is correspondence between the two sets of concepts, you may want to consider to what extent the present policies of our culture cut across the requirements stated above.

Are there ways in which our culture has institutionalized lying, for example, through management of the news, public relations and advertising? Are there similar patterns for the other requirements listed above?

If you accept this understanding of the nature of the challenge, your current thinking must change profoundly. Instead of arguing that those who believe in the "golden rule" are naïve, we will come to understand that they have a better understanding of system thinking than many academics. We can state that there is nothing wrong with "religion" except that it has never been tried.

Do you accept the ideas set out above? If so, what changes should *you* make in your lifestyle? You cannot expect to answer this question at this point, but it is certainly the basic question you should keep in mind as you read the rest of this book. In addition, it is critical that you realize that the answer you develop will be unique for you. The cooperative communications era is a period of diversity—not uniformity and equality.

What are your criteria of success?

What *are* your criteria of success?

What are *your* criteria of success?

A Fable for Tomorrow*

RACHEL R. CARSON

There was once a town in the heart of America where all life seemed
to live in harmony with its surroundings. The town lay in the midst
of a checkerboard of prosperous farms, with fields of grain and hill-
sides of orchards where, in spring, white clouds of bloom drifted
above the green fields. In autumn, oak and maple and birch set up
a blaze of color that flamed and flickered across a backdrop of pines.
Then foxes barked in the hills and deer silently crossed the fields,
half hidden in the mists of the fall mornings.

Along the roads, laurel, viburnum and alder, great ferns and wildflowers delighted the traveler's eye through much of the year. Even
in winter the roadsides were places of beauty, where countless birds
came to feed on the berries and on the seed heads of the dried weeds
rising above the snow. The countryside was, in fact, famous for the
abundance and variety of its bird life, and when the flood of migrants
was pouring through in spring and fall, people traveled from great
distances to observe them. Others came to fish the streams, which
flowed clear and cold out of the hills and contained shady pools
where trout lay. So it had been from the days many years ago when
the first settlers raised their houses, sank their wells, and built their
barns.

Then a strange blight crept over the area and everything began

* "A Fable for Tomorrow," from *Silent Spring.* © 1962 by Rachel R. Car-
son. Reprinted by permission of the publisher, Houghton Mifflin Company.

to change. Some evil spell had settled on the community: mysterious maladies swept the flocks of chickens; the cattle and sheep sickened and died. Everywhere was a shadow of death. The farmers spoke of much illness among their families. In the town the doctors had become more and more puzzled by new kinds of sickness appearing among their patients. There had been several sudden and unexplained deaths, not only among adults but even among children, who would be stricken suddenly while at play and die within a few hours.

There was a strange stillness. The birds, for example—where had they gone? Many people spoke of them, puzzled and disturbed. The feeding stations in the backyards were deserted. The few birds seen anywhere were moribund; they trembled violently and could not fly. It was a spring without voices. On the mornings that had once throbbed with the dawn chorus of robins, catbirds, doves, jays, wrens, and scores of other bird voices there was now no sound; only silence lay over the fields and woods and marsh.

On the farms the hens brooded, but no chicks hatched. The farmers complained that they were unable to raise any pigs—the litters were small and the young survived only a few days. The apple trees were coming into bloom but no bees droned among the blossoms, so there was no pollination and there would be no fruit.

The roadsides, once so attractive, were now lined with browned and withered vegetation as though swept by fire. These, too, were silent, deserted by all living things. Even the streams were now lifeless. Anglers no longer visited them, for all the fish had died.

In the gutters under the eaves and between the shingles of the roofs, a white granular powder still showed a few patches; some weeks before it had fallen like snow upon the roofs and the lawns, the fields and streams.

No witchcraft, no enemy action had silenced the rebirth of new life in this stricken world. The people had done it themselves.

This town does not actually exist, but it might easily have a thousand counterparts in America or elsewhere in the world. I know of no community that has experienced all the misfortunes I describe. Yet every one of these disasters has actually happened somewhere, and many real communities have already suffered a substantial number of them. A grim specter has crept upon us almost unnoticed, and this imagined tragedy may easily become a stark reality we all shall know.

What has already silenced the voices of spring in countless towns in America?

The Human Enterprise*

GEORGE WALD

We have come to a time of great decision not only for man but for much of life on the Earth. We are in a period which John Platt has called a crisis of crises, all coming to a head within the next fifteen to thirty years. This faces us with multiple problems. We have hard decisions to make.

We need to face and try to do things terrifying in their complexity and difficulty. We need, in fact, a revolution. I use the word in its literal sense, meaning a turn-about. We here in America, living in a democracy, still hope that we can vote ourselves that revolution, but voted or not that revolution must come if we are to survive.

All things are interrelated and we have to deal with them altogether, each one being dependent upon the others. That calls for a tremendous human effort that covers the people not only of this country but of the globe; that means that we will have to learn to work together; that in turn calls for some common acceptance of the questions that men have tried to answer throughout their history: Whence they come, what they are, and, out of these realizations, at least some hint of what is to become of us.

Fortunately for us one can find a kind of answer in the world view of science, which presents an astonishingly unified view of the uni-

* Taken from an informal speech given at the Congress on Optimum Population, June 1970. Reprinted by permission.

verse, the place of life in it, and the place of man in life. In that unified view we can find new sanctions for our beliefs in the sanctity of life and the dignity of man more credible and reliable than any that the older traditions offered us.

We know now that we live in a historical universe, one in which not only little creatures but stars and galaxies are born, come to maturity, grow old and die. That universe is made of four kinds of elementary particles: protons, neutrons and electrons; and photons, which are particles of radiation. If not the whole, then surely large parts of the universe began in a kind of plasma of elementary particles filling large sections of space. Here and there quite by accident within that plasma eddies formed, special concentrations of material, which through the forces of gravitation began to pull the particles out of the surrounding space. It grew; the more there was, the harder it pulled; it swept the material out of larger and larger sections of space and became a condensing mass of elementary particles. As that mass condensed, it heated up, and when the interior temperature reached five million plus degrees something new began to happen.

One kind of particle, protons, began joining together, four protons each approximately Mass 1 condensing to make a helium nucleus of approximately Mass 4, but in that transaction a little mass is lost and is converted into radiation.

According to Einstein's famous formula, E equals mc^2 in which E is the energy of that radiation, m a bit of mass and c is the speed of light—three times ten to the tenth centimeters per second. You square a number that big and you get a hell of a big number; multiply even a little bit of mass by that big number and you get an awful lot of energy. The energy starting to pour out of the interior of what had been a condensing mass of particles backs up the condensation. Thus this "thing" comes into an uneasy, steady state in which its further impulses to collapse in gravity are held back by the outpouring of the energy inside.

What I have just described is the birth of a star. Our own star, the sun, was born in that way about six billion years ago. It's just an ordinary run of the mill middle-aged star, with approximately six billion years more to run.

Stars live by this so-called burning of hydrogen to helium. Inevitably the time comes when stars begin to run out of hydrogen; they produce less energy; they collapse again; with that they heat up again. When the temperature in the interior reaches about a hundred million degrees something new begins to happen: the burning of helium.

Helium nuclei of Mass 4 begin to unite with one another; all simple arithmetic. Two helium atoms, four and four, make eight; that is beryllium 8, an atomic nucleus so unstable that it disintegrates within so small a fraction of a second that it has never been measured, but in these enormous condensations at these enormous temperatures there are always a few beryllium atoms. Here and there a beryllium nucleus captures another helium.

Eight and four make twelve, and what is twelve? Carbon. That is where carbon comes from in our universe. Carbon 12 can capture another helium nucleus. Twelve and four make sixteen, and what is sixteen? Oxygen. The carbon itself can begin to pick up protons, hydrogen nuclei. And Carbon 12 plus two protons equals fourteen. This is nitrogen.

These processes produce an enormous new outpouring of energy in the deep interior of the star, enough not only to back up the threat of condensation but to puff it out to enormous size.

It is now a red giant, a dying star, giant because it has puffed up to enormous size; red because it has cooled off somewhat in its outermost layers.

Red giants are in a peculiar condition, always distilling a lot of stuff off their surfaces into space. Every now and then a great streamer of material goes shooting off into space—a flare. Every now and then a little thing, a nova, threatens to blow up. Every now and then it does blow up, a supernova. In all these ways the stuff of which dying stars are made is spewed out into space. It is estimated that half the mass of our universe is in the form of gases and dust. Here and there a new eddy forms, a new knoll of material; once again by gravitation it begins to pull in the stuff from all around it and a new star is born.

These later generation stars, unlike the first generation of stars made of hydrogen and helium, contain carbon, nitrogen, and oxygen. We know that our sun is such a star because we are here. As all other living creatures we know, 99 percent of our living substance is made of just those elements I have been naming, the hydrogen, the carbon, the nitrogen, the oxygen. It is a moving realization that stars must die in order that organisms may live.

Star temperatures are too high for atomic nuclei to gather the electrons about themselves in orderly ways. That can happen only in the cooler places of the universe, on the planets. There those electrons can begin to interact with one another until the first molecules came into being. Molecules are a great new thing in the universe.

Without molecules nothing has shape or size. The world of elementary particles is the world of Heisenberg's indeterminacy principle; there are no shapes or sizes or even definable positions and motions. Those things come into the universe with the first molecules.

As soon as the Earth was formed some four and a half billion years ago the molecules began to form. The atmosphere had molecules of hydrogen, ammonia, water, and methane. In the upper layers of the atmosphere, sparked by sunlight, the molecules formed that eventually gave rise to life, organic molecules made of those four atoms: hydrogen, carbon, nitrogen, and oxygen. Over the ages they were eked out of the atmosphere into the seas. About three billion years ago somewhere, sometime, or perhaps several times in several places, an aggregate of such molecules in the ocean reached the point of being alive.

Life, too, is a great new thing in our universe. I have heard life called disparagingly a disease of matter. No, it is a culmination of matter. Give matter a chance for long enough and life inevitably appears. It is, so far as we know, the most complex state of organization that matter achieves in our universe.

Life has transformed the whole environment. Even biologists still occasionally make the mistake of thinking that the environment plays the tune to which life must dance or die, but it isn't that way at all.

The early atmosphere of this planet contained no oxygen, O_2, the stuff with which all animals respire. It was put into the atmosphere by plant organisms in the process of photosynthesis; it is held in the atmosphere now entirely by that process.

Every particle of oxygen gas in our atmosphere comes out of plants in the process of photosynthesis and goes into plants and animals in the process of cellular respiration, and so is completely renewed every two thousand years.

Two thousand years is just a day in geological time. Every particle of carbon dioxide not only in the atmosphere but dissolved in all the waters of the Earth goes into photosynthesis and comes out in respiration and is completely renewed every three hundred years.

Life is a great thing on this planet. Most of the planet is covered with water, yet every molecule of water on the Earth goes in and out of living organisms and is completely renewed every two million years; that's just a day in geological time. We have had men on the Earth for that long.

The appearance of oxygen through the process of plant photosynthesis did another thing for life on the Earth. Radiation from sunlight, produced by turning hydrogen into helium, contains short wavelength ultraviolet components that no life or large molecules such as protons or nuclear gases can tolerate. So long as that radiation poured on the surface of the Earth, life had to stay under water. There in the ocean the photosynthesis began, and nine-tenths of all the photosynthesis on the Earth still occurs in the upper layers of the ocean.

In the very upper layers of the atmosphere, sparked by sunlight, some of the oxygen formed ozone. Oxygen gas is O_2, ozone is O_3. This ozone took, and still takes, out of sunlight those ultraviolet radiations that are incompatible with life, and it is only because of that little ozone that animals and plants were able to come out from under water and populate the Earth and the air.

With the oxygen and the ozone as necessary conditions, life flourished and populated every corner of the Earth with a most extraordinary ingenuity.

About two million years ago man appeared.

You may have heard it said that a hen is only an egg's way of making another egg. In the same sense man is the atom's way for knowing about atoms, or if you wish, a man is the star's way for knowing about stars. Man is a great new thing in the universe.

We have reached a point suddenly at which our existence and continuation not only as a civilization but as a species is threatened by wholly new problems. One of the most important of those is the population problem. Biologists who liked to measure things long ago decided that the measure of fitness would be reproductive success. I suppose that man is the first species, animal or plant, on Earth to be threatened by his own reproductive success.

By all present indications unless we can cause something to happen quickly the present population of over three and a half billion will have doubled by the end of the century. Long before that we can expect famine in many parts of the world on an unprecedented scale, but those famines aren't the heart of the problem. If they were one could even feel slightly optimistic, because in the last decade the world production of food has increased a little faster than the world population.

The heart of the problem, as of all human problems, is one of meaning. Our problem isn't one of numbers but of the quality of human lives. We need that size of population in which human beings can most fulfill their potentialities; in my opinion we are already overpopulated from that point of view. Not just in places like India and China and Puerto Rico, but here and in Western Europe. With that over-population in our Western world there has been a signal deterioration in our culture all through the last century.

I don't think that the symphonies and the poems and the books and the plays and the paintings and the sculpture are anything like they used to be. Though this period is kinder to the scientists than to the arts, the life of the individual scientist has deteriorated enormously. I look back a century and envy the scientists who lived then the way they lived, the way they made their science, the amount of science they succeeded in making and its quality.

A closely related problem, also enormously threatening and important, is the way we are wasting all our remaining resources and polluting the surface of the earth; a terrible problem, to an extraordinary degree an American problem.

We are the worst offenders. With six percent of the world's population, we consume about 40 percent of the irreplaceable resources and account for about 50 percent of the world's industrial pollution. We Americans are doing those things not only to this country but to all the world.

There is a third gigantic problem: we have come into the nuclear age. This knowledge, which should come to humankind full of promise of a new degree of freedom such as men and life on Earth have never experienced before, comes upon us instead as perhaps the most serious threat we now have to face.

Why do I say a promise? There came a point for life on Earth that was absolutely critical and revolutionary. The big revolutions are the revolutions of nature; big revolutions among men are the revolutions of science. Darwin nursing his dyspepsia in a garden in Cambridge was a much greater revolutionary than Karl Marx.

When life arose on the Earth out of that aggregation of molecules leached from the atmosphere into the seas over ages of time, it leached on those molecules.

That is inevitably a losing game, because there are just so many of those molecules accumulated. Living organisms began to use them, to destroy them.

Eventually such a process would have had to come to an end, and life with it. It would have had to begin again from the beginning. However, before such an end occurred, living organisms invented photosynthesis so that using the energy of sunlight they could make their own organic molecules. They became independent of the stores of organic molecules that accumulated over previous ages in the Earth. With the coming of the nuclear age we have a similar opportunity, one of those things that happen once in several billion years. All life up till now has lived on sunlight, the plants directly, the animals by eating the plants.

Now we can make our own sunlight. But the process that the sun lives by, turning hydrogen into helium, is the way one makes hydrogen bombs—what a disgrace. Think of it. The nuclear reaction that we can now use to make our own sunlight, that we can use to make a new basis for life on the Earth, that we can use to make our own energy, is as yet only turned into a weapon that is ultimately the biggest polluter of our environment, that threatens the existence of man and of much other life on the Earth.

A biological parable may be helpful. Two hundred million years ago was the age of reptiles. Dinosaurs were the lords of the earth. They were the biggest animals that have ever existed. They were dangerous. They were well protected—by horns, teeth, claws, scales, and armor plate. They looked awfully good, those dinosaurs, but back in the shadows hiding about the roots of the trees were a small, tender, defenseless group of animals: the first mammals. They had but one thing to offer—they had rather large brains. The proportion of brains to brawn in a dinosaur is low. The mammals were doing better in that regard, and pretty soon there were no more dinosaurs. The age of reptiles gave way to the age of mammals.

The mammals kept working on the beautiful brain, and two million years ago they gave rise to man. A man standing on his own two feet with that wonderful brain, gentle, harming no one and nothing, altogether in control, is a beautiful creature, something one could love. But put him in a car—now the proportion of brains to brawn has sunk very low. Man has become a kind of medium-sized dinosaur making a roar that spits through the streets.

Cars kill more than 50,000 Americans per year. Please notice one says cars kill those Americans, not men in cars, because we realize all too well that the man isn't quite in control, having become a medium-sized dinosaur. Cars are just the beginning of it: there are trucks and trains and planes and hydrogen bombs—the proportion of brains to brawn going down fast. This time if we have an extinction it will be a "do-it-yourself" extinction, and this time there is no other creature to take over.

Mammals brought an infinitely precious thing into life on Earth;

they take care of their young. Dinosaurs laid their eggs and left them, like all the previous creatures: the fishes, the amphibians, the reptiles. But mammals carry their young inside of them. After they have given birth, they nest them for months. The word "mammal" comes from "nursing." After that they watch them play in the sun and protect them and feed them and teach them the ways of life.

Another of our problems is that we are no longer taking care of our young. We have introduced them to a world that offers them little that they want and threatens their very existence. We have become dinosaurs again, and that is our problem.

What are we to do? Please realize where we are, because whatever we do now, we have to do as men, not as dinosaurs. The temptation is great to do those things not as men but as dinosaurs. There are traps besetting us for everything we will try to do now.

Take the population problem. We are already being told that the attempt to control population is just an attempt at genocide. We are being told that it is an attempt by the well-to-do to limit the numbers of the poor; an attempt on the part of the well-to-do nations to limit the numbers in the underdeveloped nations. Yet the only hope of the poor and of the underdeveloped nations is to limit population.

So what is wrong? One has to couple that attempt to limit population with a genuine and effective taking care of all the people there are. To do the one without the other would be conscienceless. Yes, we need to limit population, but we need to take care of people better than we do now, and most of all we need to take care of children, all children everywhere, very much better than we have.

The pollution problem, too, is beset with traps. The only meaningful way to deal with pollution is to stop it at its source, but that is difficult and strongly opposed by some very powerful forces. The temptation is great to let the pollution go on but to superimpose on it a new multibillion-dollar business of anti-pollution. In these days of conglomerates it would be the same business: one division would pollute, the other division would depollute.

Here we are at the crossroads. We have to make hard choices to succeed in doing fantastic things, so difficult that if there were any alternative we would be well advised to avoid them. Those are the things that must be done for us, but much more for our children, for it is they who must inherit a good Earth, a decent place on which they can live their lives.

Cry, the Aware Elite*

GERTRUDE REAGAN—1966

Our house has cost posterity
A monumental redwood tree.
And, since a slide seemed imminent,
We walled our slope with thick cement.
Our modest runoff forms cascades,
Eroding roots of downstream glades.

Should I turn off the garden hose?
My children know that I oppose
Depleting natural resources.
I must conceal my deep remorses,
Not inflict my sons with guilt
Or other uncreative silt.

When ants by thousands penetrate
Kitchen cupboards stocked with cake,
It's all too easy to rely on
That handy nerve gas, Malathion.
(My grandson will collapse when *he* sees
Nothing but resistant species.)

* From *ZPG National Reporter,* June 1971. Reprinted courtesy of ZPG National Reporter.

I blame my coke cans for the waste
That fills the Bay with undue haste.
For smog, my husband must impute
His thirty-seven-mile commute.
Growth and congestion destroy mother earth . . .
Admonish young women not give birth!

I feel an explosion we must avert!
But now that I'm pregnant, one more can't hurt . . .

SOON TO BE ERECTED ON THIS SITE
SEQUOIA SQUARE
SHOPPING CENTER AND 300 UNIT HOTEL-MOTEL COMPLEX
KILGROW & KLINE ARCHITECTS
NOW LEASING
R. COBB
©1968 ALL RIGHTS RESERVED

Reprinted courtesy Sawyer Press, Los Angeles, California 90046.

. . . O and all the little babies in the Alameda gardens Yes . . .*

STEPHANIE MILLS

[1]

I sink I'd die down over his feet, humbly dumbly, only to washup. Yes, tid. There's where. First. We pass through grass behush the the bush to. Whish! A gull. Gulls. Far calls. Coming, far! End here. Us. Then. Finn, again! Take. Bussoftlee, mememormee! Till thousands thee. Lps. The keys to. Given! A way a lone a last a loved a long the

—JAMES JOYCE/*Finnegans Wake*

Rivers flow to the sea, clouds rise from the sea, rain falls to the earth and trickles into rivers. All of life moves, if uninterrupted, in cycles. This was Joyce's vision, and must become ours. Life ever-same and ever-changing once was ours. Or ours to lose? Man interrupts cycles, man changes life with no return to same. Man resists death, and by so doing destroys life.

This is where we are now, in this decade. Faced with a final chance to acknowledge the cycle of life and death and flow with it. Faced with the chance to rejoin nature. But faced with the coming of the worst of all possible worlds as well.

* Reprinted from *Ecotactics, A Sierra Club Handbook.* © 1970 by the Sierra Club. Reprinted by permission of Pocket Books, Division of Simon and Schuster, Inc.

The spectacle of the starving child, the sewer/river, the faceless state confronts us now, glaring at us in our corner. Why are we here now? Why must we, of all generations, live in a make-it-or-break-it era? Our world is crowded and poor. Our neighbors are hungry while we waste our food. Our brother animals are dying and we poisoned them. Ironically, our poisons seem to affect most brutally those creatures who fly, who soar and laugh at us because we cannot fly without clumsy gadgets. We earth-bound humans are only digits now, crowded into anonymity, our lives and individuality diluted by the presence of rapidly doubling billions like us.

Think of how many a billion is for a moment. Can you? Have you ever *seen* a billion things? Can you imagine a billion human beings? Three, or seven billion human beings? The neighborhood will be getting crowded in 2000.

We find ourselves overpopulated because we attempted to thwart death. Western man, through technology, has lengthened his life span by eliminating many diseases. Since the beginning of this century, missionaries of public health have brought to most of the underdeveloped nations of the world the techniques of achieving longer life. The application of these techniques, by thwarting death temporarily, upset the balance between birth rates and death rates. The growth rates of populations skyrocketed: more human beings lived long enough to produce more children, who had a better chance to survive. Etcetera. Ad infinitum.

[II]

What does it matter? What I hate is death and disease, as you well know. And whether you wish it or not, we're allies, facing them and fighting them together.

—ALBERT CAMUS/*The Plague*

These words are uttered by a doctor at the height of an outbreak of bubonic plague. Dr. Rieux has long since recognized that the plague will run its course, in spite of his efforts to combat the disease. Rieux, nonetheless, is dignified by his resistance to the inevitable.

Nobody can deny that the elimination of disease is desirable. There is a case to be made, however, against upsetting a natural balance. For balance, isn't it conceivable that birth control *could* have been employed simultaneously with death control? This is the advantage of hindsight. Yet vigorous population control is still not considered a complementary health measure—and we sink deeper into the morass of too many every day.

Birth control is regarded as tampering with nature. Death control is not. Those people who denounce contraception as interference with a Supreme Will do not, by the same token, denounce typhoid shots. For birth control is regarded as political, not medical. Swallowing Enovid is certainly more emotionally charged than popping tetracycline. But both actions involve tinkering with the natural order of things.

Acceptance of birth control is absolutely necessary for a humane solution to the population crisis. And it *is* a technical solution. The alternative "natural" solution is to eliminate death control.

There is this to be said of population at this time: the birth rates must go down or the death rates will soon go up. By the Eighties, widespread and cataclysmic death may be caused by hunger, plague, war, or environmental disaster.

Death is finiteness, and Western man rejects finiteness. We long for a limitless supply of everything: air, water, food, wilderness, time, and frontier. But our infinity is linear. We head in a straight, unswerving line for the cosmos, damning any obstacle—even scientific fact—that stands in the way. Sadly enough, as we strive for infinity, we create the irreversible limits. To acquire more electricity and more water, we dam and destroy Glen Canyon for all time. To acquire more food, we deprive the pelican of his—and destroy it, too. For all time. The roster of deaths we have caused in our rush for life is almost endless. And as more of us come into being, *more* death.

More people, we believe, means more power, more consumers, more GNP. Score three. But more people are less individual. More people are less free. A more populous nation becomes necessarily more authoritarian. And beneath the veneer roils a cesspool of chaos.

[III]

Listen! If all must suffer to pay for the eternal harmony, what have children to do with it, tell me please? It's beyond all comprehension why they should suffer, and why they should pay for the harmony.

—FEODOR DOSTOEVSKI/*The Brothers Karamazov*

Children are the first to die of hunger, children are rebirth, and children are what the concern with population is all about. Children of all ages are the solution.

Population growth intensifies the spate of problems which confront the earth today. Ignoring the population crisis precludes solving the problems of war, hunger, disease, and alienation. Numbers *per se* cause none of these, but mega-behavior and mega-societies will be fraught with all of them. Curiously enough, a recognition of the population problem and its solution—population control—is avoided by all those who have the power to effect the change.

It took a child to perceive the Emperor's nudity, since all the *loyal* subjects had their perceptions filtered politically.

Our emperors would parade their new clothes of environment, simply by announcing that the problems of environment and population will be solved. Thus far, the clothes are invisible, for meaningful solutions to the population-environment crisis must be drastic indeed. They require a revolution in consciousness.

Solving the population problem will require a reorientation of child-bearing attitudes. To encourage such a reorientation, alternative satisfactions must be provided. New modalities of family living such as communes and kibbutzes might be tried. Certainly women's roles must be expanded to encompass much, much more than the production of children. A cultural inversion must take place. The "old maid," not the mother of twelve, must be made the heroine. The childless couple should be applauded, not pitied. And the adopted baby should become the "real" baby (as he always has been).

A danger inherent in the population problem is that the state may finally assume control of reproduction if the individual doesn't. Consider a state so powerful that it controls the reproduction of its citizens. Consider, also, a nation so overpopulated that it can't survive unless drastic steps are taken to alleviate the whole complex of environmental problems.

The opportunity to assume individual responsibility is still ours, but not, perhaps, for long. If individuals abdicate this responsibility, if individuals refuse to act in their enlightened self-interest, then the state will surely take a hand in individual affairs, sooner than later.

Perhaps there is an element of self-fulfilling prophecy in such a warning. Perhaps such fears should not be voiced. Perhaps. Yet we must realize our role in the continuum of evolution. And such realization may lead us to some interesting questions. Is it our turn to become extinct as a species? Is there any point in undertaking a serious attempt to survive? Is there any wisdom in challenging what would seem the inevitable?

These questions are unanswerable; yet the image of Dr. Rieux, fighting impersonal annihilation, is inspiring. Resisting death is humane. But the death we must resist is more than the death of mankind. It is the death of the ecosystem.

[IV]

In gloomy times of bloody confusion
Ordered disorder
Planful wilfulness
Dehumanized humanity
When there is no end to the unrest in our cities:
In such a world, a world like a slaughter-house—
Summoned by rumors of threatening deeds of violence
To prevent the brute strength of the short-sighted people
From shattering its own tools and
Trampling its own bread-basket to pieces—
We wish to reintroduce
God.

—BERTOLT BRECHT/*Saint Joan of the Stockyards*

Not a bad idea. It all depends, however, on which god is reintroduced. Will it be the anthropocentric god of Genesis, or a dryad? Or can this god/godliness be so personal, so innate, that it has no name?

It's not enough to survive, hard as that alone may be. It may not be worth it to survive in a world devoid of humane beings, a world in which man's only aspiration is for biological existence. Quality of life is the concern, and life has no quality without some experience of god. The experience may not even be describable. Can you describe the wisdom of the ecosystem, the flash of awareness that comes when you perceive how the planet functions? Every organism relates to every other. God is an inadequate word.

Man's aspirations so far have been guided by the god of Genesis. For the most part, we have been proud of our subjugation of the planet. Now we are finding that our aspirations have been misguided and destructive. Where can humanity direct its aspirations, now that we see the futility of damming, grading, eroding, over-breeding?

To aspire to survival and to aspire to humanity are the paths. They are one and the same. For openers, we can turn to the humanity within us, and must to survive. All the logic, precision, and practicality in the world can't save us if we lose our own souls.

The prescription is nothing less than a revolution in consciousness. We are beginning to see it now, and must participate. It takes more than lockjawed resolution to save a world for all creatures. It takes love and joy. There can be no survival without passion. Passion for humanity, love of the earth, joy of existence, and hope for the future. A very wise man has said that "Pessimism has no survival value." Nor hate, nor elitism, nor puritanism.

. . . O and the sea the sea crimson sometimes like fire and the glorious sunsets and the figtrees in the Alameda gardens Yes and all the queer little streets and pink and blue and yellow houses and the rosegardens and the jessamine and geraniums and cactuses and Gibraltar as a girl where I was a Flower of the mountain yes when I put the rose in my hair like the Andalusian girls used or shall I wear red yes and how he kissed me under the Moorish wall and I thought well as well him as another and then I asked him with my eyes to ask again yes and then he asked me would I yes to say yes my mountain flower and first I put my arms around him yes and drew him down to me so he could feel my breasts all perfume yes and his heart was going like mad and yes I said yes I will Yes.

—JOYCE, again/*Ulysses*

Polemic: Industrial Tourism and the National Parks*

≋≋≋≋≋≋≋≋≋≋≋≋≋≋≋≋≋≋≋≋≋≋≋≋≋≋≋

EDWARD ABBEY

I like my job. The pay is generous; I might even say munificent: $1.95 per hour, earned or not, backed solidly by the world's most powerful Air Force, biggest national debt, and grossest national product. The fringe benefits are priceless: clean air to breathe (after the spring sandstorms); stillness, solitude and space; an unobstructed view every day and every night of sun, sky, stars, clouds, mountain, moon, cliffrock and canyons; a sense of time enough to let thought and feeling range from here to the end of the world and back; the discovery of something intimate—though impossible to name—in the remote.

The work is simple and requires almost no mental effort, a good thing in more ways than one. What little thinking I do is my own and I do it on government time. Insofar as I follow a schedule it goes about like this:

For me the work week begins on Thursday, which I usually spend in patrolling the roads and walking out the trails. On Friday I inspect the campgrounds, haul firewood, and distribute the toilet paper. Saturday and Sunday are my busy days as I deal with the influx of weekend visitors and campers, answering questions, pulling cars out of the sand, lowering children down off the rocks, tracking lost

* From *Desert Solitaire,* by Edward Abbey. © 1968 by Edward Abbey. Used with permission of McGraw-Hill Book Company.

grandfathers and investigating picnics. My Saturday night campfire talks are brief and to the point. "Everything all right?" I say, badge and all, ambling up to what looks like a cheerful group. "Fine," they'll say; "how about a drink?" "Why not?" I say.

By Sunday evening most everyone has gone home and the heavy duty is over. Thank God it's Monday, I say to myself the next morning. Mondays are very nice. I empty the garbage cans, read the discarded newspapers, sweep out the outhouses and disengage the Kleenex from the clutches of cliffrose and cactus. In the afternoon I watch the clouds drift past the bald peak of Mount Tukuhnikivats. (*Someone* has to do it.)

Tuesday and Wednesday I rest. Those are my days off and I usually set aside Wednesday evening for a trip to Moab, replenishing my supplies and establishing a little human contact more vital than that possible with the tourists I meet on the job. After a week in the desert, Moab (pop. 5500, during the great uranium boom) seems like a dazzling metropolis, a throbbing dynamo of commerce and pleasure. I walk the single main street as dazed by the noise and neon as a country boy on his first visit to Times Square. (Wow, I'm thinking, this is great.)

After a visit to Miller's Supermarket, where I stock up on pinto beans and other necessities, I am free to visit the beer joints. All of them are busy, crowded with prospectors, miners, geologists, cowboys, truckdrivers and sheepherders, and the talk is loud, vigorous, blue with blasphemy. Although differences of opinion have been known to occur, open violence is rare, for these men treat one another with courtesy and respect. The general atmosphere is free and friendly, quite unlike the sad, sour gloom of most bars I have known, where nervous men in tight collars brood over their drinks between out-of-tune TV screens and a remorseless clock. Why the difference?

I have considered the question and come up with the following solution:

1. These prospectors, miners, etc. have most of them been physically active all day out-of-doors at a mile or more above sea level; they are comfortably tired and relaxed.

2. Most of them have been working alone; the presence of a jostling crowd is therefore not a familiar irritation to be borne with resignation but rather an unaccustomed pleasure to be enjoyed.

3. Most of them are making good wages and/or doing work they like to do; they are, you might say, happy. (The boom will not last,

of course, but this is forgotten. And the ethical and political implications of uranium exploitation are simply unknown in these parts.)

4. The nature of their work requires a combination of skills and knowledge, good health and self-reliance, which tends to inspire self-confidence; they need not doubt their manhood. (Again, everything is subject to change.)

5. Finally, Moab is a Mormon town with funny ways. Hard booze is not sold across the bar except in the semiprivate "clubs." Nor even standard beer. These hard-drinking fellows whom I wish to praise are trying to get drunk on three-point-two! They rise somewhat heavily from their chairs and barstools and tramp, with frequency and a squelchy, sodden noise, toward the pissoirs at the back of the room, more waterlogged than intoxicated.

In the end the beer halls of Moab, like all others, become to me depressing places. After a few games of rotation pool with my friend Viviano Jacquez, a reformed sheepherder turned dude wrangler (a dubious reform), I am glad to leave the last of those smoky dens around midnight and to climb into my pickup and take the long drive north and east back to the silent rock, the unbounded space and the sweet clean air of my outpost in the Arches.

Yes, it's a good job. On the rare occasions when I peer into the future for more than a few days I can foresee myself returning here for season after season, year after year, indefinitely. And why not? What better sinecure could a man with small needs, infinite desires, and philosophic pretensions ask for? The better part of each year in the wilderness and the winters in some complementary, equally agreeable environment—Hoboken perhaps, or Tijuana, Nogales, Juarez . . . one of the border towns. Maybe Tonopah, a good tough Nevada mining town with legal prostitution, or possibly Oakland or even New Orleans—some place grimy, cheap (since I'd be living on unemployment insurance), decayed, hopelessly corrupt. I idle away hours dreaming of the wonderful winter to come, of the chocolate-colored mistress I'll have to rub my back, the journal spread open between two tall candles in massive silver candlesticks, the scrambled eggs with green chili, the crock of homebrew fermenting quietly in the corner, etc., the nights of desperate laughter with brave young comrades, burning billboards, and defacing public institutions. . . . Romantic dreams, romantic dreams.

For there is a cloud on my horizon. A small dark cloud no bigger than my hand. Its name is Progress.

The ease and relative freedom of this lovely job at Arches follow from the comparative absence of the motorized tourists, who stay away by the millions. And they stay away because of the unpaved entrance road, the unflushable toilets in the campgrounds, and the fact that most of them have never even heard of Arches National Monument. (Could there be a more genuine testimonial to its beauty and integrity?) All this must change.

I'd been warned. On the very first day Merle and Floyd had mentioned something about developments, improvements, a sinister Master Plan. Thinking that *they* were the dreamers, I paid little heed and had soon forgotten the whole ridiculous business. But only a few days ago something happened which shook me out of my pleasant apathy.

I was sitting out back on my 33,000-acre terrace, shoeless and shirtless, scratching my toes in the sand and sipping on a tall iced drink, watching the flow of evening over the desert. Prime time: the sun very low in the west, the birds coming back to life, the shadows rolling for miles over rock and sand to the very base of the brilliant mountains. I had a small fire going near the table—not for heat or light but for the fragrance of the juniper and the ritual appeal of the clear flames. For symbolic reasons. For ceremony. When I heard a faint sound over my shoulder I looked and saw a file of deer watching from fifty yards away, three does and a velvet-horned buck, all dark against the sundown sky. They began to move. I whistled and they stopped again, staring at me. "Come on over," I said, "have a drink." They declined, moving off with casual, unhurried grace, quiet as phantoms, and disappeared beyond the rise. Smiling, thoroughly at peace, I turned back to my drink, the little fire, the subtle transformations of the immense landscape before me. On the program: rise of the full moon.

It was then I heard the discordant note, the snarling whine of a jeep in low range and four-wheel-drive, coming from an unexpected direction, from the vicinity of the old foot and horse trail that leads from Balanced Rock down toward Courthouse Wash and on to park headquarters near Moab. The jeep came in sight from beyond some bluffs, turned onto the dirt road, and came up the hill toward the entrance station. Now operating a motor vehicle of any kind on the trails of a national park is strictly forbidden, a nasty bureaucratic regulation which I heartily support. My bosom swelled with the righteous indignation of a cop: by God, I thought, I'm going to write these sons of bitches a ticket. I put down the drink and strode to the housetrailer to get my badge.

Long before I could find the shirt with the badge on it, however, or the ticket book, or my shoes or my park ranger hat, the jeep turned in at my driveway and came right up to the door of the trailer. It was a gray jeep with a U.S. Government decal on the side— Bureau of Public Roads—and covered with dust. Two empty water bags flapped at the bumper. Inside were three sunburned men in twill britches and engineering boots, and a pile of equipment: transit case, tripod, survey rod, bundles of wooden stakes. (*Oh no!*) The men got out, dripping with dust, and the driver grinned at me. pointing to his parched open mouth and making horrible gasping noises deep in his throat.

"Okay," I said, "come on in."

It was even hotter inside the trailer than outside, but I opened the refrigerator and left it open and took out a pitcher filled with ice cubes and water. As they passed the pitcher back and forth I got the full and terrible story, confirming the worst of my fears. They were a survey crew, laying out a new road into the Arches.

And when would the road be built? Nobody knew for sure; perhaps in a couple of years, depending on when the Park Service would be able to get the money. The new road—to be paved, of course—would cost somewhere between half a million and one million dollars, depending on the bids, or more than fifty thousand dollars per linear mile. At least enough to pay the salaries of ten park rangers for ten years. Too much money, I suggested—they'll never go for it back in Washington.

The three men thought that was pretty funny. Don't worry, they said, this road will be built. I'm worried, I said. Look, the party chief explained, you *need* this road. He was a pleasant-mannered, soft-spoken civil engineer with an unquestioning dedication to his work. A very dangerous man. Who *needs* it? I said; we get very few tourists in this park. That's why you need it, the engineer explained patiently; look, he said, when this road is built you'll get ten, twenty, thirty times as many tourists in here as you get now. His men nodded in solemn agreement, and he stared at me intently, waiting to see what possible answer I could have to that.

"Have some more water," I said. I had an answer all right but I was saving it for later. I knew that I was dealing with a madman.

As I type these words, several years after the little episode of the gray jeep and the thirsty engineers, all that was foretold has come to pass. Arches National Monument has been developed. The Master Plan has been fulfilled. Where once a few adventurous people came on weekends to camp for a night or two and enjoy a taste of the primitive and remote, you will now find serpentine streams of baroque automobiles pouring in and out, all through the spring and summer, in numbers that would have seemed fantastic when I worked there: from 3000 to 30,000 to 300,000 per year, the "visitation," as they call it, mounts ever upward. The little campgrounds where I used to putter around reading three-day-old newspapers full of lies and watermelon seeds have now been consolidated into one master campground that looks, during the busy season, like a suburban village: elaborate housetrailers of quilted aluminum crowd upon gigantic camper-trucks of Fiberglas and molded plastic; through their windows you will see the blue glow of television and hear the studio laughter of Los Angeles; knobby-kneed oldsters in plaid Bermudas buzz up and down the quaintly curving asphalt road on motorbikes; quarrels break out between campsite neighbors while others gather around their burning charcoal briquettes (ground campfires no longer permitted—not enough wood) to compare electric toothbrushes. The Comfort Stations are there, too, all lit up with electricity, fully equipped inside, though the generator breaks down now and then and the lights go out, or the sewage backs up in the plumbing system (drain fields were laid out in sand over a solid bed of sandstone), and the water supply sometimes fails, since the 3000-foot well can only produce about 5gpm—not always enough to meet the demand. Down at the beginning of the new road, at park headquarters, is the new entrance station and visitor center, where admission fees are collected and where the rangers are going quietly nuts answering the same three basic questions five hundred times a day: (1) Where's the john? (2) How long's it take to see this place? (3) Where's the Coke machine?

Progress has come at last to the Arches, after a million years of neglect. Industrial Tourism has arrived.

What happened to Arches Natural Money-Mint is, of course, an old story in the Park Service. All the famous national parks have the same problems on a far grander scale, as everyone knows, and many other problems as yet unknown to a little subordinate unit of the system in a backward part of southeastern Utah. And the same kind of development that has so transformed Arches is under way, planned or completed in many more national parks and national monuments. I will mention only a few examples with which I am personally familiar:

The newly established Canyonlands National Park. Most of the major points of interest in this park are presently accessible, over passable dirt roads, by car—Grandview Point, Upheaval Dome, part of the White Rim, Cave Spring, Squaw Spring campground and Elephant Hill. The more difficult places, such as Angel Arch or Druid Arch, can be reached by jeep, on horseback or in a one- or two-day hike. Nevertheless the Park Service had drawn up the usual Master Plan calling for modern paved highways to most of the places named and some not named.

Grand Canyon National Park. Most of the south rim of this park is now closely followed by a conventional highspeed highway and interrupted at numerous places by large asphalt parking lots. It is no longer easy, on the South Rim, to get away from the roar of motor traffic, except by descending into the canyon. Toroweap Point in the remote northwest corner of the park, at present still unimpaired (though accessible), has not been forgotten; the plans are in the files for developing even that wild and lovely corner.

Navajo National Monument. A small, fragile, hidden place containing two of the most beautiful cliff dwellings in the Southwest— Keet Seel and Betatakin. This park will be difficult to protect under heavy visitation, and for years it was understood that it would be preserved in a primitive way so as to screen out those tourists unwilling to drive their cars over some twenty miles of dirt road. No longer so: the road has been paved, the campground enlarged and "modernized," and the old magic destroyed.

Natural Bridges National Monument. Another small gem in the park system, a group of three adjacent natural bridges tucked away in the canyon country of southern Utah. Formerly you could drive your car (over dirt roads, of course) to within sight of and easy walking distance—a hundred yards?—of the most spectacular of the three bridges. From there it was only a few hours walking time to the other two. All three could easily be seen in a single day. But this was not good enough for the developers. They have now constructed a paved road into the heart of the area, *between* the two biggest bridges.

Zion National Park. The northwestern part of this park, known as the Kolob area, has until recently been saved as almost virgin wilderness. But a broad highway, with banked curves, deep cuts and heavy fills, that will invade this splendid region is already under construction.

Capitol Reef National Monument. Grand and colorful scenery in a rugged land—south-central Utah. The most beautiful portion of the park was the canyon of the Fremont River, a great place for hiking, camping, exploring. And what did the authorities do? They built a state highway through it.

Lee's Ferry. Until a few years ago a simple, quiet, primitive place on the shores of the Colorado, Lee's Ferry has now fallen under the protection of the Park Service. And who can protect it against the Park Service? Powerlines now bisect the scene; a 100-foot pink water tower looms against the red cliffs; tract-style houses are built to house the "protectors"; natural campsites along the river are closed off while all campers are now herded into an artificial steel-and-asphalt "campground" in the hottest, windiest spot in the area; historic buildings are razed by bulldozers to save the expense of maintaining them while at the same time hundreds of thousands of dollars are spent on an unneeded paved entrance road. And the administrators complain of *vandalism*.

I could easily cite ten more examples of unnecessary or destructive development for every one I've named so far. What has happened in these particular areas, which I chance to know a little and love too much, has happened, is happening, or will soon happen to the majority of our national parks and national forests, despite the illusory protection of the Wilderness Preservation Act, unless a great many citizens rear up on their hind legs and make vigorous political gestures demanding implementation of the Act.

There may be some among the readers of this book, like the earnest engineer, who believe without question that any and all forms of construction and development are intrinsic goods, in the national parks as well as anywhere else, who virtually identify quantity with quality and therefore assume that the greater the quantity of traffic, the higher the value received. There are some who frankly and boldly advocate the eradication of the last remnants of wilderness and the complete subjugation of nature to the requirements of—not man—but industry. This is a courageous view, admirable in its simplicity and power, and with the weight of all modern history behind it. It is also quite insane. I cannot attempt to deal with it here.

There will be other readers, I hope, who share my basic assumption that wilderness is a necessary part of civilization and that it is the primary responsibility of the national park system to preserve *intact and undiminished* what little still remains.

Most readers, while generally sympathetic to this latter point of view, will feel, as do the administrators of the National Park Service, that although wilderness is a fine thing, certain compromises and adjustments are necessary in order to meet the ever-expanding demand for outdoor recreation. It is precisely this question which I would like to examine now.

The Park Service, established by Congress in 1916, was directed not only to administer the parks but also to "provide for the enjoyment of same in such manner and by such means as will leave them unimpaired for the enjoyment of future generations." This appropriately ambiguous language, employed long before the onslaught of the automobile, has been understood in various and often opposing ways ever since. The Park Service, like any other big organization, includes factions and factions. The Developers, the dominant faction, place their emphasis on the words *"provide for the enjoyment."* The Preservers, a minority but also strong, emphasize the words *"leave them unimpaired."* It is apparent, then, that we cannot decide the question of development versus preservation by a simple referral to holy writ or an attempt to guess the intention of the founding fathers; we must make up our own minds and decide for ourselves what the national parks should be and what purpose they should serve.

The first issue that appears when we get into this matter, the most important issue and perhaps the only issue, is the one called *accessibility.* The Developers insist that the parks must be made fully accessible not only to people but also to their machines, that is, to automobiles, motorboats, etc. The Preservers argue, in principle at least, that wilderness and motors are incompatible and that the former can best be experienced, understood, and enjoyed when the machines are left behind where they belong—on the superhighways and in the parking lots, on the reservoirs and in the marinas.

What does accessibility mean? Is there any spot on earth that men have not proved accessible by the simplest means—feet and legs and heart? Even Mt. McKinley, even Everest, have been surmounted by men on foot. (Some of them, incidentally, rank amateurs, to the horror and indignation of the professional mountaineers.) The interior of the Grand Canyon, a fiercely hot and hostile abyss, is visited each summer by thousands and thousands of tourists of the most banal and unadventurous type, many of them on foot—self-propelled, so to speak—and the others on the backs of mules. Thousands climb each summer to the summit of Mt. Whitney, highest point in the forty-eight United States, while multitudes of others wander on foot or on horseback through the ranges of the Sierras, the Rockies, the Big Smokies, the Cascades and the mountains of

New England. Still more hundreds and thousands float or paddle each year down the currents of the Salmon, the Snake, the Allagash, the Yampa, the Green, the Rio Grande, the Ozark, the St. Croix and those portions of the Colorado which have not yet been destroyed by the dam builders. And most significant, these hordes of nonmotorized tourists, hungry for a taste of the difficult, the original, the real, do not consist solely of people young and athletic but also of old folks, fat folks, pale-faced office clerks who don't know a rucksack from a haversack, and even children. The one thing they all have in common is the refusal to live always like sardines in a can—they are determined to get outside of their motorcars for at least a few weeks each year.

This being the case, why is the Park Service generally so anxious to accommodate that other crowd, the indolent millions born on wheels and suckled on gasoline, who expect and demand paved highways to lead them in comfort, ease and safety into every nook and corner of the national parks? For the answer to that we must consider the character of what I call Industrial Tourism and the quality of the mechanized tourists—the Wheelchair Explorers—who are at once the consumers, the raw material and the victims of Industrial Tourism.

Industrial Tourism is a big business. It means money. It includes the motel and restaurant owners, the gasoline retailers, the oil corporations, the road-building contractors, the heavy equipment manufacturers, the state and federal engineering agencies and the sovereign, all-powerful automotive industry. These various interests are well organized, command more wealth than most modern nations, and are represented in Congress with a strength far greater than is justified in any constitutional or democratic sense. (Modern politics is expensive—power follows money.) Through Congress the tourism industry can bring enormous pressure to bear upon such a slender reed in the executive branch as the poor old Park Service, a pressure which is also exerted on every other possible level—local, state, regional—and through advertising and the well-established habits of a wasteful nation.

When a new national park, national monument, national seashore, or whatever it may be called is set up, the various forces of Industrial Tourism, on all levels, immediately expect action—meaning specifically a roadbuilding program. Where trails or primitive dirt roads already exist, the Industry expects—it hardly needs to ask—that these be developed into modern paved highways. On the local level, for example, the first thing that the superintendent of a new park can anticipate being asked, when he attends his first meeting of the area's Chamber of Commerce, is not "Will roads be built?" but rather "When does construction begin?" and "Why the delay?"

(The Natural Money-Mint. With supersensitive antennae these operatives from the C. of C. look into red canyons and see only green, stand among flowers snorting out the smell of money, and hear, while thunderstorms rumble over mountains, the fall of a dollar bill on motel carpeting.)

Accustomed to this sort of relentless pressure since its founding, it is little wonder that the Park Service, through a process of natural selection, has tended to evolve a type of administration which, far from resisting such pressure, has usually been more than willing to accommodate it, even to encourage it. Not from any peculiar moral weakness but simply because such well-adapted administrators are themselves believers in a policy of economic development. "Resource management" is the current term. Old foot trails may be neglected, back-country ranger stations left unmanned, and interpretive and protective services inadequately staffed, but the administrators know from long experience that millions for asphalt can always be found; Congress is always willing to appropriate money for more and bigger paved roads, anywhere—particularly if they form loops. Loop drives are extremely popular with the petroleum industry—they bring the motorist right back to the same gas station from which he started.

Great though it is, however, the power of the tourist business would not in itself be sufficient to shape Park Service policy. To all accusations of excessive development the administrators can reply, as they will if pressed hard enough, that they are giving the public what it wants, that their primary duty is to serve the public, not preserve the wilds. "Parks are for people" is the public-relations slogan, which decoded means that the parks are for people-in-automobiles. Behind the slogan is the assumption that the majority of Americans, exactly like the managers of the tourist industry, expect and demand to see their national parks from the comfort, security, and convenience of their automobiles.

Is this assumption correct? Perhaps. Does that justify the continued and increasing erosion of the parks? It does not. Which brings me to the final aspect of the problem of Industrial Tourism: the Industrial Tourists themselves.

They work hard, these people. They roll up incredible mileages on their odometers, rack up state after state in two-week transcontinental motor marathons, knock off one national park after another, take millions of square yards of photographs, and endure patiently the most prolonged discomforts: the tedious traffic jams, the awful food of park cafeterias and roadside eateries, the nocturnal search for a place to sleep or camp, the dreary routine of One-Stop Service, the endless lines of creeping traffic, the smell of exhaust fumes, the ever-proliferating Rules & Regulations, the fees and the bills and the service charges, the boiling radiator and the flat tire and the vapor lock, the surly retorts of room clerks and traffic cops, the incessant jostling of the anxious crowds, the irritation and restlessness of their children, the worry of their wives, and the long drive home at night in a stream of racing cars against the lights of another stream racing in the opposite direction, passing now and then the obscure tangle, the shattered glass, the patrolman's lurid blinker light, of one more wreck.

Hard work. And risky. Too much for some, who have given up the struggle on the highways in exchange for an entirely different kind of vacation—out in the open, on their own feet, following the quiet trail through forest and mountains, bedding down at evening under the stars, when and where they feel like it, at a time when the Industrial Tourists are still hunting for a place to park their automobiles.

Industrial Tourism is a threat to the national parks. But the chief victims of the system are the motorized tourists. They are being robbed and robbing themselves. So long as they are unwilling to crawl out of their cars they will not discover the treasures of the national parks and will never escape the stress and turmoil of the urban-suburban complexes which they had hoped, presumably, to leave behind for a while.

How to pry the tourists out of their automobiles, out of their back-breaking upholstered mechanized wheelchairs and onto their feet, onto the strange warmth and solidity of Mother Earth again? This is the problem which the Park Service should confront directly, not evasively, and which it cannot resolve by simply submitting and conforming to the automobile habit. The automobile, which began as a transportation convenience, has become a bloody tyrant (50,000 lives a year), and it is the responsibility of the Park Service, as well as that of everyone else concerned with preserving both wilderness and civilization, to begin a campaign of resistance. The automotive

combine has almost succeeded in strangling our cities; we need not
let it also destroy our national parks.

It will be objected that a constantly increasing population makes
resistance and conservation a hopeless battle. This is true. Unless a
way is found to stabilize the nation's population, the parks cannot
be saved. Or anything else worth a damn. Wilderness preservation,
like a hundred other good causes, will be forgotten under the overwhelming pressure of a struggle for mere survival and sanity in a
completely urbanized, completely industrialized, ever more crowded
environment. For my own part I would rather take my chances in a
thermonuclear war than live in such a world.

Assuming, however, that population growth will be halted at a
tolerable level before catastrophe does it for us, it remains permis-
sible to talk about such things as the national parks. Having in-
dulged myself in a number of harsh judgments upon the Park
Service, the tourist industry, and the motoring public, I now feel
entitled to make some constructive, practical, sensible proposals for
the salvation of both parks and people.

(1) No more cars in national parks. Let the people walk. Or
ride horses, bicycles, mules, wild pigs—anything—but keep the automobiles and the motorcycles and all their motorized relatives out.
We have agreed not to drive our automobiles into cathedrals, concert halls, art museums, legislative assemblies, private bedrooms and
the other sanctums of our culture; we should treat our national parks
with the same deference, for they, too, are holy places. An increasingly pagan and hedonistic people (thank God!), we are learning
finally that the forests and mountains and desert canyons are holier
than our churches. Therefore let us behave accordingly.

Consider a concrete example and what could be done with it:
Yosemite Valley in Yosemite National Park. At present a dusty mill-
ing confusion of motor vehicles and ponderous camping machinery,
it could be returned to relative beauty and order by the simple ex-
pedient of requiring all visitors, at the park entrance, to lock up
their automobiles and continue their tour on the seats of good work-
able bicycles supplied free of charge by the United States Government.

Let our people travel light and free on their bicycles—nothing
on the back but a shirt, nothing tied to the bike but a slicker, in case
of rain. Their bedrolls, their backpacks, their tents, their food and
cooking kits will be trucked in for them, free of charge, to the

campground of their choice in the Valley, by the Park Service. (Why not? The roads will still be there.) Once in the Valley they will find the concessioners waiting, ready to supply whatever needs might have been overlooked, or to furnish rooms and meals for those who don't want to camp out.

The same thing could be done at Grand Canyon or at Yellowstone or at any of our other shrines to the out-of-doors. There is no compelling reason, for example, why tourists need to drive their automobiles to the very brink of the Grand Canyon's south rim. They could *walk* that last mile. Better yet, the Park Service should build an enormous parking lot about ten miles south of Grand Canyon Village and another east of Desert View. At those points, as at Yosemite, our people could emerge from their steaming shells of steel and glass and climb upon horses or bicycles for the final leg of the journey. On the rim, as at present, the hotels and restaurants would remain to serve the physical needs of the park visitors. Trips along the rim would also be made on foot, on horseback, or—utilizing the paved road which already exists—on bicycles. For those willing to go all the way from one parking lot to the other, a distance of some sixty or seventy miles, we might provide bus service back to their cars, a service which would at the same time effect a convenient exchange of bicycles and/or horses between the two terminals.

What about children? What about the aged and infirm? Frankly, we need waste little sympathy on these two pressure groups. Children too small to ride bicycles and too heavy to be borne on their parents' backs need only wait a few years—if they are not run over by automobiles they will grow into a lifetime of joyous adventure, if we save the parks and *leave them unimpaired for the enjoyment of future generations.* The aged merit even less sympathy: after all they had the opportunity to see the country when it was still relatively unspoiled. However, we'll stretch a point for those too old or too sickly to mount a bicycle and let them ride the shuttle buses.

I can foresee complaints. The motorized tourists, reluctant to give up the old ways, will complain that they can't see enough without their automobiles to bear them swiftly (traffic permitting) through the parks. But this is nonsense. A man on foot, on horseback or on a bicycle will see more, feel more, enjoy more in one mile than the motorized tourists can in a hundred miles. Better to idle through one park in two weeks than try to race through a dozen in the same amount of time. Those who are familiar with both modes of travel know from experience that this is true; the rest have only to make the experiment to discover the same truth for themselves.

They will complain of physical hardship, these sons of the pioneers. Not for long; once they rediscover the pleasures of actually operating their own limbs and senses in a varied, spontaneous, voluntary style, they will complain instead of crawling back into a car; they may even object to returning to desk and office and that drywall box on Mossy Brook Circle. The fires of revolt may be kindled —which means hope for us all.

(2) No more new roads in national parks. After banning private automobiles the second step should be easy. Where paved roads are already in existence they will be reserved for the bicycles and essential in-park services, such as shuttle buses, the trucking of camping gear and concessioners' supplies. Where dirt roads already exist they too will be reserved for nonmotorized traffic. Plans for new roads can be discarded and in their place a program of trail-building begun, badly needed in some of the parks and in many of the national monuments. In mountainous areas it may be desirable to build emergency shelters along the trails and bike roads; in desert regions a water supply might have to be provided at certain points—wells drilled and handpumps installed if feasible.

Once people are liberated from the confines of automobiles there will be a greatly increased interest in hiking, exploring, and back-country packtrips. Fortunately the parks, by the mere elimination of motor traffic, will come to seem far bigger than they are now—there will be more room for more persons, an astonishing expansion of space. This follows from the interesting fact that a motorized vehicle, when not at rest, requires a volume of space far out of proportion to its size. To illustrate: imagine a lake approximately ten miles long and on the average one mile wide. A single motorboat could easily circumnavigate the lake in an hour; ten motorboats would begin to crowd it; twenty or thirty, all in operation, would dominate the lake to the exclusion of any other form of activity; and fifty would create the hazards, confusion, and turmoil that make pleasure impossible. Suppose we banned motorboats and allowed only canoes and rowboats; we would see at once that the lake seemed ten or perhaps a hundred times bigger. The same thing holds true, to an even greater degree, for the automobile. Distance and space are functions of speed and time. Without expending a single dollar from the United States Treasury we could, if we wanted to, multiply the area of our national parks tenfold or a hundredfold—simply by banning the private automobile. The next generation, all 250 million of them, would be grateful to us.

(3) Put the park rangers to work. Lazy scheming loafers, they've wasted too many years selling tickets at toll booths and sitting behind desks filling out charts and tables in the vain effort to appease the mania for statistics which torments the Washington office. Put them to work. They're supposed to be rangers—make the bums range; kick them out of those overheated airconditioned offices, yank them out of those overstuffed patrol cars, and drive them out on the trails where they should be, leading the dudes over hill and dale, safely into and back out of the wilderness. It won't hurt them to work off a little office fat; it'll do them good, help take their minds off each other's wives, and give them a chance to get out of reach of the boss—a blessing for all concerned.

They will be needed on the trail. Once we outlaw the motors and stop the road-building and force the multitudes back on their feet, the people will need leaders. A venturesome minority will always be eager to set off on their own, and no obstacles should be placed in their path; let them take risks, for Godsake, let them get lost, sunburnt, stranded, drowned, eaten by bears, buried alive under avalanches—that is the right and privilege of any free American. But the rest, the majority, most of them new to the out-of-doors, will need and welcome assistance, instruction and guidance. Many will not know how to saddle a horse, read a topographical map, follow a trail over slickrock, memorize landmarks, build a fire in rain, treat snakebite, rappel down a cliff, glissade down a glacier, read a compass, find water under sand, load a burro, splint a broken bone, bury a body, patch a rubber boat, portage a waterfall, survive a blizzard, avoid lightning, cook a porcupine, comfort a girl during a thunderstorm, predict the weather, dodge falling rock, climb out of a box canyon, or pour piss out of a boot. Park rangers know these things, or should know them, or used to know them and can relearn; they will be needed. In addition to this sort of practical guide service the ranger will also be a bit of a naturalist, able to edify the party in his charge with the natural and human history of the area, in detail and in broad outline.

Critics of my program will argue that it is too late for such a radical reformation of a people's approach to the out-of-doors, that the pattern is too deeply set, and that the majority of Americans would not be willing to emerge from the familiar luxury of their automobiles, even briefly, to try the little-known and problematic advantages of the bicycle, the saddle horse, and the footpath. This might be so; but how can we be sure unless we dare the experiment? I, for one, suspect that millions of our citizens, especially the young, are yearning for adventure, difficulty, challenge—they will respond with enthusiasm. What we must do, prodding the Park Service into the forefront of the demonstration, is provide these young people with the opportunity, the assistance, and the necessary encouragement.

How could this most easily be done? By following the steps I have proposed, plus reducing the expenses of wilderness recreation to the minimal level. Guide service by rangers should, of course, be free to the public. Money saved by *not* constructing more paved highways into the parks should be sufficient to finance the cost of bicycles for the entire park system. Elimination of automobile traffic would allow the Park Service to save more millions now spent on road maintenance, police work and paper work. Whatever the cost, however financed, the benefits for park visitors in health and happiness—virtues unknown to the statisticians—would be immeasurable.

Excluding the automobile from the heart of the great cities has been seriously advocated by thoughtful observers of our urban problems. It seems to me an equally proper solution to the problems besetting our national parks. Of course it would be a serious blow to Industrial Tourism and would be bitterly resisted by those who profit from that industry. Exclusion of automobiles would also require a revolution in the thinking of Park Service officialdom and in the assumptions of most American tourists. But such a revolution, like it or not, is precisely what is needed. The only foreseeable alternative, given the current trend of things, is the gradual destruction of our national park system.

Let us therefore steal a slogan from the Development Fever Faction in the Park Service. The parks, they say, are for people. Very well. At the main entrance to each national park and national monument we shall erect a billboard one hundred feet high, two hundred feet wide, gorgeously filigreed in brilliant neon and outlined with blinker lights, exploding stars, flashing prayer wheels and great Byzantine phallic symbols that gush like geysers every thirty seconds. (You could set your watch by them.) Behind the fireworks will loom the figure of Smokey the Bear, taller than a pine tree, with eyes in his head that swivel back and forth, watching You, and ears that actually twitch. Push a button and Smokey will recite, for the benefit of children and government officials who might otherwise have trouble with some of the big words, in a voice ursine, loud

and clear, the message spelled out on the face of the billboard.
To wit:

HOWDY FOLKS. WELCOME. THIS IS YOUR NATIONAL PARK, ESTAB-
LISHED FOR THE PLEASURE OF YOU AND ALL PEOPLE EVERY-
WHERE. PARK YOUR CAR, JEEP, TRUCK, TANK, MOTORBIKE,
MOTORBOAT, JETBOAT, AIRBOAT, SUBMARINE, AIRPLANE, JET-
PLANE, HELICOPTER, HOVERCRAFT, WINGED MOTORCYCLE, ROCK-
ETSHIP, OR ANY OTHER CONCEIVABLE TYPE OF MOTORIZED
VEHICLE IN THE WORLD'S BIGGEST PARKINGLOT BEHIND THE
COMFORT STATION IMMEDIATELY TO YOUR REAR. GET OUT OF
YOUR MOTORIZED VEHICLE, GET ON YOUR HORSE, MULE, BICYCLE
OR FEET, AND COME ON IN.
ENJOY YOURSELVES. THIS HERE PARK IS FOR *people*.

The survey chief and his two assistants did not stay very long.
Letting them go in peace, without debate, I fixed myself another
drink, returned to the table in the backyard and sat down to await
the rising of the moon.

My thoughts were on the road and the crowds that would pour
upon it as inevitably as water under pressure follows every channel
which is opened to it. Man is a gregarious creature, we are told, a
social being. Does that mean he is also a herd animal? I don't believe it, despite the character of modern life. The herd is for un-
gulates, not for men and women and their children. Are men no
better than sheep or cattle, that they must live always in view of
one another in order to feel a sense of safety? I can't believe it.

We are preoccupied with time. If we could learn to love space as
deeply as we are now obsessed with time, we might discover a new
meaning in the phrase to *live like men*.

At what distance should good neighbors build their houses? Let
it be determined by the community's mode of travel: if by foot, four
miles; if by horseback, eight miles; if by motorcar, twenty-four miles;
if by airplane, ninety-six miles.

Recall the Proverb: "Set not thy foot too often in thy neighbor's
house, lest he grow weary of thee and hate thee."

The sun went down and the light mellowed over the sand and
distance and hoodoo rocks "pinnacled dim in the intense inane." A
few stars appeared, scattered liberally through space. The solitary
owl called.

Finally the moon came up, a golden globe behind the rocky fret-
work of the horizon, a full and delicate moon that floated lightly as

a leaf upon the dark slow current of the night. A face that watched me from the other side.

The air grew cool. I put on boots and shirt, stuffed some cheese and raisins in my pocket, and went for a walk. The moon was high enough to cast a good light when I reached the place where the gray jeep had first come into view. I could see the tracks of its wheels quite plainly in the sand, and the route was well marked, not only by the tracks but by the survey stakes planted in the ground at regular fifty-foot intervals and by streamers of plastic ribbon tied to the brush and trees.

Teamwork, that's what made America what it is today. Teamwork and initiative. The survey crew had done their job; I would do mine. For about five miles I followed the course of their survey back toward headquarters, and as I went I pulled up each little wooden stake and threw it away and cut all the bright ribbons from the bushes and hid them under a rock. A futile effort, in the long run, but it made me feel good. Then I went home to the trailer, taking a shortcut over the bluffs.

Drawing by Mirachi. © 1971, The New Yorker Magazine, Inc.

In awarding *Motor Trends'* Engineering Award for 1972, the editors stated that the Citröen sm deserved the prize because:

Although the sm may represent a branch of automotive engineering design that may not survive and even be widely copied, it is nevertheless the kind of mutation which must appear if automobile design is not to slip back into a dark age of total safety and utility. Furthermore, this car faces a number of fundamental automotive design problems—control of ride height and platform attitude hand-in-hand with problems of aerodynamic drag and life—in an exceptionally pleasing elegant form.

Energy, Economics, and Survival*

ROBERT HICKERSON

As one who has been trained in the physical sciences, I take what I define as a thermo-dynamic approach to history. The history of the human race may well be stated in terms of the ability of man to consume ever-increasing amounts of non-human energy. A million years ago primitive man in East Africa without the use of fire had only the energy from the food he ate. At the subsistence level this amounts to about 2,000 Kilogram calories or 100 thermal watts per person per day. One hundred thousand years ago hunting man in Europe had more food and the use of fire for heat and cooking. His per capita energy consumption was around 5,000 Kilogram calories. At about 5000 B.C. primitive agricultural man with the use of some animal energy consumed 12,000 Kilogram calories. By A.D. 1400 in northwestern Europe, advanced agricultural man with some coal for heating, some wind and water power and animals for transport had increased his per capita consumption to about 26,000 Kilogram calories. By the time of the signing of our Declaration of Independence in 1776 James Watt had so improved the steam engine that the age of power was well begun. One hundred years later in 1875 industrial man in England was consuming 77,000 Kilogram calories per capita. By 1970 in the United States the total energy

* Taken from a paper prepared for Ecology Action Educational Institute Conference on Environmental Techniques Training. Reprinted by permission.

consumption had risen to the staggering total of 65 quadrillion BTU per annum. This represents 230,000 Kilogram calories per capita per day or 11,500 thermal watts. . . . [1]

Most authors writing on this subject seem to be operating on the assumption that a continuously expanding rate of energy consumption is necessary and the problem is how to supply the energy. A few, however, have recognized that indefinite growth in energy consumption, as in human populations, is simply not possible. [3, 1] Hubbert says, "It is as true of power plants or automobiles as it is of biological populations that the earth cannot sustain any physical growth for more than a few tens of successive doublings. Because of this impossibility, the exponential rates of industrial and population growth that have prevailed during the past century and a half must soon cease. Although the forthcoming period of stability poses no insuperable physical or biological difficulties, it can hardly fail to force a major revision of those aspects of our current social and economic thinking that stem from the assumption that growth rates that have characterized this temporary period can somehow be made permanent."

Most of you have heard what an exponential rate of energy consumption will lead to. You have heard that the temperature in the Northern Hemisphere has dropped one half of one degree Fahrenheit since 1940, presumably from the particulate matter we are dumping in the atmosphere, [2, 4] and that this may soon push the Earth into a new ice age. You have heard that the energy received from the sun by the U.S. will be equaled by production of electrical energy in about 100 years if the demand continues to double every 10 years. [5] (Since the average efficiency of power plants in the U.S. is 32.5 percent [5] I leave it to your imagination what the impact of a fourfold increase in the heat added to the atmosphere will have on the global climate.) You are told that by the year 2000 power plants of all kinds will produce roughly enough heat to raise by 20 degrees the total volume of water which runs over the U.S. in a year and that in a few more years it will all be boiled away. [6] You are told that by the year 2000 the new power plants will occupy eight million acres of land with an additional one-half million acres devoted to transmission lines. [7] "By the year 2000—if not well before that time—we will be in serious environmental trouble unless the increase in power generation is slowed, and that if the increase is to be halted in time, we must begin to act immediately." [6] The scientific problem of the immediate future is how to stabilize our

rate of energy consumption and to convert from non-renewable polluting sources to renewable non-polluting sources.

How might we in the United States reduce our per capita consumption of energy and at the same time increase our real standard
of living and the quality of life? Before we begin our analysis I would
like to introduce the concept of energy cost which in the real, or
matter and energy world, is the physical cost of any goods or service. As an example, let us evaluate various transportation systems
in terms of their energy costs. We define the output of any transportation system to be the total number of passenger miles for passenger carriers and the total number of ton miles for freight carriers.
The energy input to the system is the total energy consumed by that
system whether derived from tons of coal, gallons of fuel, or KWH
of electricity for that system. The energy cost is then defined in
terms of energy per unit output. For passenger carriers it could be
expressed in terms of BTU or gallons of fuel, or KWH per passenger mile. For freight systems it would be BTU or gallons of fuel or
KWH per ton mile. Cantor has given energy costs for various systems in gallons of fuel per 100 passenger miles. [11] In order of
increasing efficiency they are: helicopter, 13 gallons per 100 passenger miles; 707, 5.5 gallons per 100 passenger miles; private
motorcar, 4.4 gallons per hundred passenger miles; bus, 0.8 gallon
per hundred passenger miles, and train, 0.36 gallon per hundred
passenger miles. He assumes about a 50 percent load factor for public transit and 1.5 passengers per motorcar. The train is then 36
times as efficient as the helicopter, 15 times as efficient as the 707,
12 times as efficient as the motorcar and over two times as efficient
as the bus. The jumbo jets should be more efficient than the 707,
but recently they have been flying with very few passengers so their
efficiency is then very low. From an energy basis we cannot afford
this sort of thing. I do not have the numbers for the Boeing SST,
but it would have to be less efficient than conventional jets. I understand that the British French Concorde is so inefficient that it cannot possibly be operated at a monetary profit.

Mr. Belding of the Bay Area Rapid Transit District in San Francisco recently gave me some figures for BART. For a load factor of
38 percent the energy cost worked out to 0.41 gallon per 100
passenger miles, but if the electricity was generated by fossil fuels,
as it probably will be, the fuel cost jumps to 1.22 gallons per 100
passenger miles.

As yet I have been unable to obtain other than estimates of the

energy costs per ton mile for freight systems. The estimates are that
the energy costs for trains is one-tenth that of motor trucks and
ships one-tenth that of trains. Pipe lines are probably more efficient
than ships. I was appalled by a recent article by Sylvia Porter in
which she reported the first Boeing 747 F jet freighter will soon be
delivered to Lufthansa, the German air line, and it is expected to
haul such goodies as automobiles, heavy drilling equipment, etc. She
reports that its profit potential is tremendous. So is its potential for
further rip-off of the planet.

Probably the outstanding example of the inability of the monetary
cost effectiveness technique to reflect physical reality is in the man-
ufacturing of aluminum. In 1960, for example, two million tons of
aluminum were produced at an energy cost of 30 billion KWH. That
represents 19,000 KWH/ton. [6] Compare this to steel plate or
wire, whose energy cost is 2,700 KWH/ton. Now how, you may
ask, can aluminum, whose physical cost is seven times that of steel,
compete with steel? The answer, of course, is that the money system
is a tremendous distorter of physical reality. It serves as a de-
coupling mechanism between mankind and the environment. The
production of aluminum was subsidized by the taxpayers of this
country when a make-work project of the depression-ridden thirties,
Bonneville Dam, 65 miles east of Portland, Oregon, on the Colum-
bia River, began its first delivery of 26,000 KW to Alcoa, the
Aluminum Company of America in 1938. The cost of this electricity to industrial customers in firm blocks is a few mills per KWH
compared to a few cents for private citizens. As of 1967 the Bonneville Power Administration marketed 8,350,000 KW, of which 39
percent went to heavy industry. By 1967, 30 percent of the primary
aluminum produced in the United States came from Pacific Northwest smelters. BPA plans for this trend to continue. By 1977 they
expect to sell 20,750,000 KW, and by 1987, 38,150,000 KW, of
which 41 percent will be produced by large nuclear reactors. And
what will all of the new aluminum be used for? It is expected that
the growing output will be used in the manufacture of more autos,
trucks, buses, and containers, all uses that were served by steel at
one-seventh of the energy cost. . . .

It is becoming evident to increasing numbers of people that
something is going wrong with the U.S. economy. The admission
that the Nixonomic game plan was not working. Federal Reserve
Chairman Arthur Burns' admission on nationwide TV that "the economic system does not appear to be working the way we thought it

did." (This is an open admission that our leaders don't know what
they are doing.) A balance of payments deficit in the third quarter
of 1971 of 12 billion dollars. The fact that the total U.S. debt, public,
private, and corporate, has reached 2.1 trillion dollars and that Federal obligations to Social Security, federal deposit insurance, etc.,
has risen to 2.6 trillion dollars. The presence of 60 billion of Euro-
dollars on deposit in European Central Banks that Europe does not
known what to do with. (It is entirely possible that U.S. industries
in Europe may be confiscated in payment for those Euro-dollars.)
These are all signs of a possible impending collapse of our money
system that will make the 1930's look like a picnic. . . .

I have met some in the environmental movement who have suggested that we should return to the 2,000 Kilogram calorie energy
level, that this might be a good thing. What they are suggesting is
that 99.9 percent of our population should die a very unpleasant
death. They might just as well propose an all-out nuclear war. The
end result would be the same. While I admit that both of these ca-
tastrophes are possible, I find them equally unacceptable. What we
must do is evaluate our present position and then decide where we
want to go. Then we must plan how to get there. . . .

A steady state economy, as opposed to our present inherently
wasteful linear economy, must be designed as a closed loop system.
A feedback loop must be provided for so that all materials in the
economy that become unserviceable are fed back into the production process and reappear as new products. The actual physical
wealth of our society would be determined by our materials inventory and, because of the bountifulness of nature in North America,
could be set high enough that Robert Theobald's economy of
abundance could be achieved. [9] (Theobald states, "The key economic reality to which our thinking is geared is scarcity—we believe that there is not enough of anything to go around. Our lives
are ordered by a pursuit of material goals because we are afraid
that not enough can be produced to satisfy our needs, which we assume are insatiable. We have not understood that abundance is feasible and could already exist if we would reorganize our socio-
economic systems.") Within the limit of a fixed materials inventory
the standard of living and the quality of life would be higher if the
rate of flow of materials were lower. This is so because more materials would be in use by the people and less in the recycling feedback
loop. This maximizing of materials in use could be accomplished by

increasing the durability of individual commodities. It has the additional inherent advantage of reducing the expenditure of energy in the recycling and industrial processes. And it reduces the number of man-hours and hence the number of jobs in the industrial process. . . .

One of the most massive forces that stands in the way of any attempt to move from our anti-survival to a survival system is the entire cultural hangup known as the "Protestant or work ethic"— the pernicious idea that hard work and suffering are somehow, per se, desirable. This idea is embodied in the neo-Keynesian commitment to full employment and the idea that incomes must be provided by job holding. It is assumed that somehow a man is able by his personal services to render to society the equivalent of what he receives, from which it follows that a person's income shall be in accordance with the services rendered and that those who do not work must not eat. . . .

I am convinced that even without pressure from environmentalists there is no way that society can provide enough jobs for all who need them. All the evidence points to increasing unemployment. If society cannot supply enough jobs for everyone to certify himself as a consumer, we have no choice but to find other means of certification. We must remove the connection between income and work and recognize the principle that each individual has an inalienable right to live—a right to which no conditions are attached and which implies the right to the high standard of living it is technically possible for our society to achieve. [12] *Environmentalists should push for a guaranteed income for all citizens* as a birthright. As Theobald says: "The destabilizing impact of automation and cybernation will increase in the future because it was consistently denied throughout the sixties. During the last decade Americans should have faced the fact that the goal of full employment had become obsolete and needed to be replaced by the goal of full unemployment. We shall now pay for our failure to recognize that the goal of full employment is obsolete. A substantial proportion of the population is committed to a backlash against what they consider to be the causes of unemployment"—technology and the environmentalists. Theobald goes on to cite the trend among middle management to resist the installation of computers which threaten their jobs, deliberate acts of sabotage by bored and frustrated automobile assembly line workers, the dramatization by ecology groups of their hatred for technology by purchasing cars and then breaking them up with sledge-hammers, the misuse of Ellul's book, *The Technological Society,* as a rationale for a policy of destruction and violence. He goes on to state that, "The neo-Luddite revolt rests, in part, on the belief that it is desirable to break the present society down because its lifestyle is unattractive or intolerable. It is argued, correctly, that American society would collapse if its production, transportation, and communications systems were crippled.

"Neo-Luddites do not realize, however, that their approach works against their stated goal of diminishing the effectiveness of machines and the linear mode of thinking. Social systems inevitably continue to evolve in the same direction unless they are attracted in a different direction by clearly defined alternative routes. In order to create new patterns of attraction, it is necessary that those who have already perceived the need for change *create attractive options for the culture.* Any breakdown in communications and transportation nets necessarily hampers such an effort. The neo-Luddite revolt, therefore, has the ironic consequence of making a total cultural and ecological collapse *more* probable." [10] I suggest that environmentalists *clearly define alternative routes and create attractive options for the future.* I have listed five ideas which might be used in developing alternatives.

1. Substitution of energy cost effectiveness technique for monetary cost effectiveness. Example: we have truth in lending laws, truth in packaging laws, etc. Push for truth in pricing laws which require that all goods and services must show energy cost as well as dollar costs. Buy products and services with lowest energy cost.

2. Push for an Energy Commission to replace the AEC. Oppose nuclear reactor construction and Project Plowshare. The plan of AEC is to set off 700–900 bombs in Colorado to release natural gas, etc. Argue for increased energy conversion efficiency and conversion away from more energy-costly systems to less energy-costly systems, such as ships and rail instead of 747 F's and trucks. Show how our energy needs can be reduced and QOL (Quality of Life) increased. Support development of renewable energy sources.

3. Insist on certification of all citizens as a birthright. Then push for shutdown of all industries and elimination of all jobs which represent a threat to our survival (auto industries, most freeway construction, excessive packaging, throwaway bottles, etc.). Oppose any new technological development until its impact on the ecosystem can be evaluated.

4. Develop the general specifications for the type of society you want in the future, survival oriented; cooperative instead of competitive; education for living instead of how to make a living; physical and economic security instead of insecurity. Then take these specifications to the biologists, the systems ecologists, the new economists, anyone who has the systemic approach, and insist that they come up with a design for the new society that meets your specifications and the plans to implement it. Some suggested people are Barry Commoner, Paul Ehrlich, John Goffman, Ken Watt, Arthur Tamplin, Snell and Gail Putney. History has shown that major breakthroughs often come from completely unexpected sources, those not bound up by the conventional wisdom or the traditional approach. Perhaps your group could organize a conference with such people to get it together. . . .

5. Go to the heads of essential industries and services: BART, Greyhound, SP, PG&E, garbage and sewer services, Safeway, PT&T, etc., and ask to see their contingency plans in case of an economic collapse. If they don't know what you are talking about, spell it out for them. Ask them how they intend to instill a sense of social responsibility in their key people to stay on the job when their pay checks stop. I have already been told by one telephone plant engineer that Safeway doesn't give out groceries for love and he intends to split if things get bad.

Paul Ehrlich and Richard Harriman have written in their book, *How to Be a Survivor, a Plan to Save Spaceship Earth,* "The 1970's is the decade of decision. In this decade, mankind will either take the necessary action to preserve his species on the surface of this planet, or he will so erode, overtax and exploit his only habitat that he will destroy himself.

"This is no longer a matter for debate. There is no longer any question about the destructive potential of our course. The only question is, can we change that course?

"The only acceptable answer is yes. But the changes required are so massive that some blind themselves to the need for change, and some will not believe the course can be altered. Allow enough of them and we will all be non-survivors.

"So it is up to those with knowledge, guts, and resources, to recognize what is needed and to convince and carry the rest of the world. There is nothing small about this plan. This is a plan to save the world, to keep it alive for the next thirty years. If we can do that, mankind will have a chance." [8]

Bibliography

1. Cook, Earl, 1971. The Flow of Energy in an Industrial Society. *Scientific American,* September 1971.
2. Singer, S. Fred, 1970. Human Energy. Production as a Process in the Biosphere. *Scientific American,* September 1970.
3. Hubbert, M. K., 1969. Energy Resources. In *Resources and Man.* NAS–NRC Committee on Resources and Man, pp. 157–242. W. H. Freeman and Co.
4. Bryson, R. A. and W. M. Wendland, 1970. Climatic Effects of Atmospheric Pollution. In *Global Effects of Environmental Pollution,* pp. 130–138. S. F. Singer (Ed.), D. Reidel.
5. Summers, C. M., 1971. "The Conversion of Energy," pp. 149–160, *Scientific American,* September 1971.
6. Committee for Environmental Information, 1970. The Space Available. *Environment,* March 1970, pp. 2–9.
7. Tallman, V., 1971. The Problem of Power. *Parade,* November 7, 1971, pp. 18–19.
8. Ehrlich, P. R. and R. L. Harriman, 1971. *How to Be a Survivor.* New York: Ballantine.
9. Theobald, Robert, 1970. *The Economics of Abundance.* New York: Pitman Publishing Co.
10. Theobald, Robert, 1972. *Habit and Habitat.* Englewood Cliffs, New Jersey: Prentice-Hall.
11. Cantor, K. P., 1970. Warning: The Automobile is Dangerous, etc. *The Environmental Handbook.* New York: A Ballantine Book, pp. 197–213.
12. Fromm, Erich, 1968. *The Revolution of Hope: Toward a Humanized Technology.* New York: Harper & Row.

In Forty Words, or Less

J. M. SCOTT

I have forty words allotted to me.
The object is economy.
That enemy of poedantry.
Of prolix poets the enemy.
A friend to life and ecology.
The subject is economy.
Limited use, so that all may be free.
I find I've got one less.
Or more.

Will Man Make It?*

WILLIAM VANDUSEN WISHARD

Quo vadis America? Where are we heading? Behind the cacophony of the candidates and prophecies of the pundits, that is what is bugging Mr. & Mrs. Average Voter. What kind of a country is America going to be, and who, if anybody, has a large enough vision of the future to move us all forward?

The political season brings forth voices that equate the American condition with Rome or Greece after they passed their zenith of power and glory. Other voices say we are on the edge of a new era of development and wonder, and can only dimly perceive the outlines of a fantastic future. Some say we have lost the moral foundations which constituted the fabric of society, while others proclaim the emergence of a new value system.

In short, we are either at the twilight of greatness or the edge of a new greatness, depending on with whom we talk and the perceptions they hold.

But what is the truth? Where are we? I suggest that there is no *one* view of our condition; that elements of truth exist in the perceptions of all of us.

The presence of widespread anxiety cannot be denied. The sense of hope that once characterized America has yielded to a sense of uncertainty. Cynicism has replaced optimism, doubt has replaced

* Reprinted with permission.

anxiety, suspicion has replaced trust. The reality of our circumstances, however, favors optimism, expectancy and trust.

A Watershed of History

We are learning how to live in an era which appears to be a watershed of human history. The problems we face are caused not simply by the desire of one nation to dominate another, nor by the desire of a people to be free of all domination. Nor are our problems caused solely by the advance of science and technology.

Throughout history, man has been controlled by and subject to the evolutionary process of life. Now, for the first time, we can control and determine part of that process. This is forcing us to redefine our relationships to nature, to the universe, and to our fellow man. We are having to redefine our relationship to every belief and institution which has been the foundation of civilization.

In one sense, we have not lost our way at all. The roads of the past have come to an end and we have not yet discovered a path to the future. The quarter century from 1960 to 1985 may mark the overlap of different ages—the past separatist period and the global period ahead.

Periods of transition through history have usually been imperceptible. Change came gradually. Communications, commerce, and travel were of a pace that permitted people to assess the newest development and adjust to its impact. Slowly new developments became an established part of life, allowing life to progress in an orderly fashion. Progress has always been constant, but it came at a pace which permitted understanding and adjustment.

Gradual change has now given way to accelerated change and man is denied the time to adapt. It is thrusting on us a new kind of growth and maturity which is being forced against our instincts, under greater pressure than man has heretofore experienced and in the face of conditions which, if miscalculated, could obliterate the human race.

Simultaneous Revolutions

In truth, we are experiencing simultaneous revolutions—the knowledge revolution, the computer revolution, the space/time revolution, the black revolution, the youth revolution, the genetic revolution, the population revolution, the revolution of rising expectations. Any one of these is enough to cause upheaval in the stablest of societies. Coming together, they have shredded the fabric of established patterns of life and behavior. It is not that the values and concepts which held our society together are no longer right. It is rather that the structure of life we live in is so different that everything must be rethought and formed anew.

One of the first areas to feel the impact of these simultaneous revolutions is that of authority. Webster defines authority as "the power to influence or command thought, opinion, or behavior." Historically, that power has been exercised by relatively few people in society as a whole—and certainly by few people relative to those people whose thought, opinion, or behavior were to be influenced.

The effect of these simultaneous revolutions is to dissipate power and fragment authority. It is a universal trend, be it in the military, the family, the police, the church, educational institutions, business, and not least of all, the government. It has come about in some measure because of the unprecedented extension of education and information. Information and education breed independence and power which tend to fragment authority. The effect is that part of the inherent authority of the institution is being transferred to the individual. It means that the institution can no longer simply hand down decisions and expect subordinates to blindly follow. Increasingly, the individuals affected by the institution want to be taken into the decision-making process if they are to support and implement the decision. Somehow the individual must achieve both an enlarged awareness of the total need, and an increased sense of responsibility.

Changing Politics

The world of politics, both domestic and global, has felt the impact of these simultaneous revolutions. On a world scale, the old ideologies of communism, nationalism, socialism, neutralism, and isolationism as static concepts have passed into irrelevance. The world is in a new frame of reference. This is not to say that a nation will no longer seek its own economic or political advantage. That is not the same, however, as the nineteenth century nationalism where the nation-state concept constituted the outer limits of a people's political consciousness. What we are experiencing now is not nationalism as a cultural-political concept, but nationalism simply as a struggle for power and economic advantage.

On a national scene, much the same holds true for traditional concepts of conservative, liberal, moderate, independent, and even to some extent Democratic and Republican. They do not hold much relevance for the people and the problems of the future. Life has moved beyond them all.

Throughout history man's political consciousness and self-identification have constantly expanded. It has grown from the family, to the tribe, to the village, to the region, to the nation. Now we are experiencing the emergence of a global society. While electronics and technology are fragmenting established patterns of thought and action, they are at the same time drawing the world together. Communications and space exploration are creating a global culture. Though national boundaries remain the same, cultural, political, and economic boundaries are ever expanding. A global information grid is developing. Banks and multinational corporations have operated on a global scale for some time.

We are developing a global awareness and consciousness. Daily through TV, we feel and experience the events that touch the lives of the peasants in Asia, the students in France or the tribesmen in Africa. More of our problems, for instance, ecology, will require a global action to solve them. Obviously, if pollution is as serious a problem in Russia and Japan as it is in the United States, it will require a global authority to solve the problem. With increasing overproduction on one side of the world and increasing overpopulation on the other, it requires a greater degree of global coordination in order to satisfy the needs of the human family.

Effect on Government

One of the most vital areas affected by the change we are experiencing is that of government.

For a variety of reasons, America is facing a crisis in government at every level. Are we, in fact, able to govern ourselves? The process of government is becoming more difficult, slower, more cumbersome, and, in some respects, less effective. City governments face bankruptcy. National programs appear ineffectual. Even the process of financing established operations is taking so long that it is putting those operations in jeopardy.

What is creating this crisis? The first point to come to mind, the bureaucratic structure, is such a highly documented subject that there is little which could be added here. Suffice it to say that compartmentalization, fragmentation, inflexibility, lack of direction, lack of excitement or expectancy leave a massive bureaucratic machine inching forward at its own pace.

Some say there is a crisis of confidence in government, an erosion of the public trust. Possibly it is more accurate to say there is an erosion of public trust in some of the politicians who govern. This is not too surprising when we consider the erosion of trust between some of the politicians themselves. At the center of this lack of public confidence is government's inability to solve our most urgent problems. Part of the reason for this is that we have not yet delineated what government can do and what we as individuals should do ourselves. We've developed an automatic reaction that expects government to do everything.

The impact on government of television and the information explosion must be considered. In former times the public generally conceded that it didn't have the facts or background on a given issue, that the government did, so people were likely to leave the decision on an issue in the hands of the government. Not any longer. Television has created an instantaneous information delivery system which equips everyone with at least enough facts so they think they are qualified to have some judgment on vital issues. The public no longer concedes that the government has any monopoly on knowledge, and as Vietnam clearly demonstrates, it is all too ready to oppose the government viewpoint, and even to reject the factual basis for government decisions.

An absence of a consensus of "national interest" plays a part. In simpler times many a problem was solved by pleading the "national interest." Today, however, that sense of national interest, shared even by a minority of our people, no longer exists, and we lack a common concept of nationhood.

We have experienced an unparalleled extension of economic independence and political freedom. The outcome: individuals are surer of the way to go and how to get there. These factors, plus the broader dissemination of information, have had the effect of fragmenting traditional political and ideological concepts, thus multiplying the number and variety of viewpoints that need to be considered on any given issue.

Certainly rapid change is one permanent feature of our lives. This transition from the stability of life as we have known it in the past to an era of continual change as we will experience it from now on tends to create a national atmosphere of uncertainty and insecurity in which it is more difficult for government to govern. All this forces us to rethink the process of government—how can it best serve its purpose in the midst of change, speed and complexity?

Varied Reaction

What has been our reaction as a nation to all this—to the emergence of an age of continual change? The greatest single reaction has been simply to continue doing what we have been doing. The job still has to be done, the family has to be fed, life has to be lived. Add to that the complexity of the changes taking place, and the average person is left wondering what he can do that could possibly make any significant impact.

Some simply drop out—and the dropouts are in every age group. The older generation found ways of dropping out long before the discovery of dope or communes.

Others view our circumstances as a disintegration of society and a collapse of the established order. Their reaction is to try to hold things together, perhaps even to stick the broken pieces together again. To do this they reach for concepts which have been the foundation of the best of the past. This is understandable, but is it enough? Is not our need actually to re-create moral precepts, to re-create a social framework? The question goes beyond the social order. It concerns the individual, what he thinks and believes within himself.

People react to change. Change creates insecurity. People naturally cling to the security of the known. But if one thing is certain, it is that we are living on the edge of the unknown in every area of life. The great task of our time is to explore that unknown area and lay the foundations of a new civilization. It requires that we learn to live with a certain amount of insecurity while maintaining a balanced tension of mind and spirit.

Perspective and Purpose

Integral to the way we react to change and new circumstances are our perspective and purpose. Talk abounds calling for a new purpose, both for individuals and for the nation. But is not our national purpose the same as man's purpose has always been—the understanding of his world and, given that understanding, the development of the highest form of society and culture possible? We must continue to pursue that purpose while continually re-evaluating what it requires. Certainly as knowledge and awareness expand and with that expansion the complexities of life increase, it will demand more of man to achieve his purpose than in former times. Man's spirit, will, and flexibility will have to grow faster than the difficulties he faces if he is to survive. Such a step in growth is coming. Perhaps mankind is already in the midst of a transition from an epoch of competition and individualism to an epoch of cooperation and interdependence.

Our perspective as a people is all important in this process. Some people are focused on the past, and they long for the simplicity of a bygone era. Some are focused on the future with a fixation that ignores present realities. Still others are absorbed with our present problems and would fail to remind us how far we have come and what are the possibilities of the future. The communications/time-space revolution is partly responsible for the tendency to lack perspective, but it can easily be balanced.

Age of the Individual

A nation's purpose and perspective are, of course, the sum total of the purposes and perspectives held by its citizens. In this respect, the future very much depends on the individual.

Contrary to what one hears about a "mass society" or a "corporate state," this is the age of the individual. Never has the individual had so much freedom to think what he pleases, say what he pleases, do what he pleases. People are less inclined to act as a member of a bloc—as a "Catholic," a "black," a "worker." People act as individuals, and you will get as many different viewpoints on any given question from the so-called "youth" as you will from the so-called "senior citizen."

The United States may be experiencing something that no other country has yet gone through. We may be experiencing the first full flowering of democracy. In the sixteenth century an idea that had lain dormant was reborn: the belief that the responsibility of the individual is the ultimate criterion of politics and religion. The renewal of that concept made democracy possible on a scale larger than that of the Greek city-state. Its full impact, however, was never felt by the majority of people, but remained largely a concept of the educated. Perhaps the United States, which was the first country to make material plenty available to most of its people, is now the first country to face the consequences of the fact that widespread prosperity universalizes the revolution of individualism. America is attempting to provide for the masses in terms of education, prosperity and political freedom what throughout history has been the privileged right of a minority of people.

New Choices

As uncomfortable as it may be, the individual is being forced to consider issues he has never confronted before, as well as issues he has taken for granted. The individual is used to considering the economy, social needs, poverty, foreign trade, war or peace—issues that are the product of the industrial era. These are tangible topics. But the intangibles have become the imperatives. It might be worth considering—especially in an election year—the following and what impact they are already having on our lives:

—The decline of a sense of nationhood. What elements do we have in common to hold us together? Do we share a sense of a common heritage and culture? How do you govern a nation when various differences become enlarged beyond the point of any national or common interests? In his farewell address, Washington advised that, "Of all the dispositions and habits which lead to political prosperity, religion and morality are indispensable supports. . . . It is substantially true that virtue or morality is a necessary spring of popular government." If this is true, what is the future of popular government in America in view of what is certainly a changing morality and some would describe as a decline in morality?

—Freedom. What is the relationship among freedom, license, control, and responsibility? Is freedom automatically self-renewing? What engenders freedom? What is the relationship between an individual's freedom and the needs of society? What are the consequences of today's widespread political and economic freedom—a freedom the extent of which has never been achieved by any society in history? History tends to indicate that if freedom is made absolute, anarchy or tyranny soon follows. Concurrently, as the complexities and interdependence of life increase, the question of control will come into sharper focus. Simple societies require limited control, complex societies demand more control. It would seem that the only alternative to both the tendency of anarchy to follow freedom and complexity requiring control is for a heightened individual responsibility on a widespread scale. Can it be achieved?

—Are we considering the basic issue involved in the question of law and order? Clearly, law reform, prison reform, judicial reform, more and better paid policemen, more judges are needed. But if law is based on morality and traditions, and if increasingly there are divergent opinions of what constitutes morality or the worth of our traditions, is not the fundamental question what are the basic concepts and ground rules we as a people will agree to live by and accept as a basis of law? This is not to suggest that the present basis is wrong, but only that a growing number of people are in disagreement with that basis.

—The breakup of the family structure. The family has historically been the basic unit of government and a training ground for children to learn how to live in society. Have we abdicated the function of a family? Are families needed in today's world? What is the purpose of the family? How will children be prepared for life in the future?

—Television. What is its effect on our society? How is it being used? What is the effect of TV's dissemination of information? Are we producing children who grow up with a TV-induced appetite for excitement and entertainment? If so, what does that do to their initiative and creativity?

—The communications revolution. The ability to communicate faster doesn't necessarily guarantee communication on a deeper level. Is our communications based on substance or images? What are the values we are communicating?

—What is affluence doing to us as a people? What is the effect of success? Are we really addressing the vivid imbalance between the extremes of poverty and plenty? How do we balance expectations that rise faster than buying power?

—What should be America's relationship to the rest of the world? What is the right balance between global awareness and responsibility on the one hand, and not being the world's policemen on the other? We Americans tend to swing from one extreme to the other. Part of our growing-up process as a nation is a mature balance of initiative and reserve.

—What has been our traditional morality and what moral values are emerging? As our moral values are reconsidered, are we asking more of ourselves or less? Is the Protestant Ethic declining, and if it is, how will that affect our ability to work and produce? How is the wider moral sense of social responsibility evolving? What will move us as people to demand of ourselves the greatest degree of morality possible, and to subordinate personal or group interests to the larger interest of the whole? How do attitudes toward sex fit into the overall scheme of moral thought?

—There is the decline of formal religion and concurrent experiences which question the very existence of God. Man now has the ability to perform acts heretofore attributed only to God. Heart transplants and synthetic body parts raise the question: What is life? What is death? Brain transplants raise the question of who is who. How does an increased understanding of God fit into our expanded consciousness of life and this world? What has been the impact on religion of man's growing awareness of his miniscule place in the cosmos?

—How to put it all together. For two hundred years our own national purpose has been expansion and growth—within a framework of freedom. A larger objective now is how to achieve the right balance of all our needs, such as growth and the awareness of its effects and limitations; change; exploration; unprecedented individual liberty; economic imbalance; new lifestyles and patterns; competing demands for limited resources—how to put all these things together so there is a harmonious totality to life for all our people.

—What is the nature of the age we are in; where are we in our evolution? In the midst of constant and rapid change, what gives the individual a sense of balance, of continuity, of perspective and direction?

We can appropriately ask if these are relevant questions, and, if so, whether as a nation we are adequately considering them. Perhaps these are among the kinds of issues we ought to be discussing this election year.

Either Way

The American experiment clearly can go either way—to new heights of life and culture or to stagnation and fragmentation. The outcome may depend on what thousands of Americans decide. The possibility of a new civilization with undreamed of achievement and fulfillment is before us. And the means to realize it are at hand. The question mark is man himself—whether we as individuals will rise to new heights.

Man has always faced a succession of greater challenges. In one sense the story of history is the story of the expansion of man's knowledge and freedom, and man's capacity to cope with the problems that expansion creates. As each new phase has unfolded it has forced man to find an increased maturity and growth within himself which expressed itself in new developments and culture. Now again man faces the eternal challenge of his own inner growth.

Perhaps one of the motivational keys to that growth is the need for new dreams and hopes. Today hope and expectancy are out of vogue while cynicism is in fashion. Pessimism and cynicism, however, are not the stuff of which a new age is built.

It might be argued that dreams are the element that move men to action. To deny a people their dreams and visions is to rob them of the most powerful force to urge them forward. The ancient prophets used to say that where there is no vision the people perish.

Yet America is disillusioned with her dreams. Here is the paradox. America is on the verge of fulfilling the dreams humanity has held for centuries, yet we seem to have lost the capacity to hold new dreams. Part of this is the result of the sixties—a decade that started with dreams and ended with ashes. One might be forgiven for reminding us, however, that the sixties also ended with man reaching for the stars and accomplishing one of his greatest achievements thus far.

The time is ripe now for new dreams; dreams tempered with realism, dreams molded by maturity, dreams in the light of experience. But exciting and compelling dreams nonetheless. These dreams will not be the product of rhetoric nor the empty words of the phrase maker. Instead, they can be the dreams of a people who know that a better quality of life can result only if they demand a higher quality in themselves; a people who know that there are no instant solutions, and that to build a new age requires perseverance, energy, and hope; people who know that the only thing that is going to save mankind is for enough people live their lives for something or someone other than themselves.

As a nation we have emerged from the shell shock of the sixties. The past four years have given us respite, allowed us to pull ourselves together and reassess our approach to the future. We have not solved our problems, but we have come a long way. Judged by most social measurements, the America of 1972 is a long way ahead of the America of 1962.

But the hour of respite is coming to a close, and soon we will need to find something that will give us a new thrust forward. We will have to ask ourselves again, to what are we committed? A fresh sense of commitment will not be a glib concept fanned by charisma and oratory. Instead, it may be something that emerges out of the spirit of us as a people—the will to create, the compassion to fulfill. The elimination of poverty, the protection of the environment, the securing of peace are all part of it. Yet, it goes beyond that. What sort of nation do we want America to be? What do we really consider important? What price are we willing to pay? Will we re-linquish personal and group interests for the larger interest? These are the questions that decide what our commitment is. Perhaps a new commitment is already growing within us.

And perhaps, too, we are achieving a new understanding of what America is all about. America is not meant to be a fixed goal or pattern. Rather, it should be a flexible framework within which men can live, grow, change, develop, prosper, and constantly reach for a higher effort in life.

It might be worth recalling the words of Woodrow Wilson: "We know our task to be no mere task of politics but a task which shall search us through and through, whether we be able to understand our time and the need of our people, whether we be indeed their spokesmen and interpreters, whether we have the pure heart to com-prehend and the rectified will to choose our high course of action."

The outcome rests with us.

There is a massive backlash against authority in the world today. People are no longer willing to be given orders: they are demanding the right to control their own lives. A massive argument is now developing as to whether we can live without any form of leadership or whether there must be leadership.

The next piece suggests, in an unusual context, that there will always be a necessity for leadership. It also suggests that leadership can be provided by different people depending on the circumstances.

If this is true, those who have the knowledge and skills to lead should always use them. But they must understand that the ability to lead effectively depends on their transferring the ideas and leadership which form the basis of their leadership.

There are two temptations which beset the potential leader. The most commonly accepted today is that the individual accepts the role of leader and then demands obedience without understanding. The other danger is that he will refuse to use his greater knowledge to help those who have need of it.

Leadership is a reality. But leadership can be the way by which society grows toward its potential.

Sociality*

JOHN N. BLEIBTRAU

There exist among the rotting leaves on forest floors a class of creatures known technically as the *Acrasiales* (from the Greek, meaning *unmixed*) and popularly as the slime molds.

As they perform their ecological function of contributing to the decay sequence, they live as amoeba, freely, each wandering separately over its chosen area ingesting bacteria by *phagocytosis,* by surrounding and enclosing its prey animal, incorporating it literally into its flesh. The following description of its behavior, while gen-

* Reprinted with permission of the Macmillan Company from *The Parable of the Beast.* © 1968 by John N. Bleibtrau.

erally true of all the eight or nine species of this class, refers particularly to the species *Dictyostelium disocideum,* which was identified in 1935 by a soil chemist named Kenneth B. Raper, who worked at that time for the United States Department of Agriculture in Washington. Raper found that this particular species of slime mold (unlike many others) submitted easily to conditions of captivity, flourishing under a wide range of humidity and temperature gradients. Because of this it soon became the primary animal used by laboratory students of its behavior.

This behavior is unique, and as a result fascinating, to a variety of biological disciplines—to cytologists, embryologists, geneticists, and others. It should be the object of study for sociologists as well, since this tiny brainless, nerveless animal has evolved a complex system of social interactions; yet for some strange reason it has remained neglected. Perhaps it is because animal sociology still remains in its infancy and seems to be progressing backwards down the ladder of biological complexity, from the more easily observed and presumably more easily comprehended social behavior of vertebrate forms to the social behavior of more simply constructed beings.

While in their free-living state, each amoeba lives alone, moving about along the substrata either by elongating and then contracting its entire body, or else by extending and then contracting extruded portions of itself called *pseudopodia.* Its form is always in flux.

When food is plentiful and other conditions appropriate, every amoeba multiplies by simple cell division once every three or four hours. Eventually this geometrically expanding population exhausts the available local supply of bacteria, and as this happens the amoeba commence the enactment of an incredible series of activities. These activities are a literal metaphor for the organization of cells in a multicelled individual, or the organization of individuals into a social unit, whether that unit be an ant colony, a baboon troop, or a human society.

As their food gathering becomes more difficult, the wandering amoeba begin as individuals to cease their feeding and begin to form communal aggregations: first a few individuals clustering around a dominant (or attractant) individual, and then this group joining other groups until (as seen on an agar dish) clumps of organisms discernible to the naked eye form themselves, giving the surface of the dish a stippled effect. Now the clumps begin still another aggregation—they begin to join one another, clump to clump. They form straggling streamers of living matter, which now begin to orient themselves toward central collection points. At this stage the dish seems to be covered with numerous, regularly spaced, many-armed swastika-shaped patches of slimy mold. At the hub of each central aggregation point a mound begins to form as groups of amoeba mount themselves atop other groups, which have already arrived at the central hub. This hub gradually rises first into the shape of a blunt peg, and then into a distinctly phallic erection. When all the incoming streams of amoeba are almost completely incorporated into this erected cartridge-like form, it topples over onto its side, now looking like a small, two-millimeters-long, slimy sausage. This slug begins now to migrate across the forest floor to a point where, hopefully, more favorable ecological conditions will prevail. At this point the communal mass that forms this slug is known as a *migrating pseudoplasmodium*. It seems to possess a discrete envelope, almost a skin; but this is a sheath of slime, and as it migrates it leaves behind a trail of slime. It looks exactly like a minute garden slug, except that it lacks the extensible horns of these snails.

As the slug migrates, it continues to attract scattered solitary amoeba, which had not participated in the original aggregation. These join the mass and become immediately incorporated within it. Estimations about the size of the population that comprises the average slug vary, but generally it is thought that perhaps some half a million amoeba are involved.

When he discovered that this animal thrived in the laboratory, Raper experimented with directing the course of the slug's migration and found that it responded to light and warmth; such little light, as a matter of fact, as that provided by the luminescent dial of a wristwatch shining in the dark, and such little heat as 5/10,000 of a centigrade degree. He found he could lead the slug around over a smooth surface by the light of a watchface just as one can lead a donkey with a carrot on a pole. Raper also noted that the slug narrowed quite obviously into a point at its front end. "During migration," he writes, "the point, the apical tip, as it has been termed, is constantly to the fore and apparently guides the migration of the entire body." Raper cut this tip off the slug and found that when the community was thus deprived of its leadership, migration stopped dead in its tracks. "When the anterior portion of a migrating plasmodium is removed," he writes, "the decapitated body ceases migration, nor does it respond to light. The amoeba comprising it crowd forward to the line where the excision was made, and there collect in a rounded body. . . . In only a few isolated cases has a pseudoplasmodium thus decapitated been observed to form a new apical tip with accompanying directive center."

After migrating for a variable period of time (which can be two minutes or two weeks) in the direction of light and warmth, this slug, this wandering community, now ceases its movement and enters into another phase of its communal history called "culmination" or "the formation of the fruiting body." Exactly what causes migration to stop is not yet known, but as it ceases its forward motion, the slug gradually erects itself once again into its phallic shape until it is standing on its tail. John Tyer Bonner, a zoologist at Princeton who has spent the major part of his working life studying these fascinating creatures, describes what happens: "In the apical tip of the pseudoplasmodium, a group of cells near the tip becomes rounded off and enlarged. The whole group is either round or oval in shape, and its outer limit is smooth, bounded by a visible wall. . . ." This oval shape gradually assumes the form of a candle flame, bellied at the bottom and coming to a point at the top. As the belly forms, a waist also appears between the base, the tail of the now-erect slug, and the candleflame section which is forming directly above it. This waist gradually lengthens and becomes a stalk, pushing the candle-flame section ever upwards into the air. This brittle stalk continues to rise, carrying the candleflame section, which now tends to become more spherical in shape, up and up, either in a straight line or in a wavering direction, depending on certain conditions. Normally the end of this culminating stage produces a brittle form which looks exactly like an old-fashioned hatpin except that it is smaller—only half an inch or so high. The candleflame pod atop the stalk is known as the spore mass. As this process unfolds over the course of some two or three hours, it seems as though the stalk, growing from the bottom upward, lifts the sorocarp or fruiting body into the air. But what actually happens (as Bonner demonstrated by staining certain cells and noting the direction of their movement) is this: Amoeba from the apical tip migrate downward through the forming fruiting body, thus erecting the stalk. As the process actually occurs, it resembles a slow motion movie of a rising water fountain run backwards. Bonner describes it somewhat differently: ". . . to accomplish this transformation, the slug first points its tip upward and stands on its end. The uppermost front cells swell with water like a bit of froth and become encased in a cellulose cylinder which is to form the stalk. As new front cells arrive at the tip of the stalk, they add themselves to the lengthening structure. . . . Each amoeba

in the spore mass [the fruiting body] now encases itself in cellulose
and becomes a spore. The end result is a delicate tapering shaft
capped by a spherical mass of spores. When the spores are dis-
persed (by water, or contact with some passing creature such as an
insect or worm) each can split open to liberate a tiny new
amoeba."

Thus the cycle of the community begins again, with the amoeba
population thriving and growing on their newly located bacterial
food, until this food supply is exhausted and the cycle of aggregation
and culmination begins anew. This microscopic, brainless creature
enacts in the course of its life history the parable of all communities.
As they do in all communities, certain members of this microcosmic
society seemingly take upon themselves the responsibilities of leadership, initiating the activities of the group.

Just how this happens was demonstrated by a young Cambridge
zoologist named Bryan M. Shaffer, who went to the United States
in 1956 and worked first at Bonner's laboratory in Princeton and
then in Raper's laboratory, which had by this time been moved to
the University of Wisconsin. To prevent aggregating cells from
mounting one another in clumps, thus obscuring what each cell was
doing, Shaffer devised what he called a "sandwich" technique, a
complicated arrangement of oil and water films floating between
glass slides, which forced the amoeba to aggregate in a single layer
without clumping. In this way he discovered the existence of what
he called "founder" cells. He wrote in his description that "a founder
varied somewhat in appearance [from ordinary amoeba] at the time
it became active. In many cases it was oval or almost completely
circular in outline and stationary. . . . Because it was less expanded, it frequently appeared smaller than most or even all of the
cells that responded to it, and also darker. . . . It abruptly began
to affect its neighbors over a considerable area. These elongated
toward it within a few minutes. . . . The first to reach the founder
began to encircle it, either in one direction, or, becoming temporarily Y-shaped, in both. Whether it was able to surround it de-
pended partly on their relative sizes and partly on how soon further
cells arrived, for these competed for the founder's surface. Such
intimate contact was established that a two or three celled center
could sometimes be mistaken for a single giant cell. Occasionally,
perhaps five or ten minutes after starting to attract, a strong founder
became less circular and less refractive [dark] and stopped attract-
ing. The responding cells became less elongated and tended to pro-

duce pseudopodia from other parts of their surfaces; and then perhaps five minutes later, the founder rounded up again and the others moved toward it."

Shaffer wondered whether their role as founders was predetermined by their particular genetic heritage, or whether any amoeba could become a founder, whether it was mere chance that determined which amoeba would first feel the pinch of food shortage and become impelled to disseminate the signal for assembly.

The nature of this signal was chemical—a gas. This had been determined several years previously by Bonner, who had designed a series of experiments which systematically excluded possible non-chemical signals, such as electrical fields or other chemical communication systems, like contact or molecular trails left by amoeba in the course of their travels. Though unable to isolate the chemical molecule which comprised the gas, he named the substance *acrasin,* a coinage from the technical class-name of the animal which produced it.

There are no clear-cut conclusions to be reached as a result of the experiments Shaffer subsequently conducted. He seeded a culture, permitted it to flourish for a period, and then deprived it of food until a founder cell formed. "If this," he writes, "was immediately killed, and the culture at once returned to darkness, the residual cells did not re-aggregate. But if it was left in the light, a new founder eventually did appear."

However unhappily inconclusive this work may have been, the presumption remains from other evidence that varying social roles may be assumed by many members of the population. As early as 1902 biologists were bringing slime molds back to their laboratories and doing what almost any child would do—seeing what would happen if a migrating slug were cut into several sections. And what happened was this: Each section ceased its migration and promptly entered into the culminating stage, producing a fruiting body that was somewhat smaller than normal in size, but seemingly perfectly normal in all other respects. From its spores perfectly normal new populations would spring.

Among the slime molds the question of whether differences of behavior pre-exist in differing members of the population, or whether any behavior can be assumed by any member of the population, is still open. If the migrating slug is cut apart, new migration leaders will not appear. Migration as an activity ceases. But leaders that initiate other specialized social roles do appear. Stalkbuilding, a social role which would be normally assumed by the leadership cadre at the apical tip, is now assumed by other amoeba quite distant from the tip. In the case of the slug which is cut into three sections, certain amoeba in the terminal section far removed from the apical tip will nonetheless commence filling themselves with water, encasing themselves in cellulose and beginning to migrate backwards through the mass of their fellows in order to form the stalk. Under normal circumstances these animals would not form the stalk, but would remain anonymous members of the sorocarp; each one would have transformed itself into a spore, not a bit of stalk.

It is also curious that in the slime molds the individual members of the community that form the leadership group are nonreproductive. Only those animals that form themselves into spores contribute genetically to subsequent generations. The amoeba at the apical tip seemingly perform a totally sterile role in the future of the community, by bearing the mass of their fellows aloft, raising the community away from the contact with the earth, thus assuring the community more favorable possibilities for dispersion. This is curious, for it has a relationship to human societies; it overleaps the evidence of most vertebrate communities where the dominant animals, particularly males, have greater sexual opportunities and generally pass on their genetic characteristics differently—in a larger statistical degree—than low-ranking, nondominant individuals. Often in human societies many of the most valuable members are nonreproductive; members of celibate religious orders, ascetics, homosexuals, and so on. Reproduction flourishes on the lower levels of societal competence; the marginal members often reproduce disproportionately large numbers of themselves.

Marvelously instructive as this parable of the slime molds will very likely be—in furthering our understanding of how cells aggregate to form the fetal stage of multicelled organisms, how our understanding of slime mold behavior can contribute to our understanding of human growth and wound-healing and many other related phenomena—it is somehow still surprising how little is known about the actual process itself.

In part the problems inherent in the study of slime mold sociology derive from the microscopic scale of observation; it is very difficult to distinguish individuals within the group, difficult to mark them as individuals and follow them in the course of their social activities. No such scale difficulties involving technical problems impede our understanding of vertebrate sociology. There the problem is of a different order—one that may perhaps be considered to result from a barrier erected by human vanity. For it is vanity that identifies the self as unique and separate from all that is nonself. The human mind, working through the eye, is a synthesizing instrument. When we look, for example, upon a piece of cloth, we see a fabric and not an ordered collection of individual fibers. An earthenware pot exists in the mind of the human beholder as a plastic form in space and not a collection of particles of clay.

And so it was quite late that Western man came to understand that social orders exist in vertebrate communities other than his own. The order that exists in insect communities could not be denied. But humans observed schools of fish, flocks of birds, herds of antelope, and saw them as totalities in much the same disinterested way as one might view a cloud of insects around a street lamp on a summer evening. No one apparently deemed it a fit concern of science to attempt to distinguish the individuals from within such a collective and study their interactions with other members of the aggregation. As far back as the Pleistocene period, human hunters doubtless perceived that very often such a collection of vertebrates as a herd of deer, or a school of fish, or a flock of birds might contain a leader, an individual who stimulated and directed the group's activities. Modern zoologists also realized this, but what they did not realize was that the leader arrived at his (or her) position by ascending a graduated ladder of social responsibility. Social recognition comes to animal leaders in much the same way as it does to human leaders, by the community's consent to the leader's competence. Within each stable animal society there exists a scale of interlocking social relationships, and since the acquisition of leadership (or dominance) requires that these relationships be manipulated, animal leaders are equally as political as human leaders.

This fact, which is now considered obvious, was first noted by a Norwegian zoologist named Thorlief Schjelderup-Ebbe. It was in 1913 that he first announced to his parochial Norwegian community of zoologists that political hierarchies existed in barnyard chicken coops, and later (in 1922) he announced these findings in German to the world at large. He demonstrated to his fellow scientists by designing a series of hard, statistics-laden experiments, which were widely reproduced, the existence of a condition that had been well known to every farm boy since the domestication of a barnyard fowl. He demonstrated the obvious fact that every chicken and every rooster in a barnyard flock is an individual; and that the flock only becomes transformed into a society when the membership comes to recognize one another as individuals and acknowledges a graded hierarchy of social rank. Schjelderup-Ebbe writes of that peculiar vanity that blinds humans to the recognition of individuals. The human self only recognizes other, similar-appearing selves as being potentially unique, being individuals. Schjelderup-Ebbe begins one of his most important papers with the statement: "Every bird is a personality. . . . This may sound odd, but it is only because the individual and social psychology of birds has been regarded too superficially. No attempt has been made to know each individual bird in a given flock. So to know them, however, is the most important prerequisite for the full understanding of the general and comparative psychology of birds. The ability to distinguish each individual provides the key for the solution of a series of problems which we should otherwise be unable to solve, and which are not only of ornithological interest but also of importance for the understanding of the general continuity that prevails in all life.

Horatio Alger is seen as an author who glorified immediate success and who believed that anybody could rise to the top whatever his circumstances. In fact, his vision was broader. Alger's hero, Walter Conrad, shows this in the following* where he reflects on his future:

Though his [Walter's] life for a few months had been an active one, he had by no means lost his relish for study, nor had he given up his intention of resuming his studies at some time. In case he should realize five per cent. on the mining shares, this would amount to five thousand dollars, a sum with which he would be justified in continuing his preparation for college, and a four years' collegiate course. He estimated that his expenses as a student would not average more than five hundred dollars a year, and as the interest would amount to considerable—three hundred dollars the first year—he concluded that he could educate himself, and have considerably more than half his capital left to start in life with, when his education was complete. I mean, of course, his college education, for, strictly speaking, one's education is never complete, and those who attain eminence in any branch are willing to confess themselves perpetual learners.

* Reprinted from *Strive and Succeed*. Horatio Alger. Pp. 21–22.

Problem/Possibility Focuser on Ecology*

It is generally agreed that the combined effects of industrialization, technological change, urbanization, affluence and rapid population growth are resulting in the degradation of the environment. Simple sense data confirm this. The air is obviously dirty; sometimes it hurts our eyes. Silence is a thing of the past. Open space is vanishing. The media provide daily crisis reports—a fish kill here, oil spill somewhere else, massacres of endangered species; possibility of famines or epidemics still elsewhere. There is virtually no disagreement that environmental degradation is a problem.

There is a great deal of disagreement as to whether this degradation is a cost of development that must be borne; whether it can be survived at all; whether it can be solved by conventional political means, and how serious a problem it is in light of other global and national concerns. Perhaps the most fundamental question is whether or not environment can or should be considered as an *issue,* separate from other issues.

Ecology is a new science, and the knowledge required to assess environmental problems and provide their solutions is just now be-

* This document is not copyrighted. However, it would be appreciated if those reprinting it checked with Problem/Possibility Focuser, Swallow Press, 1139 S. Wabash Avenue, Chicago, Illinois 60605, to see if a later version has been developed. Comments should be sent to the same address.

ginning to be gathered. Though ecological wisdoms and perceptions have existed in different cultures throughout human history, there are enormous gaps in our practical understanding of the way natural systems work. Estimates of the amount of stress ecosystems can endure are speculative, and predictions of crises are partly subjective, depending on the optimism or pessimism of the predictor.

Basic Ecology

Ecosystems comprehend pyramids of organisms having varying degrees of sophistication, ranging in complexity from one-celled plants and animals to highly evolved creatures like dolphins and humans. In general, the greater the diversity of elements in an eco-system, the greater will be its stability. Cycling is characteristic of natural systems. Materials that are used are transformed in their passage through organisms and are returned to the earth-source in an ongoing process of birth-death resurrection. A healthy diversified ecosystem is homeostatic, in dynamic equilibrium permitting evolu-tionary change.

Man Apart

Prior to civilization, man was part of the fabric of natural systems. He hunted and gathered, exercising his intelligence and consciousness through shamanism and mysticism. But humans are verbalizers, makers of tools. Perceiving these unique capacities led mankind in-evitably to a sense of otherness. With agriculture, man initiated a process of changing and reshaping the environment to serve his purposes. This developing sense of otherness led to the divergence of cyclic and linear, holistic and atomistic concepts of time and the world.

To Reflect/Atavism

Some argue that human beings are obliged to respect the evolu-tionary destinies of other forms of life; that human survival depends on maintaining a high degree of diversity and genetic variability in the world. Some ecologists urge that man see himself once more as an interconnected member of the ecosystem whose role should be stewardship of resources and other life forms.

Prometheus

Harnessing energy permitted humanity to make great advances in science, invention, production, transportation, and resource extraction. These new capabilities seemingly freed humans from the constraints and threats of nature. The history of energy use has been one of steady increase, and, it is argued, must continue to be if humanity is to provide a reasonable standard of living for its increasing numbers. However, it is impossible to produce power without some environmental impact, be it visual, chemical, radiological, or thermal, in the micro sense of a specific environment, like a river heated in the process of cooling a nuclear pile, or in the macro sense of a perceptible increase in atmospheric temperature.

Possibilities for averting some form of energy crisis include developing settlement patterns which are less energy consumptive, discovering methods of utilizing solar and wind energy, and developing nuclear fusion, potentially much cleaner than the fission reaction which we now use for nuclear power generation and which produces radioactive wastes having half-lives of up to 24,000 years, causing a formidable waste disposal problem.

Centralization/Simplification

The progress of agriculture has steadily decreased the amount of land required to support an individual human, and permitted the accumulation of surpluses. With these developments came urbanization and centralization, which trends have culminated in the mega-farms and megalopoli of the present. Some of mankind's needs are served by such created environments, but evidence points to the fact that as they are presently functioning, megalopoli and mega-agricultures are stressing natural systems with their enormous demands for power and transportation. Mega-cities and mega-farms are simplified systems, with little resilience or self-sufficiency. Each produces by-products that the other needs (farms provide greenery and quiet, cities produce human intelligence and labor and organic wastes), but both are of such a scale and so removed that these useful things go to waste, resulting in a dangerous fragility for both.

Overpopulation

Agriculture, urbanization and industrialization allowed human numbers to exceed the hunting and gathering survival base. Recent improvements in public health have decreased infant mortality rates and lengthened lifespans. All this has resulted in the exponential growth of human numbers which, it is generally agreed, is ultimately unsupportable. The natural checks on the growth of any population of organisms are exhaustion of food supply, disease, destruction of habitat, and stress due to overcrowding. Human progress has somewhat allayed these.

Food

Food supply is the most immediate limit on human population growth. Some experts maintain that this has been exceeded already, on the grounds that millions of people starve to death annually. Possibilities exist for increasing the available food supply. Two general drawbacks to all of these are that humans are conservative about their diets, and farmers are conservative about their methods (this may not be such a bad thing, in light of the failures of modern agriculture).

Cultivating more land, improving grain stocks, better storage, and elimination of waste in processing would yield more food. Monocropping, however, which is required for cultivation of the miracle grains, creates a simplified vulnerable ecosystem and requires lavish use of pesticides and chemical fertilizers, as does the cultivation of marginal land. The hybridization of grains is presently reducing the available genetic variability (new species supplant old, old germ plasm is not preserved). Integrated methods of pest control which use chemicals, naturally resistant plants, and predators to control pests are promising, as is the practice of a labor-intensive multicrop agriculture, like Japan's.

Consuming second and third level consumers of solar energy (eating chickens which are fed on fish meal, which was nourished by plankton) is inefficient and wasteful. Eating lower on food chains would leave more food available.

Farming the sea on a sustained-yield basis will require a hitherto unknown degree of cooperation among the nations which draw on the oceans, and will mean temporarily fishing less to allow presently depleted species to multiply. Aqua-culture—farming fish in ponds on land—could provide much valuable protein. Thus there are possibilities of increasing food supply, but they are not infinite.

Solving Overpopulation

The population problem and alleviating it are probably the most threatening and emotionally charged aspects of the ecological predicament. What is implied is either a reappearance of natural checks on population growth, in the form of famine, plagues, and war (indeed, some experts maintain that it is already impossible to solve the problem, and that nature should be allowed to take its course),

or a vast change in reproductive behavior, which is, in fact, suscep-
tible to rapid change. The means and incentive to change are hotly
debated. Some feel that advances in birth-control technology will
affect reproduction significantly. Others hold that these would be irrelevant without providing meaningful reasons for humans to reduce
the number of births. Some of the reasons for large family size are
high infant mortality rates which require many births to assure a
few survivors, traditional agrarian cultures, which need numbers of
offspring to work the land, and lack of social security, which requires that children be a hedge against uncertain old age.

One school of thought maintains that development, which would
change these conditions, is sufficient in and of itself to stabilize population. Difficulties with this idea of demographic transition are that
the time required to bring it about would permit several more doublings of population, that injudicious development could result in
the same raft of environmental problems that the developed nations
are now suffering, and finally that the reliability of the demographic
transition has never been proved.

Population control is sometimes regarded as a red herring dragged
across the trail of a global redistribution of wealth. If development
and the provision of greater security are seen as essential to motivate
people to reduce births, then there is no way that the population
crisis can be stopped without a global redistribution of wealth.

Economics of Ecology

Extravagant consumption of resources and an ever-increasing demand for consumer goods as emblems of accomplishment have been
institutionalized in the contemporary American value system by
advertising and built into an economic system which equates growth
with health. Such a system requires continually increasing consumption and numbers of consumers, thus opposing conservation of
resources. Though an increase in demand does not necessarily constitute increased ability to purchase goods and services, and though the
purchasing of goods and services is not automatically an improvement in the quality of life, there are many, particularly those concerned with the poor, who claim that we must pursue economic
growth and then be concerned about ecological damage: there is
strong disagreement between those who see economic growth as an
urgent need and those who argue that the ecosystem cannot tolerate
abuse on the scale which would result from such a policy, and that
we must limit growth now. Some feel that the gross national product

is merely gross, and an insufficient index of progress, health, or social achievement. Growing numbers of hospital admissions for lung cancer increase the GNP, as does terminal depletion of nonrenewable resources.

Some invaluable resources are not "ownable," and are thus unaccountable in our present economics. Clean air and water are among these, plus other less definable "goods" like the overall health of the global ecosystem and its continued ability to function. Other considerations of a psychological and aesthetic nature such as silence and the integrity of the landscape are in similar economic limbo.

Damage to environmental "goods" held in common is not presently reckoned into production costs, and the public sector is indirectly subsidizing the private sector by permitting manufacturers to use the air and water as dumping grounds for effluents. Some manufacturers maintain that including these costs in the price of their goods (passing the economic burden of the cleanup on to the consumer) would drive them out of business. Thus the specter of unemployment is often raised in response to the plea to stop pollution. In the short run, the exploiter of a "commons" seems to have everything to gain and nothing to lose.

Irreversibles

Much environmental degradation can be reversed. Species and wilderness extinction cannot, and they are two effects of development (as it is presently conceived) that are increasing rapidly. When a species is destroyed, it cannot be replaced; with each extinction, the earth loses more of its diversity and necessary genetic variability. When man changes or "develops" a wilderness area, its wildness is gone forever. Mankind, for all his genius and skill, is incapable of creating a system with as much complexity and interrelationship as a forest or tundra. We plan cleverly, but we cannot plan to replace the last giant redwood or last golden eagle. Moreover, we cannot predict which element of an ecosystem is the crucial one, the one without which it dies. The debate about the value of these nonrenewable resources—wild places and creatures—depends on the importance of immediate human desires relative to the needs of the global ecosystem, viewed in a time perspective which considers the eons of earth's lifetime before man.

The ability of human beings to tolerate environmental stressing is a crucial question. Little is known about possible synergies (synergy is when the whole is greater than the sum of the parts)

which could result from the interaction of external and internal
stresses, such as the continuous exposure of humans to new, un-
tested chemicals, and exposure to increasing levels of noise, artificial lights, and totally man-created environments. We have not
yet considered what might be the best environmental mix of natural
and man-made for humanity.

The Hope

It is argued that spectacular technological advances could circum-
vent the need for a careful use and renewal of ecosystems. Certainly
such advances could buy time in which to make the necessary re-
organizations in our culture. There are drawbacks to this brave hope
for technological salvation though. Each new technological break-
through has environmental costs—in power, resources, or landscape.
And these breakthroughs may have unforeseen side effects on the
environment which could cause damage in one part of the ecosystem
while relieving it in others. Some feel that our technology and means
of production are merely flawed, and that refining them would solve
most of our problems. Others believe that a total reconsideration
of them, our culture, value system, and planetary behavior is required; that such a consideration might evolve into a new, low-
profile technological ethic suitable to a bio-renaissance.

The range of environmental problems, possibilities, questions,
and disagreements is infinite. The possibility implicit in the problem of planetary survival is that humans can perceive the earth as
a whole system, and themselves as related within it.

We may yet reconsider our present order of priorities in light of
the task of survival, and see that the status quo—nationalism, anarchy among those nations, a commitment to warfare and the re-
finement of hideous weaponry—must be changed; that preserving
these values in a damaged environment whose human inhabitants
are mostly ill-housed, ill-clothed, and ill-fed is a suicidal waste of
potential. The greatest possibility is that through cooperation and
intelligent concern we may survive, and progress thereby.

This focuser is only a second draft, and it's slightly less in focus
than the writer would like. The subject matter is the whole world;
where and how we are in it, and what we're doing to it. Earth is the
primordial system; to paraphrase John Muir, no matter how we try
to consider any aspect of this planet separately, we discover it to be
hitched to everything else in the universe. So it is with writing a

basic statement about ecology—it's impossible to out*line* a net.
Apologies then to the reader for the order or lack of it in this draft.

In sketching the broad outlines of ecology, and the sources of
environmental deterioration, some important specifics have necessarily been omitted—discussion of the automobile and alternatives
to it, examination of the impact of different political philosophies
on the environment, and so on. Should these be included in the next
draft?

The Need for New Myths*

GERALD CLARKE

The latest incarnation of Oedipus, the continued romance of Beauty and the Beast, stands this afternoon on the corner of 42nd Street and Fifth Avenue, waiting for the traffic light to change.

—JOSEPH CAMPBELL

That statement, fanciful as it sounds, is simply a shorthand way of saying that everyone is a creature of myth, that the ancient legends and tales of the race are still the master keys to the human psyche. The science-minded Victorians who sneered at myths as superstitious twaddle were guilty of a kind of scientific superstition themselves: the belief that reason could explain all human motives. Aided by psychoanalysis, anthropology and three-quarters of a century of archaeological discovery, modern scholarship has replaced the Victorians' sneers with respect and even awe. Mythology, its partisans are now claiming, tells as much about humanity—its deepest fears, sorrows, joys, and hopes—as dreams tell about an individual. "Myths are public dreams," says Joseph Campbell, who is probably the world's leading expert on mythology. "Dreams are private myths.

* Reprinted by permission from *Time,* the Weekly Newsmagazine. © Time, Inc., 1972.

232

Myths are vehicles of communication between the conscious and the unconscious, just as dreams are."

The trouble is, Campbell asserts, that this communication has broken down in the modern Western world. The old myths are no longer operative, and effective new myths have not arisen to replace them. As a result, he maintains, the West is going through an agony of reorientation matched only by a period during the 4th millennium B.C., when the Sumerians first conceived the concept of a mathematically ordered cosmos and thus changed utterly man's concept of the universe around him.

Campbell's words carry extraordinary weight, not only among scholars but among a wide range of other people who find his search down mythological pathways relevant to their lives today. A professor of literature at Sarah Lawrence College in Bronxville, N.Y., Campbell has written and edited some 20-odd books on mythology. They include a massive four-volume work entitled *The Masks of God; The Flight of the Wild Gander,* and the book for which he is most famous, *Hero With a Thousand Faces,* a brilliant examination, through ancient hero myths, of man's eternal struggle for identity. *Hero,* which has had sales of more than 110,000 copies, an impressive figure for a scholarly book, has become a bestseller on campus. After 37 years of teaching in relative obscurity, Campbell, at 67, has now become a well-known and respected figure in academe.

What is a myth? In Campbell's academic jargon, it is a dreamlike "symbol that evokes and directs psychological energy." A vivid story or legend, it is but one part of a larger fabric of myths that, taken together, form a mythology that expresses a culture's attitude toward life, death, and the universe around it. The Greek myth of Prometheus, the Titan who stole fire from Olympus and gave it to man, thus symbolizes the race's aspirations even when they conflict with the powers of nature. The almost contemporary Hebrew myth of the trials of Job, on the other hand, symbolizes man's submission to a power above nature even when that power seems cruel and unjust. The two myths are, in effect, picture stories that tell the philosophies of two totally divergent cultures. The Greek stresses man's heroic striving for human values and civilization; the Hebrew emphasizes, rather, man's humble spiritual surrender to God's will. Abraham's willingness to sacrifice Isaac is the supreme symbol of this attitude.

Though not true in a literal sense, a myth is not what it is considered to be in everyday speech—a fantasy or a misstatement. It is rather a veiled explanation of the truth. The transformation from fact to myth is endlessly fascinating. The battle of Achilles and Hector, for example, is symbolic, but there was a Trojan War in which great heroes fought. The psychological duel between Faust and the Devil is a philosophical and psychological metaphor, but Georg Faust, a German magician who was born about 1480, did live and did make claims to superhuman power, including the ability to restore the lost works of Plato and Aristotle and to repeat the miracles of Christ. Yet it was not until poets like Christopher Marlowe and Goethe took up the legend that Faust became famous—and mythic. The Faust story appealed to Marlowe and to Goethe because the times in which they lived, eras in which faith and reason were in basic conflict, called for such a symbolic struggle.

What should a mythology do? In Campbell's view, a "properly operating" mythology has four important functions:

▶ To begin with, through its rites and imagery it wakens and maintains in the individual a sense of awe, gratitude, and even rapture, rather than fear, in relation to the mystery both of the universe and of man's own existence within it.

▶ Secondly, a mythology offers man a comprehensive, understandable image of the world around him, roughly in accord with the best scientific knowledge of the time. In symbolic form, it tells him what his universe looks like and where he belongs in it.

▶ The third function of a living mythology. is to support the social order through rites and rituals that will impress and mold the young. In India, for example, the basic myth is that of an impersonal power, Brahma, that embodies the universe. The laws of caste are regarded as inherent features of this universe and are accepted and obeyed from childhood. Cruel as this may seem to Westerners, the myth of caste does give Indian society a stability it might otherwise lack and does make life bearable to the impoverished low castes.

▶ The fourth and, in Campbell's view, the most important function of mythology is to guide the individual, stage by stage, through the inevitable psychological crises of a useful life: from the childhood condition of dependency through the traumas of adolescence and the trials of adulthood to, finally, the deathbed.

The churches and synagogues still provide mythological guidance for many, Campbell argues; for many others, however, this guidance fails. The result is that, where once religion served, many have turned to psychoanalysis or encounter groups. "All ages before ours believed in gods in some form or other," wrote Carl Jung, whose theories of the collective unconscious have most profoundly influenced Campbell's thinking. "Heaven has become empty space to us, a fair memory of things that once were. But our heart glows, and secret unrest gnaws at the roots of our being." In search of something that they can hold on to, many people in the West, particularly the young, are either returning to Christian fundamentalism through the Jesus Revolution or turning to the religions of the East, chiefly Buddhism and Hinduism. "The swamis are coming from India, and they're taking away the flock," says Campbell. "They're speaking of religion as dealing with the interior life and not about dogmatic formulae and ritual requirements."

For the vast majority, Campbell believes, the West's general lack of spiritual authority has been a disaster. Forty years in the study of eternal symbols have made Campbell a conservative of a rather dark hue. Though he is optimistic about the long range, he finds the present bleak indeed. "We have seen what has happened to primitive communities unsettled by the white man's civilization," he observes. "With their old taboos discredited, they immediately go to pieces, disintegrate, and become resorts of vice and disease. Today the same thing is happening to us."

Many Oriental and primitive societies even today have working mythologies, and Communist countries have at least the basis of a mythology in Marxism. The Marxist dream of the withering away of the state, after which each man will give according to his abilities and receive according to his needs, echoes numerous religious beliefs of a paradise on earth or a Second Coming. The Chinese Communists have, in addition, the myth of the "Long March" in the '30s and the subsequent sanctuary of Mao Tse-tung and his followers in the caves of Yenan. The events were real enough, but for this generation of Chinese, and probably for generations to come, they will have much the same deep mythological significance that the Trojan War had for the Greeks.

In the West there have been desperate attempts to provide at least fragments of a modern mythology. Churchill brilliantly recreated the myth of St. George and the dragon during World War II: the picture of little Britain, a citadel of justice, besieged by the evil Nazi hordes. The situation, of course, was much as he painted it—Britain was besieged and Hitler was evil—but a Neville Chamberlain would not have been able, as Churchill was, to light up his people with the basic themes of their culture. Charles de Gaulle, both as wartime leader and as President of the Fifth Republic, quite consciously resurrected the ghost of Joan of Arc. "To my mind," he wrote, "France cannot be France without greatness." The founders of Israel similarly evoked, and still evoke, mythic images of the Bible's chosen people to enable Israelis to survive in their hostile environment.

Often, such attempts add up merely to rhetoric or incantation. John Kennedy sought to revive the American myth that the U.S. was a country with a messianic mission. "Now the trumpet summons us again," he said in his Inaugural Address, "to a struggle against the common enemies of man: tyranny, poverty, disease and war itself." A post-Viet Nam U.S. can no longer quite believe in such an American mission. And Martin Luther King Jr. worked to provide the nation's blacks with a myth of their own. "I've been to the mountaintop and I've looked over, and I've seen the promised land," King said the night before he was killed, echoing the Bible's story of Moses on Mount Sinai.

For centuries Americans were emboldened by the myth of the endless frontier, the notion that a new life could always be started out West, whether the West was Ohio or California. That version outlasted the frontier itself, but no one believes in it today. Campbell hopes that the landings on the moon will reinvigorate that mythic tradition. Only a handful of people can go to the moon, and no one would want to stake out his 160 acres there, but the excitement of the journey itself is infectious, a re-enactment on the TV screen of Prometheus' stealing fire from the gods. Beyond that, Campbell believes, there is an even more durable myth: the "American Dream." That is the idea, grounded in fact, that a man is judged on his own ability rather than on his family or his place in society. "This pessimistic optimist thinks that the myth still works," he says. "The fact that Nixon was a poor boy and was yet elected President is a good example."

In the final analysis, however, it is wrong in Campbell's view to ask for one grand mythology that will guide people today. Instead there must be many different mythologies for many different kinds of people. "There is no general mythology today," Campbell says, "nor can there ever be again. Our lives are too greatly various in their backgrounds, aims, and possibilities for any single order of symbols to work effectively on us all." The new myths must be internalized and individual, and each man must find them for himself. Some, in fact, are following mythological paths today, unconsciously and without design. The hippie who leaves society and goes off to a commune, for example, is being guided by a mythological map of withdrawal and adventure laid down by Christ in the desert, the Buddha at Bodh-Gaya, and Mohammed in his cave of meditation at Mount Hira.

The man in search of an ideal could at least begin, Campbell thinks, by searching through the myths of antiquity, religion, and modern literature. For the elite who can read and understand them, T. S. Eliot, James Joyce, Thomas Mann, among modern writers and poets, and Pablo Picasso and Paul Klee, among modern artists, have updated the ancient mythological motifs. Campbell and the other mythologists are, in a sense, providing the workbooks for the poets—the modern Daedaluses in turtlenecks. "It doesn't matter to me whether my guiding angel is for a time named Vishnu, Shiva, Jesus, or the Buddha," Campbell says. "If you're not distracted by names or the color of hair, the same message is there, variously turned. In the multitude of myths and legends that have been preserved to us—both in our own Western arts and literatures, synagogues and churches, and in the rites and teachings of those Oriental and primitive heritages now becoming known to us—we may still find guidance."

The mythologists are not providing myths, but they are indicating that something is missing without them. They are telling modern man that he has not outgrown mythology and will never outgrow it so long as he has hopes and fears beyond the other animals.

Technological Progress

BERNARD KARSH

Technological progress is as old as man. The history of all societies is a history of invention. But if inventions and changes in industry are not new, what is new is the increasing rate at which they are occurring.

J. Lewis Powell describes this acceleration in interesting terms. For the sake of graphic presentation, he compressed the 50,000 years of mankind's recorded history into fifty years, and on this basis develops the following chronology: (1) Ten years ago, man left his cave for some other kind of dwelling; (2) Five years ago, some genius invented the first writing; (3) Two years ago, Christianity appeared; (4) Fifteen months ago, Gutenberg developed the printing press; (5) Ten days ago, electricity was discovered; (6) Yesterday morning, the airplane was invented; (7) Last night, radio; (8) This morning, television; (9) The jet airplane was invented less than a minute ago.

The Future*

DAVID LOYE

Some say these grey years
are the golden age,
that ahead lie more tears,
more hate, more rage;
and then like sink water
circling round and round
the drain looms near
and we're gulped down.
Others say we're only crushed
within the tortuous vortex of
birth and will be pushed
into a new world of love.
It is clear to some
that the choice then
is to be garbage, to be kitchen flotsam,
or be men.

* Reprinted courtesy of David Loye.

PART IV.

Changing Personal
Success Criteria

UP TO this point we have been dealing with changes in our overall thinking about the economy and society. These changes have implied major transformations in our views of personal success criteria, but these have not been spelled out as yet. What are the direction and magnitude of the changes which are needed in our ways of thinking?

The necessary reexamination is extraordinarily difficult because most of us are largely unaware of the values which control our views of "success." Our views about what we should do were inculcated in us during our youth; we have usually failed to change them as conditions have altered. One of the more tragic realities in today's world is that people believe it is possible to change their views about appropriate economic, socio-economic, and ecological behavior without having to change their private and public behavior to accord with their intellectual understandings.

We are only just beginning to understand fully how this apparent illogicality can persist. Most of our behavior patterns are unconscious—or at best semiconscious. Even when we think we have made a decision which would move us toward more human lifestyles, our competitive goal-oriented, industrial era values remain with us and prevent significant change in behavior. It appears that our only hope of breaking out of past behaviors is to be *fully* aware of how we are all booby-trapped by our earlier experiences and to realize how long it will take us to break out.

If we fail to remain conscious of our past values, we are particularly likely to be controlled by them. Many of the most exciting experiments in creating new values and new styles of living have broken apart because of our failure to realize how difficult the transition from a competitive goal-oriented culture to a cooperative process-oriented culture must inevitably be. Indeed, we are still only at the beginning of the process of finding out what behaviors and lifestyles will be viable in the coming communications era.

Any shift in values is always difficult. We are, however, engaged in a meta-transformation: a transformation not only of our values but of the ways we think about our values. During the industrial era, we came to value a system which would promote sameness and uniformity. We acted as though we should eliminate our individuality and become a replaceable cog in a bureaucratic machine. We measured success in terms of our ability to meet apparently objective educational norms, to gain promotion within organizations and thus achieve higher incomes. The adequacy of the income was measured against the various ways of life which were considered appropriate for different income levels; one's income never rose as fast as the standard of life to which one was expected to aspire.

These past criteria of success are no longer seen as acceptable by large parts of the population. People no longer want to be equal but rather to have the opportunity to discover their own identity. This can be seen in the drive of ethnic minorities—whether they originated in Africa, Asia, or Europe—to discover their own lifestyles. Increasingly these groups are arguing that their educational and socialization systems should reflect their own values rather than "American" values. The drive against bussing reflects, in large part, this ethnic revival.

The movement toward diversity is not a short run, reversible phenomenon. It is a minimal requirement for human survival. Just as ecological systems are vulnerable when they contain only a limited number of organisms, so are human societies. The drive toward uniformity during the industrial era destroyed so much diversity as to put the survival of the human race in doubt. We need to redevelop the widest possible range of "cultural genes" as a method of ensuring the development of many ideas as we move forward.

Nevertheless, this diversity must be informed by a basic sense of world citizenship. We must be prepared to give up our belief that "we" are good and "they" are evil. In our small, interdependent world, there is no room for this belief which has persisted throughout history and is the basic cause of violence and wars. Paradoxically, such a shift toward realizing the humanness of others will require a greater sense of our *own* self-worth—for only when we are sure of our own value will we be prepared to tolerate lifestyles other than those we value for ourselves.

Behind all of these shifts lies an even more basic alteration in our thinking. We usually consider reality as objectively determinable. The cooperative communications era is replacing this belief with an understanding that reality is personal—that each one of us has his own vision of how the world works which results from his past experience, his present goals, and his dreams for the future.

The future is ours for us to "art." But artistry requires knowledge, imagination, and perseverance. Will we generate these qualities in sufficient measure to save the world? If we fail to do so, the destruction of the human race is certain. If we should succeed, none of us has sufficient imagination to perceive the potential of our future.

Who was that early sodbuster in Kansas? He leaned at the gatepost and studied the horizon and figured what corn might do next year and tried to calculate why God ever made the grasshopper and why two days of hot winds smother the life out of a stand of wheat and why there was such a spread between what he got for grain and the price quoted in Chicago and New York. Drove up a newcomer in a covered wagon: "What kind of folks live around here?" "Well, stranger, what kind of folks was there in the country you come from?" "Well, they was mostly a lowdown, lying, thieving, gossiping, backbiting lot of people." "Well, I guess, stranger, that's about the kind of folks you'll find around here." And the dusty gray stranger had just about blended into the dusty gray cottonwoods in a clump on the horizon when another newcomer drove up: "What kind of folks live around here?" "Well, stranger, what kind of folks was there in the country you come from?" "Well, they was mostly a decent, hardworking, lawabiding, friendly lot of people." "Well, I guess, stranger, that's about the kind of folks you'll find around here."

CARL SANDBURG

A New World City: Syntropy and Learning*

JAMES SCHABERG AND STEPHEN SILHA

?
How do you plan to spend eternity
Do you often think far into the future
Is it futuristic to think in anything but the here and now
Is futuristic thinking worth it
?

That should start a good inner dialogue. But you are more than your thoughts, or your plans for the future, or the cucumber you had for dinner last night. You are, in fact, your whole now-then ecosystem, and unless we see that we're all in this together, we're not & it's not, even though it is. The earth's knot. ? Do you believe we can invent the future together ?

? Who are we ? With you, we are two rather young pale-faced earthians who have done a lot of thinking about the future. Unfortunately, our sense of awareness is still mostly in the eyeball-waking state of consciousness—so our account with reality is rather incomplete. But we continue to expand, and hope to celebrate and communicate with those of you who are still near our level. To find ways to new-see, flowing ever beyond where we are now.

* Used by permission.

246

Assume we have survived until the year 1990. . . . And we are living in a city of 250,000 somewhere in Minnesota. When this "experimental city," Syntropia, began to materialize in 1974 we never imagined we'd ever live there. . . . Because cities were the worst place a person could live during the seventies—real technological abortions of the industrial age. But some people decided they could steer changing technologies to create a city for people, physically and emotionally geared for change. . . . And though Syntropia went through much initial opposition and internal upheaval, people have found there is a way they can live/learn/work/love together in nongeographical communities with shared values.

The American culture has changed fundamentally in four major areas since 1972:

1) scarcity systems replaced by abundance systems in communications and resource allocation

Beginning with the cable TV and videotape transformation of the seventies, an unlimited number of air/laser channels became available to all the people of Syntropia. An abundance economy— with a guaranteed yearly income—greatly altered patterns of human needs and resource allocations.

2) sapiential authority systems displace bureaucracies, build communities

Decision-making/authority systems shifted from the prestige-based structural authority of the past to a pattern where people who were most informed and competent in a given area were naturally listened to.

3) free flow of credible information

While media instruments had been controlled by corporate interest, people now used communications tools for being honest— not manipulating information for exploitative purposes. All relevant viewpoints were released on the cables and airwaves. Ideas and information instead of money and laws were defined as power.

4) overload yields to underload: future shock defused

No longer inundated with reams of rotting information, people were able to screen, sort out, and feed back ideas important to them. Decentralized, close-knit communities found new ways with computers to cut across the time formerly needed to gain knowledge in an interest area. As the globe-munity cut down on repeated information and as new communication modes helped to get previously disconnected people together, new information was created.

Many macro-community myths and assumptions were central to the actualization of these conditions. Organized by a dynamic, self-screening process, Syntropia residents built their communities, life-styles and perceptions of reality with many of the following shared mind-ways.

Syntropy World View

As Western man tried yesterday to explain his "laws of entropy and energy," he had concluded that the universe was a great death machine. Since every action contributed to the entropy of the running down of the universe, man's efforts to survive were futile. However, the seventies germinated a new era—a new world view of hopeful evolutionary potential. A spiritual energy, rising out of the rags of entropy—creative and often "invisibly" emergent—was identified as syntropy. This regenerative spontaneous action was agreed to be increasingly conscious and the result of the evolution of awareness, spirit, and consciousness. Thus, a synergetic myth for mankind to transform Mother Earth and explore the realms beyond her womb was the essential perception behind her survival.

Dynamic Knowledge

As most static assumptions and "solutions" of the past were defined out of existence, all learners in the city participated as creators of knowledge. "Knowing" became increasingly viewed as metaphorical, the practical/conceptual dichotomy of the past homogenized.

Everyday Mysticism

Learning was seen simply as syntropic energy generation based on the individual's flowing expression and intuition. This process orientation was naturally self-paced. The mystery of laughing at yourself while exploring astral fields.

Nonmanipulation

Since it was assumed that all people have different learning styles and are inherently curious, freed people found ways to learn what they needed to know when they needed to know it. Motivation and rewards were primarily internalized, though many friends had ritualized knowledge-sharings.

More with Less

It was not recognized until recently how "performance per pound" extensions of technology had guaranteed the power of the individual to find his place in space. As uses of the world's resources were miniaturized and cybernated, what a person wanted to do and what the culture required of him were increasingly the same.

Enoughness

As rounder realization of the world's resources gave them enough to go around, people became uninterested in the accumulation of things. And as a finite, functioning system, they became more aware of their changing limitations and potentials. For example, "aggressions" which had been used for competitive and greedy ends in the past served more creative uses.

Global Requirements

Syntropia was often viewed as a spaceship as it grew, a microcosm of the planet which housed it. It became one of the transnational models for the simultaneously growing membrane of Earth-interrelated awareness. Its life-support systems were seen as a part of the complex dynamism which enlivens the Earth. And as people, like residents of Syntropia, began to perceive in whole Earth patterns, they listened and learned the art of creative surrender, always remembering the words of the last Whole Earth Catalog: "We can't put it together. It is together."

Systemic Thinking

Replacing the linear thinking of the industrial era, the electronic environments and computers helped people think in a more altogether way. Perceiving in long-term patterns and watching the secondary and tertiary consequences of a given action, people in the seventies saw there was no inevitability about the future. Thinking in terms of alternatives, change was steered first by planners and futurists, then by everyone.

New Definition of Culture

"Where our fathers defined their culture in objects to be sold at auctions and shown in museums, we today see the only meaningful definition of culture as all the things that connect one mind with another, as openness to new ideas, as communication itself." (Alex Gross in *Radical Software No. 1*) Decentralized media, including cable TV, satellites, and videotape, cut through bureaucratic and corporate interests. In the new view of survival, although diverse cultures kept their geographical characteristics to some degree, no culture could survive independently of the others. Collective survival—a world culture—was seen as the only way to individual survival.

Wow.

This is getting a little Utopian even for us. So how was this great cultural change accomplished? Who changed? How did this all happen?

Obviously, there are countless possible trips into the future. And this is only one of them, even if rather wishful. Still we are concerned with what we could make happen. A vision we believe is essential, because we can't deal well with sophisticated realists—neopessimists. So, a closer look at "education" in Syntropia, 1990:

> Only one school was ever built in the city. Nearly everyone realized as the seventies moved on that schools were terribly destructive and a waste of resources. This one school had soon become a relic of the nationalistic past and was one of the most popular museums in 1990. So there was no need in Syntropia for the kinds of schools which had perpetuated power structures in corporate states.

> Now, with new channels of communications and technological opportunities, there is no "education system." Some call it synergetic anarchy.

> *Frequency matching.* There are computerized reference services listing people (their interests, skills, how they can be reached, and anything else one cares to put on the computer) and other resources (conditions of access, etc.). The wide diversity of people, lifestyles and new technologies provides infinite learning possibilities.

> *Process and cope-ability skills are shared.* Problem solving, learning to learn, and nonlinear perceptions are highly developed as "learners" conduct their own educational adventures. Sometimes they meet in places like gaming centers, where they might simulate infrastructure or synergetic-energetic geometry, or play the World Game.

> *Youngest members of the community are especially well cared for.* Future parents are well informed on nutrition and other dynamics of prebirth and early child rearing. It is widely recognized that the precious mental instrument each person carries is formed very early and delicately. Everything the child feels, hears, experiences

is all-important to his growth. Bertrand Russell said that one generation of fearless women could transform the world by bringing into it a generation of fearless children. Bucky Fuller believed, "There is no such thing as genius. Some children are less damaged than others."

Dialogue, in new communication styles, has evolved as a prime means for communities to invent their futures. With the assumption that change is constantly situational, social synergy has occurred increasingly as communities have found and extended their common realities and minimized meaningless debates. The new view of self-interest, change-threat, and personal power evolves new languages out of which possibilities emerge to temporarily stabilize imbalance.

"Disciplines" are no longer categorized as before. The old disciplines uncatch and remesh as people move in and out of problem-possibility institutes which create new information for implementation. No one is coerced into any learning situation. Problems are studied within the competence of the learner.

The city itself has become a self-regenerative organism. The abundance and authority systems assure that very few decisions are locked in. Continual feedback—virtually ignored during the one-way industrial era—is the built-in screening/checking mechanism for "mistakes" and bad vibes. Disorientation and reorientation (building new responses and directions) methods were found necessary at first, and later were demanded by many new residents.

Beyonding. Beyond the "common sense" hyperrationality of industrial man, citizens freely pursue their creative imaginations, dreamworlds, new levels of consciousness—psychic and simulsensory exploration in cosmic perceptions. Beyond the "self-actualization" needs of the sixties and seventies, these are journeys into the subjective sciences of a higher self. The ego manipulation, the symbols, the games, the masks, and the dreams of social self are seen and enjoyed in their proper perspective. Beyond survival, people look for new ways of being, seeing, and becoming, in search of greater potentialities for themselves as part of the Human Unity. A transforming metaphysic.

Simplicity and sharing are evident in most lifestyles. Expressions of people's relation to the cosmos in many forms—crafts, sculpture, theater, telepathy, health, privacy, silence. Creative uses of automation have freed the "housewife" and many assembly line workers; however, both sexes find life-support activities soulful exercises. Organic farmers are nuclear physicists.

We hope your inner dialogue has been tasty and your mouth is full of questions. The "who decides . . ." and "will there be . . ." type questions. . . .

? WHO DECIDES WHAT AMOUNT OF WORK NEEDS TO BE DONE ? ? WILL THERE BE CENTRALIZED PLANNING OR COMPLETE LOCAL AUTONOMY ? ? WHAT ABOUT 1984 AND BIG BROTHER ? ? WILL THERE BE BIOLOGICAL CONTROL ? ? WON'T ULTRAINTELLIGENT MACHINES BE SMARTER THAN PEOPLE BY THEN ? ? WILL THE CITY BECOME A WHITE, MIDDLE CLASS REFUGE FROM URBAN PROBLEMS ? ? WHO WILL MONITOR GUIDANCE SYSTEMS ? ? WILL THERE BE PRIVATE CORPORATIONS ? ? HOW MUCH HIERARCHY IS NEEDED IN A COMMUNITY ? ? WILL SOMEBODY HAVE THE POWER TO PUNISH ? ? HOW DO YOU TURN THE MASSES ON TO ALL THIS ? ? WILL TRANSCULTURAL COMMUNITIES WORK ? ? IS THIS SO MUCH MORE FRONTIER MYTHOLOGY ? ? AND ARE CITIES OBSOLETE ?

And so on. It seems that everyone is talking about how far we aren't and how far we have to go. We know so little about how we can make the world work, how people learn and adapt to changing conditions. But asking the right questions about the future, challenging all previous assumptions, and recognizing the possible is one way of getting there.

> . . . there are a thousand hacking at
> the branches of evil to one who is
> striking at the root, and it may be
> that he who bestows the largest
> amount of time and money on the
> needy is doing most by his mode of
> life to produce that misery which he
> strives in vain to relieve. . . .
>
> HENRY DAVID THOREAU

Postscript

"What can't be said, can't be said, and it can't be whistled either."

RAM TIRTHA

Trying to give another person a vivid sense of belonging in the ecosystem, trying to convince another person of the rightness of the working of the ecosystem, leads either to frustration or loving: to the mystery.

Sharing the experience of an eagle's artless design, seeing the un-planned genius of evolution making practical miracles of snail's homes, knowing that could and should are often the same in the natural world—these are insights. You can only have your own. Those of others may not fit.

There is a world out there, outside your mind in this book, be-yond your front door. It is a not-man-made world that functions creatively and progressively, without premeditation, where the value system is trial and error, making diversity.

This world works well, can continue to do so, with us quite in it if perhaps we can fine-tune our own value systems to harmonize with what's beautiful out there.

> In beauty I walk
> With beauty before me I walk
> With beauty behind me I walk

253

With beauty above me I walk
With beauty above and about me I walk
It is finished in beauty
It is finished in beauty

NAVAJO INDIAN

If you wish to select an idea of success which will work in our world, please go walk in its beauty.

Walk silently. Look at the beauty of its diversity, knowing that your eye bringing you that blessing is made by the same process which colors wood iris variously for insects, pollination, and the next profusion of colors of wood iris.

Walk. Move yourself through the beauty perceiving. Use your sense of wonder to hear water moving also. Know that water is much of the basis of you, of our lives on this planet.

Earthly life has integrity, reason, and genius, if only we behold it. The world out there is not raw material any more than we are. And there is a continuum from out there in here. In your perceiving mind's intricacy is the whole history of trial and error out there. If we understand the out there in here, if we harmonize, we may succeed and be a way station on the continuum of Earthly beauty and evolution.

But this is quite enough whistling for not saying. Go out. Walk in beauty. Whistle beauty of your own.

If a pickpocket meets a holy man,
he will see only his pockets.

—HARI DASS BABA

One basic weakness in a conservation
system based wholly on economic motives
is that most members of the land community

have no economic value. Wildflowers and
songbirds are examples.

—ALDO LEOPOLD

**Lives based on having are less free than lives based either on doing
or being.**

—WILLIAM JAMES

Our society views dying as being in questionable taste despite the
fact that ten out of ten still do it.

—HOWARD LUCK GOSSAGE

The essence of civilization consists not
in the multiplication of wants but in
their deliberate and voluntary renunciation.

—GANDHI

It comes in any color you want, so long as it's black.

—HENRY FORD

While cars get faster and longer, lives get slower and shorter. While
Chrysler competes with Buick for the getaway, cancer competes
with emphysema for the layaway. This generation is indeed going
to have to choose between humans and the automobile. Perhaps
most families have too many of both.

—ROBERT and LEONA RIENOW

Even though we know we are being taken, we are being taken.

—WILLIAM F. FORE

There is a quality even meaner than outright ugliness or disorder, and this meaner quality is the dishonest mask of pretended order, achieved by ignoring or suppressing the real order that is struggling to exist and to be served.

—JANE JACOBS

When our rewards go to people for thinking alike, it is no surprise that we become frightened at those who take exception to the current consensus.

—WILLIAM O. DOUGLAS

It is always a little hard to find a convincing answer to the man who says, "What has posterity ever done for me?"

—KENNETH BOULDING

Usually, terrible things that are done with the excuse that progress requires them are really not progress at all, but just terrible things.

—RUSSELL BAKER

Every gun that is made, every warship launched, every rocket fired signifies, in the final sense, a theft from those who hunger and are

not fed. . . . Under the cloud of threatening war, it is humanity hanging from a cross of iron. Is there no other way the world may live?

—Dwight Eisenhower

Nations are such an artificial construct from an ecological point of view that any further energies poured into them are almost certain to do more long-term harm than good.

—Keith Lampe

My young men shall never work. Men who work cannot dream, and wisdom comes in dreams.

—Smohalla

O thou who art trying to learn the marvel
of love from the copybook of reason, I
am very much afraid that you will never
really see the point.

—Hafiz

A flower is relatively small; everyone
has many associations with a flower—the
idea of flowers. You put out your hand
to touch the flower—lean forward to smell
it—maybe touch it with your lips almost
without thinking—or give it to someone
to please them. Still—in a way—nobody
sees a flower—really—it is so small—
we haven't time—and to see takes time
like to have a friend takes time.

—Georgia O'Keeffe

Bibliographies

EDITOR'S NOTE

This book cannot be more than a beginning.

Where you go from here is up to you!

If you can work with print media, the following three bibliographies will give you the resources you require to go further.

We are still looking for those with whom we can work to compile similar lists for the spoken and visual media.

Societal Change and Implications for Education

MICHAEL MARIEN

Bennis, Warren G. and Philip E. Slater. *The Temporary Society.* New York: Harper & Row, 1968.
Six separate essays by one or both of the authors "to force into view certain changes affecting vital aspects of our key institutions: organizational life, family life, interpersonal relationships, and authority." In the first essay, democracy is seen as inevitable—the necessary social system of the electronic era. In the second essay, Slater looks at change and the democratic family, noting that "experiential chasms between age cohorts serve to invalidate parental authority." (p. 24) The topics that follow concern the new style organizations beyond bureaucracy, social consequences of temporary systems, new patterns of leadership for adaptive organizations; and in the final chapter on the temporary society, the necessary education is prescribed for the art and science of being more fully human: how to get love, to love and to lose love; how to enter groups and leave them; how to attain satisfying roles; and how to cope more readily with ambiguity. "For the most part we learn the significant things informally and badly, having to unlearn them later on in life when the consequences are grave and frightfully expensive, like a five-day-a-week analysis." (p. 127)

Berghofer, Desmond E. *The Future: Its Challenge to Twentieth Century Man. A Review of Key Works on Social and Educational*

Futures. Edmonton: University of Alberta, Faculty of Education, January 1972. Mimeo.

An excellent integration of many works with the intent of demonstrating the dynamic relationship of education with other activities, all of which are interacting to shape the future of mankind. "Running through the works reviewed in this paper has been the theme that a potentiality currently exists for a shift away from a vision of reality that has dominated the thinking of Western man for several centuries." (p. 33)

Blakely, R. J. *Toward a Homeodynamic Society*. Boston: Center for the Study of Liberal Education for Adults, 1965. (Notes and Essays on Education for Adults, No. 49.)

"This essay is an attempt to answer two big questions: 'What are the important social trends? What are their implications for education?' . . . The major trend of the present age is to increase knowledge and power. The major problem is the widening gap between knowledge and power and our ability to control them. The major implication is that our learning to control knowledge and power must overtake our learning to increase knowledge and power." (p. iii) In going on to advocate the homeodynamic, inventive society, Blakely distinguishes between three types of learning (hereditary-cultural, adaptive-cultural, and inventive-cultural), and the necessary learning for the adult as parent, citizen, and worker.

Carroll, James D. "Noetic Authority," *Public Administration Review*, 29:5, September–October 1969.

"This paper suggests that the state is withering away in a psychological sense because of an increase in awareness in contemporary society and a growing questioning of authority. It also suggests the state is withering in a technological sense because of a failure to use organized knowledge to satisfy expectations and values. It then suggests that a new form of the state, the 'innovative state' characterized by a new form of authority, may in time emerge." (Abstract) "Noetic" refers to "the increase in awareness-consciousness—of man's social and physical environment—that is occurring throughout much of the world." (p. 492) Noetic politics is the politics of knowledge and awareness in an increasingly complex society that is shifting to a mental base of operations and a collegial form of authority. The implications for educating institutions are not discussed, but are obviously profound.

Chase, Stewart. *The Most Probable World*. New York: Harper &
Row, 1968.
A popular overview considering the consequences of technological
change. The final chapter, "No Path But Knowledge," outlines a
desirable curriculum for the education of future leaders, and pro-
poses a supranational agency "to evaluate and screen the consequences of large technological innovations *before* they go into mass
production, seriously to affect the culture." (p. 209)

Commoner, Barry. *The Closing Circle: Nature, Man and Technology*. New York: Alfred A. Knopf, 1971.
This well-received popularized volume by a leading ecologist is one
of many recent books on our growing ecological crisis. There are
two important implications for SF/TF education that can be drawn.
First, Commoner argues that the cause of the environment crisis is
technology and the resulting ignorance of fundamental concerns such
as the ecosphere. "The natural tendency to think of only one thing
at a time is the chief reason why we have failed to understand the
environment and have blundered into destroying it." (p. 26) And
our fragmented subdisciplinary thinking has resulted from the manner in which our educating institutions are organized. Secondly,
Commoner estimates an annual cost of survival of about $40 billion
per year—which would necessarily require economies in other sectors
of society, including education.

The Conference Board. *Information Technology: Some Critical Implications for Decision Makers*. Conference Board Report No.
537. The Conference Board, Inc., 845 Third Avenue, New York,
N.Y. 10022. 1972. $25.00 for Nonassociates; $5.00 for Associ-
ates and Educational.
A report developed by 42 experts serving on 8 panels devoted to
information technology, the individual, business, antitrust policy,
education, government and politics, and the changing information
environment. The chapter on education by Marvin Adelson discusses topics such as the shift in education from the communication
of knowledge to the utilization of knowledge, libraries as the core
of the education process, the trend to transform portions of education into a "goods" industry by the creation of media packages, the
distinction between "real" and "informational" environments, and
possible initiatives for government and education. The final chapter by John McHale provides a variety of topologies of potential

impacts of the new information environment, while discussing global aspects and the need for planetary policies.

Drucker, Peter F. *The Age of Discontinuity: Guidelines to Our Changing Society.* New York: Harper & Row, 1969.
An important book focusing on four major discontinuities: new technologies, the world economy (including a chapter on "The Global Shopping Center"), a society of large organizations (including a chapter on "The New Pluralism"), and the changed position and power of knowledge such that we are becoming a knowledge society—"the greatest of the discontinuities around us." This final section on knowledge (Chapters 12–17) is of immense importance to educators.

Drucker forecasts that the knowledge industries will account for one-half of the total national product in the late 1970's (p. 263), and argues that knowledge, rather than agriculture and mining, has now become the primary industry supplying the essential and central resource of production. Under these circumstances, "It is not that we cannot afford the high costs of education; we cannot afford its low productivity" (p. 334), and economic necessity will therefore force a revolution. "In a knowledge society, school and life can no longer be separate." (p. 324) The diploma curtain is seen as a problem, as is the prolongation of adolescence by the schools and the inherent conflict between extended schooling and continuing education.

Because of our knowledge needs, "We face an unprecedented situation in which we will have to set priorities for new knowledge," (p. 365) and the existing disciplines will not remain appropriate for long, if knowledge is to have a future.

Educational Policy Research Center at Stanford. *Alternative Futures and Educational Policy.* Menlo Park, California: Stanford Research Institute, EPRC Memorandum Report, January 1970.
Tentatively summarizes the findings of a preliminary set of alternative future histories prepared at EPRC/Stanford, and suggests implications for educational policy. Of some two score future histories ranging from Manifest Destiny and Exuberant Democracy to Authoritarian Recession, "1984"/Theocracy, and Collapse, "there are very few which manage to avoid one or another kind of time of serious troubles between now and 2050. The few that do, require a dramatic shift of values and perceptions with regard to what we

came to term the 'world macroproblem.' This macroproblem will be the predominant concern of the foreseeable future, for all the alternative paths. It is the composite of all the problems which have been brought about by a combination of rampant technology application and industrial development together with high population levels." (p. 6)

"The overall message is clear. It is not yet time to redesign education for ecstatic individuals in a carefree world. To the extent that one believes that the analysis of the roots of the 'world macroproblem' holds up, to that extent he will believe that the paramount educational task for the developed world is the radical altering of the dominant basic premises, perceptions, images, and values of the culture and that the paramount task for the nation is the development of a sense of purpose and unity. To that extent, also, it will seem essential that we reexamine all our present educational institutions, practices, and commitments to determine how their priority is altered in view of these future outlooks." (p. 42)

Ferkiss, Victor C. *Technological Man: The Myth and the Reality.* New York: George Braziller, 1969.
An overview of the vast changes transforming society and necessary cognitive changes in man involving a new naturalism, a new holism, and a new immanentism.

Gardner, John. *No Easy Victories.* New York: Harper & Row, 1968.
A collection of excerpts from Gardner's speeches and writings with important insights about the future of our society and the necessary directions for effective action. Particular attention is paid to education (pp. 67–112), for it is felt that "in terms of our national future, teaching is the most important profession." (p. 95) The comments concerning lifelong learning, which has "no adequate reflection in our social institutions," are especially of interest.

Lundberg, Ferdinand. *The Coming World Transformation.* Garden City, New York: Doubleday, 1963.
A broad and long-term assessment of social trends, with major attention paid to learning needs and brainpower as a matter of national survival such that continuing adult higher education will become the largest segment of the educating system.

Michael, Donald N. *The Unprepared Society: Planning for a Precarious Future.* Foreword by Ward Madden. The John Dewey Society Lecture No. 10. New York: Basic Books, 1968.

An excellent introduction to explaining the need for looking at the
future, who does it, how it is done, and problems encountered. The
final chapter, "Some Challenges for Educators," discusses implications for education, e.g.: "We must educate so people can cope efficiently, imaginatively, and perceptively with information overload."
(p. 108)

Muller, Herbert J. *The Children of Frankenstein: A Primer on Modern Technology and Human Values.* Bloomington, Indiana: Indiana University Press, 1970.
After providing historical background, the impact on society and
culture is explored in separate chapters on war, science, government,
business, language, higher education, natural environment, urban
environment, mass media, the traditional arts, religion, and people.
The chapter on higher education observes the consequences of spe-
cialization and "the spell of scientific methods," with the view that
"most college graduates—whatever their specialty—have too limited
an understanding of our technological society for potential leaders."
(p. 230)

Organization for Economic Cooperation and Development. *Information for a Changing Society: Some Policy Considerations.*
Paris: OECD, 1971.
Report of an ad hoc Group on Scientific and Technical Information,
convened to deal with the present fragmented state of information
systems at a time when information is increasingly "the key to the
wise management of the future." Many recommendations are made;
of particular interest is the one "that the re-evaluation of educational requirements of modern societies take full account of the
need for information transfer systems better adapted to the continuing re-education of adults. Totally new institutional arrangements
must be evolved, involving opportunities and motivation for education concurrent with daily activities. Research to foresee and pre-
pare for these developments is urgently needed." (p. 47)

Platt, John. "What We Must Do," *Science,* 166: November 28,
1969.
A concise and powerful overview of the multiple crises that we are
confronting, with the view that "it has now become urgent for us
to mobilize all our intelligence to solve these problems if we are to
keep from killing ourselves in the next few years." Two overview
charts are provided (for the U.S. and the world), indicating the

priority of problem areas and the estimated time to crisis, broken down in three future periods (1–5 years, 5–20 years, and 20–50 years). For the U.S. the problem areas, in order of priority, are total annihilation, great destruction or change (physical, biological, or political), widespread almost unbearable tension (slums, race conflict), large-scale distress (transportation, urban blight, crime), tension producing responsive change (water supply, privacy, drugs, marine resources), other problems important but adequately researched (military R&D, new educational methods), exaggerated dangers and hopes (mind control, heart transplants), and noncrisis problems being overstudied (man in space and most basic science). It is concluded that "The task is clear. The task is huge. The time is horribly short. In the past, we have had science for intellectual pleasure, and science for the control of nature. We have had science for war. But today, the whole human experiment may hang on the question of how fast we now press the development of science for survival."

Schon, Donald A. *Beyond the Stable State.* New York: Random House, 1971.
An important work on the central problem facing Western civilization today: rapidly accelerating change. As an alternative to perpetual disruption, Schon argues that businesses, governments, and social institutions must become "learning systems."

Theobald, Robert. *An Alternative Future for America Two,* revised and enlarged edition. Chicago, Illinois: Swallow Press, 1970.
Two-thirds of the book incorporates new material, including a "working appendix" listing various organizations studying alternative futures. Education (pp. 157–182) is defined as "the process of providing each individual with the capacity to develop his potential to the full." Four levels of learning are viewed: the first level is the simple perception of a fact; the second occurs when two facts are interrelated; the third (to which present systems of education are geared) makes it possible to improve our level of performance within our present perceptions of the state of the universe. "We are beginning to perceive the need for fourth-level learning—learning which permits us to change our perceptions about the nature of the world in which we live . . . the styles which make possible fourth-level learning are profoundly contradictory to those needed in third-level situations."

Theobald, Robert. *Habit and Habitat*. Englewood Cliffs, New Jersey: Prentice-Hall, 1972.
A broad and challenging overview of the transition from the industrial era to the communications era, and from linear thinking to systemic thinking, where one perceives connections, interdependencies, and reciprocal relationships.

Toffler, Alvin. *Future Shock*. New York: Random, 1970.
A well-known popularized overview on social change, with several appropriate comments on SF/TF learning: "Long before the year 2000, the entire antiquated structure of degrees, majors, and credits will be a shambles." (p. 241) "Failure to diversify education within the system will simply lead to the growth of alternative educational opportunities outside the system." (p. 243) "This dispersal in geographical and social space must be accompanied by dispersal in time. The rapid obsolescence of knowledge and the extension of the life span make it clear that the skills learned in youth are unlikely to remain relevant by the time old-age arrives. Super-industrial education must therefore make provision for life-long education on a plug-in/plug-out basis." (p. 361)

Wagar, W. Warren. *Building the City of Man: Outlines of a World Civilization*. A World Order Book. New York: Grossman, 1971.
The first volume in the World Order Models Project, sponsored by the World Law Fund, Wagar describes a viable world society of the twenty-first century in which "the world citizenry will devote at least half of its active hours to learning, both inside and outside the formal educational structure. . . ." (p. 122)

Ways, Max. "Don't We Know Enough to Make Better Public Policies?" *Fortune,* April 1971.
Asks whether modern society is "in danger of rattling apart because the progress of knowledge is so uneven in its application to the world of action." "There is considerable evidence that the more we learn the more we need to know. Few scientists think they are running out of questions. And it is the common observation of nonscientists that society in action faces more 'problems' now than it did fifty years ago." p. 66)

Forecasting business activity and the impact of government policy, despite the advances of economics, has not become easier or more successful because "The wild cards multiply even as economists raise their skill in dealing with the determinable elements." (p. 67)

One of the reasons for this paradox is that contemporary society confronts new and formidable areas of ignorance, leading to "a new kind of inertia" where change is resisted because we cast about for a higher degree of certainty. "Such, however, is the inescapable context of all policy making in a truly complex and rapidly changing society. Either we accept the framework of acting on the basis of very incomplete knowledge or else we condemn ourselves to retaining unchanged those institutions, like the present welfare system, for which we have lost respect." (p. 118)

Perceiving the Communications Era*

Geoffrey Ashe. *Camelot and the Vision of Albion*. New York: St. Martin's Press, 1971. A study of man's myths, intended for the British reader. However, it is valuable for all because of the way it traces the recurrence in man's experience of the "golden age" theme.

Isaac Asimov. *I, Robot*. New York: Fawcett World Library, 1970. This book relates a series of short episodes about the first robots in the solar system. They change, make mistakes, and become more human.

Ben Bagdikian. *The Information Machines: Their Impact on Man and the Media*. New York: Harper & Row, 1971. Primarily concerned with the impact of technology on journalism, but also tackles the development of communications technology and the history of social change.

Ruth Benedict. "Synergy," in *Psychology Today,* June 1970. Ruth Benedict originally used the word synergy to describe the attributes of cultures that were nonviolent. Her work has opened the way for current thinking about a "good society" and how it might be achieved.

* Compiled by Futures Conditional, an Information System, Box 1531, Wickenburg, Arizona 85358. Used by permission.

Carlos Castenada. *The Teachings of Don Juan: A Yaqui Way of Knowledge.* New York: Ballantine, 1971. This book explores the world of a Yaqui wise man.

Barry Commoner. *The Closing Circle.* New York: Alfred A. Knopf, 1971. The damage man does to his environment and what he must do to live within ecological realities.

R. Buckminster Fuller. *Operating Manual for Spaceship Earth.* New York: Pocket Books, n.d. *Utopia or Oblivion.* New York: Bantam, n.d. Inconceivable abundance for all mankind or unlimited catastrophe. These are the choices the author sees for mankind in the next decade. In these books Fuller develops his concepts of how mankind might achieve the first of the two alternatives.

Tom Hanna. *Bodies in Revolt.* New York: Harper & Row, 1970. Posits a radically different world and states that we're on the way to becoming radically different kinds of human beings.

Robert Heinlein. *Stranger in a Strange Land.* New York: Berkley Publishing Corp., 1968. Valentine Michael Smith is a human, born and raised on Mars. He comes back to earth and begins to learn what it means to be human.

I Ching (Book of Changes). New York: New American Library, n.d. This book contains much of the knowledge of Old China. It is to be consulted as an old friend.

Anthony Jay. *Management and Machiavelli.* New York: Bantam, 1971. A satirical look at the realities of management.

R. D. Laing. *The Politics of Experience.* New York: Ballantine, n.d. Laing takes a second look at people who are labeled insane and placed in asylums. He asks whether some of them can teach us.

David Loye. *The Healing of a Nation.* New York: W. W. Norton & Co., 1971. Suggests that personal intensive communication is one of the routes to handle the issues caused by racism in the United States.

Abraham Maslow. *Toward a Psychology of Being.* 2nd ed. New York: Van Nostrand Reinhold Co., 1968. Maslow breaks with the long-standing trend in psychology of concentrating on pathology. He attempts to develop a psychology for healthy human beings.

Marshall McLuhan. *Gutenberg Galaxy. Understanding Media.* New York: New American Library, 1971. *The Medium Is the Message.*

New York: Bantam, 1970. McLuhan shows how the industrial era fractured man and forced him into linear thinking. McLuhan then discovers what he believes are trails leading toward a new world that promises a more human future.

John Platt. *The Step to Man*. New York: John Wiley & Sons, 1966. Platt is generally known as a scientist. In this volume he applies the knowledge of science to current social realities.

Pierre Teilhard de Chardin. *Phenomenon of Man*. New York: Harper & Row, 1959. Teilhard develops a new world view. Through his thinking we can see the world on an evolutionary journey, developing increasingly more complex physical forms and increasingly higher levels of consciousness.

Robert Theobald. *An Alternative Future for America Two*. Chicago, Illinois: Swallow, 1970. The present situation is the starting point for this book. An overall framework is developed that makes it possible to examine the trends in American society.

————. *Futures Conditional*. New York & Indianapolis: Bobbs-Merrill, 1972. Shows that there are three major ways of looking at the nature of time and experience; permits the reader to work through his own present ideas and to develop new thinking.

————. *Habit and Habitat*. Englewood Cliffs, New Jersey: Prentice-Hall, 1972. This volume shows the extent of the changes that will be required in social, economic and political thinking if humanity is to survive the ecological crises of the seventies and eighties.

————, ed. *The Dialogues Series*. New York & Indianapolis: Bobbs-Merrill. The following titles are in the series: *Dialogue on Poverty, Dialogue on Education, Dialogue on Women, Dialogue on Violence, Dialogue on Technology, Dialogue on Science*. Important primarily for their attempt to introduce a new style of document: the dialogue focuser. Each volume $1.25.

———— and J. M. Scott. *Teg's 1994: An Anticipation of the Near Future*. Chicago, Illinois: Swallow Press, 1972. A story about a girl, Teg, who wins an Orwell Fellowship in 1994. The Fellowship enables her to discover the significance of developments over the past 25 years and the directions in which further change is required.

William Irwin Thompson. *At the Edge of History*. New York: Harper & Row, 1971. A companion book to Ashe's, starting from recent American experience.

Alvin Toffler. *Future Shock*. New York: Bantam, 1971. Toffler notes the increasing speed of social changes in recent years and talks about the possible effects on man and culture. He argues that we have yet to reach the high point of the industrial era.

Kurt Vonnegut, Jr. *Player Piano*. New York: Avon, 1971. This book explores some logical conclusions of the Protestant work ethic: what can we expect in present circumstances if we apply the idea that each person must hold a job?

W. Warren Wagar. *Building the City of Man: Outlines of a World Civilization*. New York: Grossman, 1971. Argues that there is a "totalizing crisis" in civilization and that a new world order is necessary. Believes, however, that this cannot be achieved without a world war.

Norbert Wiener. *The Human Use of Human Beings*. New York: Avon, 1969. Wiener examines some of the moral implications of man's technological advances.

Gene Youngblood. *Expanded Cinema*. New York: E. P. Dutton, 1970. This book moves our thinking beyond the linear mode of existing art. An unintentional mixing of communication styles often obscures the author's meaning. Nonetheless, this material stems from a truly fundamental rethinking of "art" and "reality."

Theory for the Communications Era*

MARC ROSENBERG

1. Communication Theory

Jurgen Ruesch & Gregory Bateson. *Communication: The Social Matrix of Psychiatry.* New York: W. W. Norton, 1968. Bateson's a genius, the Einstein of contemporary communication theory. If you're into communication theory or interaction analysis, read this.

Claude Shannon and Warren Weaver. *The Mathematical Theory of Communication.* Urbana, Illinois: University of Illinois Press, n.d. Weaver's essay is a short and readable version of Shannon's technical work. A seminal work in information theory.

Ray Birdwhistell. *Kinesics and Context.* Philadelphia, Pennsylvania: University of Pennsylvania Press, n.d. If you've read any of the popular works on "body language," then read this as well. Birdwhistell is the man who started it all, and he's better than his popularizers.

Colin Cherry. *On Human Communication,* 2nd ed. Cambridge, Massachusetts: M.I.T. Press, 1968. A good general introduction.

Watzlawick, Beavin & Jackson. *Pragmatics of Human Communication.* New York: W. W. Norton, 1967. Students and colleagues of Bateson. A synthesis of Bateson's varied work.

* Used by permission.

Frank Herbert. *Whipping Star.* New York: Berkley Publishing Corp., 1970. Another science fiction novel from the man who brought you *Dune.* Very far-out.

2. Anthropological Perspectives

Edward Hall. *The Silent Language.* New York: Fawcett World Library, 1969. A more basic and general work on communication and culture than *Hidden Dimension.*

Erving Goffman. *The Presentation of Self in Everyday Life.* Garden City, New York: Doubleday, 1959.

————. *Interaction Ritual.* Chicago, Illinois: Aldine-Atherton, 1967. Face to face communication. Life as drama and ritual.

Claude Levi-Strauss. *Triste Tropique.* New York: Outerbridge & Dienstfrey, 1964. The founder of structural anthropology has done his field work. This is it. A beautifully written book. A prose poem.

————. *Structural Anthropology.* New York: Basic Books, 1963. A collection of theoretical essays on structuralism, culture, communication. A very important book.

Dorothy Lee. *Freedom and Culture.* Englewood Cliffs, New Jersey: Prentice-Hall, 1959. Only a few anthropologists know what culture is all about. Dorothy Lee is one of them.

Jules Henry. *Culture Against Man.* New York: Random, n.d. Anthropology applied to the contemporary scene. Know your environment.

Edmund Carpenter. *They Became What They Beheld.* New York: Ballantine, 1970. If you dig McLuhan, read this. Similar material, but a slightly different perspective.

Carlos Castenada. *The Teachings of Don Juan.* New York: Ballantine, 1971. Turning on with an expert.

3. McLuhan and His Sources

Marshall McLuhan. *The Gutenberg Galaxy.* New York: New American Library, 1971. McLuhan's best-documented work. Perceptual changes and the technology of print. Particularly good for those who are into history or literature.

————. *Understanding Media.* New York: New American Library, 1971. McLuhan's most important book, embodying his theory of media hot and cool.

Harold Innis. *The Bias of Communication*. Toronto: University of Toronto Press, 1964. Innis is McLuhan's guru. Not an easy book to read, but well worth the time and effort required.

Siegfried Giedion. *Mechanization Takes Command*. New York: W. W. Norton, 1969. "Anonymous history"—technology and the shape of our lives.

Jacques Ellul. *The Technological Society*. New York: Alfred A. Knopf, 1964. Technology as a bummer.

William Ivins. *Art & Geometry*. New York: Dover Publications, 1946. Modes of perception in Classical and Renaissance art.

4. Life Sciences

Pierre Teilhard de Chardin. *The Phenomenon of Man*. New York: Harper & Row, 1959. Biomysticism.

John Bleibtrau. *The Parable of the Beast*. New York: Crowell, Collier & Macmillan, 1969. Together ethology.

Alan Watts. *Nature, Man & Woman*. New York: Pantheon, 1958. Anything by Watts is well worth reading.

Rene Dubos. *So Human an Animal*. New York: Charles Scribner's Sons, 1968.

Clifford Grobstein. *The Strategy of Life*. San Francisco, California: W. H. Freeman, 1965.

Garrett Hardin. *Nature and Man's Fate*. New York: New American Library, n.d.

J. T. Bonner. *The Ideas of Biology*. New York: Harper & Row, 1962.

Theodosius Dobzhansky. *Mankind Evolving*. New Haven, Connecticut: Yale University Press, 1962.

(Any of the above five books provides a good introduction to biology. They are listed in approximate order of thoroughness and difficulty.)

John Lilly. *Man and Dolphin*. Garden City, New York: Doubleday, n.d. An introduction to inter-species communication.

————. *The Mind of the Dolphin*. Garden City, New York: Doubleday, 1967. Further research on nonhuman intelligence and communication.

5. Visions of Today and Tomorrow

Alvin Toffler. *Future Shock.* New York: Random, 1970. A documentation of accelerating social change along a variety of dimensions.

Arthur Clarke. *Profiles of the Future.* New York: Harper & Row, 1963. The science and technology of the future. Pretty far out, but not so far away.

Nigel Calder, ed. *The World in 1984.* Baltimore, Maryland: Penguin Books, n.d. Experts from a variety of fields forecast the futures of their specialties.

Wall Street Journal Editors. *Here Comes Tomorrow.* Homewood, Illinois: Dow Jones-Irwin, 1967. An attempt to predict the shape of America's immediate future.

Charles Reich. *The Greening of America.* New York: Random, 1970. Take it with however many grains of salt are needed to satisfy your taste.

Theodore Roszak. *The Making of a Counter Culture.* Garden City, New York: Doubleday, 1969.

Jesse Kornbluth, ed. *Notes from the New Underground.* New York: Viking Press, 1968. A good collection of underground documents.

Richard Kostelanetz, ed. *Beyond Left and Right.* New York: Apollo Editions, 1968. At the edge of the conceptual revolution. Heavy thinkers from Buckminster Fuller and Marshall McLuhan to Herman Kahn, Paul Goodman, and Leslie Fiedler.

6. Generalists

Ludwig von Bertalanffy. *General Systems Theory.* New York: George Braziller, 1969. Nature is one. We break it up to study it. General Systems Theory tries to put it together again.

Kenneth Boulding. *The Image.* Ann Arbor, Michigan: University of Michigan Press, 1956. An easy-going introduction to general systems, and more.

Arthur Koestler. *The Ghost in the Machine.* New York: Crowell, Collier & Macmillan, 1968. Is the human brain a maladaptation? Koestler thinks it is.

Buckminster Fuller. *Utopia or Oblivion*. New York: Bantam, n.d. A collection of Bucky's essays, old and new. Synergetics, geodesics, and other integral musings.

———. *Operating Manual for Spaceship Earth*. New York: Pocket Books. The Earth is a machine, but it didn't come with an instruction book on how to use it. *Operating Manual* attempts to remedy that oversight.

7. Inner Space Exploration

Masters & Housten. *The Varieties of Psychedelic Experience*. New York: Holt, Rinehart & Winston. "The revolution in the study of mind is at hand . . . we doubt that extensive work in this area can fail to result in eventually pushing human consciousness beyond its present limitations and on towards capacities not yet realized and perhaps undreamed of."

Aldous Huxley. *The Doors of Perception & Heaven and Hell*. New York: Harper & Row, n.d. Exploring the frontiers of the mind.

Alan Watts. *The Joyous Cosmology*. New York: Pantheon, 1962. Subtitled "Adventures in the chemistry of consciousness." Some nice photos, too.

Timothy Leary. *High Priest*. New York: College Notes & Texts, 1968. Tales of a head.

8. Formal Approaches

Bertrand Russell. *Introduction to Mathematical Philosophy*. New York: Simon & Schuster, 1971. A very readable book. Good chapters on the theory of logical types and mathematical structure.

G. Spencer Brown. *The Laws of Form*. Rutherford, New Jersey: Fairleigh Dickinson University Press, n.d. Often incomprehensible, often brilliant, always thought-provoking.

Whyte, Wilson & Wilson, eds. *Hierarchical Structures*. New York: American Elsevier Publishing Co., 1969. A collection of essays dealing with hierarchies in nature, artifact, and thought.

L. L. Whyte, ed. *Aspects of Form*. Bloomington, Indiana: Indiana University Press, 1961. The concept of form as used in biology, psychology, esthetics, etc.

9. Cybernetics

Norbert Wiener. *The Human Use of Human Beings.* New York: Avon, 1969. A nontechnical overview of control systems.

W. Ross Ashby. *An Introduction to Cybernetics.* New York: Barnes & Noble, 1969. How to do cybernetics. A very formal, but understandable, introduction.

————. *Design for a Brain.* New York: Barnes & Noble, 1966. A cybernetic analysis of the living organism.

Date Due

PRINTED IN U.S.A.   CAT. NO. 24 161   BRODART